To:

From:

Date:

366 DEVOTIONS

AMAZING GRACE

God's Love to Rescue and to Restore

Christian Art
PUBLISHERS

Visit Christian Art Gifts, Inc., at www.christianartgifts.com.

Amazing Grace: God's Love to Rescue and to Restore

Published under license by Christian Art Gifts, Inc.

First edition 2025.

Written by Solly Ozrovech.

Designed by Christian Art Gifts, Inc.

Cover and interior images used under license from Shutterstock.com.

ISBN 978-1-63952-665-9

Printed in China.

30 29 28 27 26 25
11 10 9 8 7 6 5 4 3 2

"My grace is all you need.
My power works
best in weakness."

~ 2 Corinthians 12:9 NLT

Contents

January

Gathering the Flock

"I am the good shepherd.
The good shepherd lays down
His life for the sheep."
~ John 10:11

Loving, timeless God of yesterday,
today and tomorrow,
to You be all praise, honor and worship
as we venture out on unfamiliar paths.
We thank You for being our Savior
and showing us the way.
Thank You, Lord Jesus,
for coming to this sin-torn world to lead us
from our wanderings back to the Father's House.
Help us to follow You not only
when we can clearly see the road before us,
but also when we go through dark valleys.
Grant that our faith in Your guidance will never falter.
Thank You that You were sent to make us part of
God's flock; that You are the Good Shepherd who
wants to lead us beside green pastures and quiet waters.
Let us start this month with our hand firmly
in Your loving hand and grant that we will willingly
and obediently follow wherever You might lead us.
In the name of our Savior and Master.
Amen.

God Gave

"For God so loved the world that He gave His one and only Son, that whoever believes in Him shall not perish but have eternal life." (John 3:16)

To truly and intimately know someone, you need to meet with that person, speak to him and even live with him. There are people who have pen pals in far-off countries. Having a pen pal means that you tell him all about yourself through the letters that you write.

You might send a photo of yourself. If you are able to phone each other you will get to know each other's voices. If you know of someone who is going to visit near where your pen pal lives, you might ask that person to visit your pen pal or to deliver a gift. Your pen pal will continually gather knowledge about you. Hopefully the day will come when the two of you can meet face-to-face and then you will truly and intimately know each other.

When Jesus came to earth, God Himself arrived. Messages were no longer necessary. It was an individual, face-to-face, interpersonal relationship. Jesus did not only come for Peter, James and John, but for every person in the universe.

When Neil Armstrong landed on the moon, he said, "We came in peace for all mankind." When Jesus Christ came to earth, God's message for humanity was, "I come in love for all mankind!" A cardinal truth became known through this event: God is pure, sincere, self-sacrificing love! This is the greatest truth ever.

Wonderful God of grace, let all of humanity come to know Your undying love. Amen.

Read John 3:1-21

God's Love Becomes Visible

"For God so loved the world that He gave His one and only Son, that whoever believes in Him shall not perish but have eternal life." (John 3:16)

If you study the people of Israel in the Old Testament you will discover that a fear of God is evident. Scripture tells us about individuals who tried to flee from God and hide from the mighty Jehovah. Their lives were filled with fear. We discover that Abraham was willing to sacrifice his son because his reverential fear lead to obedience.

Through Jesus Christ, God affirmed that He is not only a God to be revered and feared, but that He is, in essence, a God of love. Jesus brought the love of God to humankind through His life and sacrificial death. He paved the way for a new relationship with the Almighty God.

Even today people find it difficult to accept that God is not simply a feared Judge who has various ways to punish our transgressions. As a result their spiritual lives become dead and their worship is ruled by fear rather than a true desire to worship.

Even though we will all be held accountable for the way we lived our lives, Jesus Christ came to this world to bring God's love to you and to lead you into a personal, loving relationship with Himself. Live unceasingly from within the source of His love and experience the abundance of life through Jesus Christ (see John 10:10).

Holy Lord Jesus, in Your love I find fulfillment and hope for the future. Amen.

How Far Does Love Reach?

This is how we know what love is: Jesus Christ laid down His life for us. And we ought to lay down our lives for our brothers. (1 John 3:16)

Human love is often a case of, "I'll love you as long as you love me." Even the love between parents and children can be strained, especially when the child is the "black sheep" or when the parents let the child down.

Through Jesus Christ, God's love reached new depths. Before Christ, people knew that God loved them and expected them to keep His commands. But before Christ, they didn't know *how much* God loved them.

Jesus taught people what the love of God meant. His parables about the Prodigal Son and forgiveness of the guilty speak about this. His deeds revealed God's love: His healing of the sick, feeding of the hungry and love for the outcast. Through these acts, the love of God was demonstrated.

But it was Jesus' death on the cross that proved that there are no boundaries to God's love. With this one sacrificial deed God said to humankind, "This is how much I love you. As unlovable, rebellious, weak and unfaithful as you are, I seek to save you and to win your trust through this act of unrequited love. You deserve death and your sins separate you from Me. I died in your place. Won't you repent, believe and love Me in return?"

God's love is not sentimental. It sets the final standard of love. How is this standard of love being upheld in your life?

God of Love, grant me a love as endless as Yours. Amen.

Read John 3:1-21

Sent to Save

"For God did not send His Son into the world to condemn the world, but to save the world through Him." (John 3:17)

Jesus Christ came on a mission to save and He was sent for this specific purpose. His coming to this world, His service and teaching, His healings and friendships, and His death and resurrection were all for one single purpose: He came to save!

In what respect must you be saved? Firstly, you must be saved *from* sin. This means that you must first receive forgiveness for your sins. Confess that you have sinned and wandered away from God, and then accept God's forgiveness. You will then enter into a living and permanent relationship of trust and submission to Jesus. You will also seek His help and inspiration to fight and overcome the sinful things you were involved in before, and to lead a sinless life as far as possible.

Then you must be saved *to* a new life of honoring and glorifying God, of accepting His leadership, and of becoming actively involved in serving your fellow man. Your experiences with other believers will encourage you and so you will be united with the community of believers.

You were saved by Jesus to serve Him. You then become an agent in the saving work of Jesus, which you yourself received. You have been saved to a life which must grow in the likeness of Christ.

Ask yourself honestly before God: Have I been saved?

Gracious God, thank You for the salvation that Jesus brought. Amen.

True Life

This is how God showed His love among us:
He sent His one and only Son into the world
that we might live through Him. (1 John 4:9)

When you are young you are encouraged to study so that you can use your talents and accumulate knowledge to help you get the best out of life. Young people often wonder, "Will I be successful? Will I be happy? Will I be rich?" They believe that this is what life is about.

The Christian faith suggests something completely different. It regards success, happiness and wealth as secondary goals. But if you follow these goals alone, you will miss the really important things in life, namely to know and to serve God. God's view of life is so important that Jesus came to live and die to make it known to you.

His life was "true life" and not mere "existence," because His life was driven by love. Love originates in God. This love is made personal through Jesus Christ, "I have come that they might have life, and have it to the full" (John 10:10). We receive this life and then pass it on.

Christ's way of life is also a source of joy. The certainty of knowing that we are loved is the source of a positive feeling of joy, praise and worship. This kind of life enables us to handle the dark side of life. It offers forgiveness and redemption to the guilty, healing to the sick, and the prospect of a new life after death. For human weakness He offers His strength. In the darkness He gives light. It is truly an enriching "life" that God grants us through Jesus Christ.

Lord Jesus, thank You for the enrichment of my life. Amen.

Read 1 John 4:7-21

A Godly Initiative

This is love: not that we loved God,
but that He loved us and sent His Son as
an atoning sacrifice for our sins. (1 John 4:10)

We all think that we know precisely what love means. Even so, human love is a strange mix of wonder, sympathy, selfishness, lust, caring and sacrifice. In our love relationships we experience mere glimmers of what God's love is like.

God's love always supersedes our love. He loved us before we loved Him. He loved us before we were born. He loved our parents before He loved us. He loved humankind before He brought it into existence.

Humans became living beings through God's love. We didn't ask God to love us, He took the initiative. All other loves come from His love and they are brought to life through His love.

Our love for God and each other is molded on His love. Despite His great love for us, we ignore and neglect Him. By doing this, we distance ourselves from Him.

But God loved us even more and His great desire to win our love led Him to offer His Son. Through this sacrifice we are forgiven.

When we accept that God has adopted us, unworthy as we are, then His love becomes the most valuable thing in our lives. It saves, heals, restores, motivates and enables us to grow in the likeness of our Savior, Jesus Christ.

How do you respond to God's great love?

Holy Father God, how can I ever thank
You enough for loving me first? Amen.

Abundance or Want?

"I have come that they may have life, and have it to the full." (John 10:10)

Many people don't live life to the full; they simply exist. Howard Rutledge, a U.S. Navy Captain, had his plane shot down over Vietnam during the early stages of the Vietnam war and spent several years in a Vietnamese prison cell. There he discovered how little he had to cling to. Before the war he had been "too busy" to spend time with God. He said that, "It took time in prison to make me see how empty my life was without God."

The essential reason why Jesus came was so that people who trusted and followed Him could experience life in all its fullness.

Faith in Jesus brings joy—not a superficial, carefree life without depth, but a deeply rooted, quiet joy that meets the harsh realities of this world with a calm confidence borne from the knowledge that God is in control.

Faith in Jesus gives you purpose because you know that you are important to God, that He loves you, and wants to travel with you on life's journey. Faith in Jesus gives you hope when circumstances are hard. Faith in Jesus helps you to get your life in order when you otherwise would have fallen apart. Faith in Jesus motivates you to love others and to overcome your own self-centeredness.

Do you want to live a life of abundance or want? Jesus is the only answer—and the choice is yours.

Lord Jesus, I plead that You will give me the fullness of life that was Your purpose in coming to this world. Amen.

Read John 10:1-10

How Do You React to Life?

"I have come that they may have life,
and have it to the full." (John 10:10)

People react differently to the stresses and demands of life. Some see life as an intense battle and become aggressive, others are apathetic and quietly accept everything that comes their way without rejoicing or moaning. Most people react emotionally to life and live imprisoned by their attitudes; they allow their feelings to rule their lives.

It's your choice whether something that happens in your life will bless you or hurt you. When painful things happen, the emotional and spiritual scars can remain and you can lose faith. But with God's help you can control your reactions and strengthen your faith and endurance.

Don't approach life with an attitude of self-pity, frustration, impatience or anger. Life does not get hurt through these things—but you do. Different age groups react differently to life. Young people seem to react with a naïve charm, while older people often react with self-reproach. Everyone reacts to life—one way or the other.

As a Christian, you know that you have been made in the image of God and are of priceless worth. Because you have been reconciled through the blood of Christ, you can approach the Father with confidence and enjoy peace with God. You have assurance in life's difficulties, knowing that you have been brought near to the Father, and the Spirit will help you learn to react to life's challenges with both strength and wisdom.

Savior, thank You for equipping me with
the Holy Spirit, to help me to deal with life. Amen.

Live United with Christ

See that what you have heard from the beginning remains in you. If it does, you also will remain in the Son and in the Father. (1 John 2:24)

Many things can cause you to backslide in your faith. Sickness and depression might make you feel that God has rejected you. Family issues might discourage you. Failure in a business undertaking might make you doubt God's goodness. Conflict in your congregation can gnaw at your faith. Doubts about whether God even exists can slip into your life. In situations like these your faith in God can wane.

It is essential to be aware of any temptation that can rob you of your faith. Don't allow these things to cause you dismay. Be firm in your faith and cling to it like a drowning person clings to a life buoy. In the end you will be thankful you did. Remember Paul's words to the Romans, "I am convinced that neither death nor life, neither angels nor demons, neither the present nor the future, nor any powers, neither height nor depth, nor anything else in all creation, will be able to separate us from the love of God that is in Christ Jesus our Lord" (Rom. 8:38-39).

Believers have good and bad days, just like everyone else. Regardless of circumstances you should always stay in Christ Jesus; He will never forsake you. He knows you and intercedes for you with the Father. Praise the Lord!

Lord Jesus, hold me in Your love so that I might never lose my faith in You. Thank You for interceding for me with the Father. Amen.

Read 1 John 2:18-27

Christ's Promise to You

This is what He promised us—even eternal life. (1 John 2:25)

Many young Christians make premature promises to God. They promise to serve and obey Him to the end. They promise to live pure and righteous lives and to pray every day. From time to time Christians renew the promises they made to God. But many of us keep our promises for a while and then we neglect them.

Our promises to God are our reaction to the amount of love God has shown us. On God's end of the agreement is the promise of an endless future. He promises us everlasting life. This is the gift of quality of life for us, but it also points to a future dimension on the other side of human existence. It offers us life after death. The "Jesus quality" of life means that death does not have the final say for any disciple of Jesus Christ.

It opens the door not only to eternal life, but also to a more glorious life on the other side of the grave. Eternal life is a life with God in His unquestionable glory and sovereignty. It is unrestrained communion with God and eternal joy and peace in His presence. It is a life of love and beauty, unblemished by human weakness. There will be no more suffering or grief and we will have glorified bodies.

Above all, it is a life in Christ with His truth, glory and love surpassing all. It surely is a future to long for!

Thank You, Lord Jesus, for the promise of
eternal life for Your faithful children. Amen.

Are You Losing Your Shine?

"Yet you refuse to come to Me to have life." (John 5:40)

It is easy to get caught up in beliefs or movements that may initially seem compelling, but ultimately undermine the centrality of Christ and His teaching. Historic creeds can be useful, but only insofar as they help us remain faithful to Jesus and the teachings of Scripture. Christianity that loses Christ isn't Christianity at all.

The Christian life involves a set of rules that are based on the teachings of Christ. It is basically a way of life that must be lived in the power of the Holy Spirit. Jesus came to give new life to all who accept Him. This new life is a direct outpouring of the Holy Spirit in a person's life as promised by Jesus.

Many have called themselves Christians and were once excited about Jesus' teachings. But, as time passed, their excitement waned, and what once appeared to be a robust faith has grown cold. True Christianity is not a flash in the pan, but a lasting trust in Jesus. It may not always burn bright, but as it is stoked with prayer and meditation on God's Word, it will always give warmth and light to our lives.

To maintain a Christ-centered faith, nothing must come between you and the Master. In this regard Paul prays that you might "know this love that surpasses knowledge—that you may be filled to the measure of all the fullness of God" (Eph. 3:19). Your faith can never lose its shine as long as you stay focused on Jesus.

Holy Savior, keep my thoughts focused on
You so that my faith will keep shining. Amen.

Read John 11:17-32

A Firm Trust

"I am the resurrection and the life. He who believes in Me will live, even though he dies." (John 11:25)

These words spoken by the Master might seem like a contradiction. Indeed, many of Jesus' teachings seem inexplicable when we try to understand them intellectually.

The Holy Scriptures and the experiences of dedicated Christians demonstrate that trust, faith and submission to God always form the basis of miraculous events that challenge human logic.

Through the ages, people have had to deal with dangers and testing in a variety of forms. It has always been those with a strong, unshakable faith in Jesus Christ who were able to withstand and overcome the attacks.

Today our faith is still tested. It might be through persecution, financial difficulties, sickness or some kind of personal setback.

Whatever your situation, always remember that God is with you to support you and to carry you through your time of difficulty. "So do not fear, for I am with you; do not be dismayed, for I am your God. I will strengthen you and help you; I will uphold you with My righteous right hand" (Isa. 41:10).

Cling to the presence of the Living Christ in your life. He will inspire you to a life of trust and firm faith in all circumstances.

My Savior, in You I discover unending joy,
love and true life. I thank You for this. Amen.

Using Crises as a Turning Point

Jesus said, "For judgment I have come into this world, so that the blind will see and those who see will become blind." (John 9:39)

We usually perceive a crisis as a time of difficulty. But a crisis can also be a turning point where we move forward in a new and more productive direction. It can create an opportunity that we would never have had if things had stayed the same.

When Jesus said that He came to judge, He meant that His coming would cause a crisis in the lives of people. It placed them in a dilemma where they were forced to choose either for Him or against Him. Reacting to Him in faith brought insight and light to the people, just like it did for the man who was born blind. By refusing to believe in Him they brought upon themselves the darkness of rejection, they were separated from God and placed under judgment.

Whether or not you live in light or in darkness depends on how you respond to Jesus. When He comes to you it places you in a crisis because a personal experience with Jesus is the most critical moment in your whole life. You must either say "Yes" or "No" to Him. You can believe in Him, entrust yourself to Him, worship and obey Him. If you do this you will walk in the light and you will begin to see more and more of the light.

Your meeting with Jesus either becomes a golden opportunity or a dire crisis that you will regret for the rest of your life. God says to you today: Choose life!

Jesus, I choose You as the Savior and Light
of my life, for now and evermore. Amen.

Read 1 John 5:1-12

The Gift of Eternal Life

This is the testimony: God has given us eternal life, and this life is in His Son. (1 John 5:11)

People's life expectancy is increasing and today the average person is expected to live well into his seventies. Developments in medical science have resulted in people being able to live longer than ever before. In biblical times people didn't live as long and there was a greater consciousness of the brevity of life.

In order to satisfy the human yearning for a long life, many religions offered the promise of eternal life. If you believed, you could live the same kind of life as the idol you worshiped. But only Jesus Christ can truly keep this promise. Eternal life is the life of God, because God alone is eternal. God can give you eternal life because He grants it to all who believe in Him and share in His life.

Because God is a God of peace, eternal life looks forward to a tranquility that calms the frustrations of life. Likewise, God is a God of holiness, and He gives us strength to resist temptation. While we experience this blessing in part now, we look forward to a day where we will experience eternal life in full, where our striving and stressing cease entirely.

God is love and He fills your heart with His love that can remove all bitterness, vengeful thoughts and hate. God's life is everlasting, and in Him you have a quality of life that overcomes death. God's life within you is indestructible. Praise God because He is good. There is no end to His love.

Eternal God, fill my life with eternal life that only belongs to You. Amen.

Life is About Jesus

He who has the Son has life; he who does not have the Son of God does not have life. (1 John 5:12)

What is life all about? For some it is about satisfying their hunger for wealth and possessions: cars, houses and other valuable treasures. For others it's about money: the more you have, the better you live. For some, life is just about pleasure. Others value prestige, power or self-fulfillment.

The Bible has a clear message: Life is about Jesus Christ! If you have Him, you have life, and if you don't have Him, you don't have life.

Knowing Jesus might bring you prosperity—but it might not. Following Jesus brought power to a small group, but for many it led to humble service without any remarkable authority or the slightest reward.

When Jesus enters your life, He begins a healing process. You find your priorities changing, and you become excited about things you had never thought of before. Through the forgiveness of sins, you have peace with God and will grow in your relationship with Him.

Jesus opens your eyes when you welcome Him into your life. You see everything for what it is—yourself, God and the World. You find perspective on all aspects of life and existence. These things happen to you when Jesus becomes the Savior of your life.

Savior and Redeemer, I have only one short earthly life to live. Help me, through Your grace, to make it the best that I can. Amen.

Read Galatians 3:21-29

Become Part of God's Family

You are all sons of God through faith in Christ Jesus. (Galatians 3:26)

When we read the Bible and see Jesus as the "Son of God," we are overcome by the majesty of Christ—unless we are totally emotionless.

On the level of human relationships as we know them, it is difficult to understand how the Son of God could live on this earth as a human being. Sometimes it seems incomprehensible to us. Perhaps that's why some people say that it is impossible for us to follow the example of Jesus, because He wasn't a normal person—He was divine: the Son of God.

Never let this way of thinking keep you from giving yourself to the service of the Master. Remember that through God's limitless grace, you have been called to become His child through your faith in the reigning of Christ in your life. God's family is universal and everyone who accepts Jesus as Redeemer and Savior is welcomed in Jesus' family as a child of God.

Serve God by walking with Christ, and obediently and diligently following His example. As you grow in grace, you will become more and more aware of God as our Father. You will realize that He watches over you and that through the Holy Spirit, He equips you to fulfill your role in this world as His child.

O Lord my God, I delight in knowing that, through Jesus Christ, I may call You Father. Amen.

So That All Might Believe

He came as a witness to testify concerning that light, so that through him all men might believe. (John 1:7)

When you become a child of God, you become part of a worldwide community. This experience is so intensely personal that we sometimes speak of Jesus or God as our own private possession. We sometimes hear people say, "My Jesus!"

The New Testament people had passion. They lived to make Jesus known across the whole world. The mindset that God was the God of the Jews alone and that other people had their own gods was totally refuted by the life, teachings, death and resurrection of Jesus Christ.

When the Holy Spirit came at Pentecost, the disciples left Jerusalem. Jesus said, "You will receive power when the Holy Spirit comes on you; and you will be My witnesses in Jerusalem, and in all Judea and Samaria and to the ends of the earth" (Acts 1:8).

Today there are approximately eight billion people on earth. About two billion are Christians. A further one billion have heard about Jesus Christ, but have not made a commitment to Him. Half of the world's population has not even heard about Jesus yet. The work that John the Baptist started still has a long way to go.

No matter how challenging the task may seem, Christians today have the same mission. This mission will never be completed if we leave it to the theologians. We each need to be an effective witness for Jesus.

Lord Jesus, grant that Your followers will attempt to bring others to faith in You. Amen.

Read John 1:1-18

The Word Became Flesh

The Word became flesh and made
His dwelling among us. (John 1:14)

Actions speak louder than words" is a well-known saying which means that your deeds are more significant than the things that you say. We also refer to people who just talk and don't do anything as "all talk and no action."

The Bible doesn't share this distrust in our words. According to the Scriptures, words contain great power. The Word of God is seen as exceptionally powerful. When God spoke through the prophet, He said, "So is My word that goes out from My mouth. It will not return to Me empty, but will accomplish what I desire and achieve the purpose for which I sent it" (Isa. 55:11). God's words or messages became mighty deeds that spoke louder than human words.

A word is a sound or thought that comes from deep within a person's being and becomes a reality that we call speech. But God's words are weaved into a life that is far more than just sounds and thoughts. He speaks to us from a heart that beats with love, in actions that heal, in miracles that overrule evil, in parables that us tell what God's kingdom is like, in the building of a community of followers and in death and triumphant resurrection.

We mustn't overflow with words, but lack in deeds. We must strive to follow our words with God-honoring actions. God's words must be visible in our actions. Jesus must be seen and heard in our words and actions.

Let Your Word speak clearly through
my life and actions today. Amen.

Light for a Dark World

"While I am in the world, I am the light of the world." (John 9:5)

To be in the dark without a light is a scary experience. You don't know where you are, you walk into things and you can even injure yourself. Without a light your activities come to a stop. If a power failure caused the darkness, then your activities will cease till the power comes back on. Light is essential for everyday life and we often take it for granted.

When Jesus said He was the Light of the World, there were few sources of artificial light. People relied on the light of the sun. Just as the sun brought light, so too did Jesus. People who lived in His light saw the world in a completely new way. It was as if they were blind before. A new world opened up for them that enabled them to know, to see and to give and receive guidance.

Jesus can bring light to any dark area of your life, whether it be doubt, depression, feelings of guilt or failure. Sometimes people live in darkness because they are confused by false teachings which present themselves as truthful and good.

Allow Jesus to bring light to the darkness in your life. Make Him your Savior and submit to His plan for your life—you will discover a new beam of light shining in your life. It will enlighten your thoughts, guide your footsteps and focus your life on God's love.

I pray for those who are still walking in darkness,
Lord guide them to the light. Grant that Your light
might be switched on in their hearts and minds. Amen.

Read 1 John 1:1-10

Everlasting Light!

The life appeared; we have seen it and testify to it, and we proclaim to you the eternal life, which was with the Father and has appeared to us. (1 John 1:2)

Have you ever made peace with the fact that life is short and the older you get, the shorter life gets? When people you went to school with begin to pass away, the brevity of life becomes a stark reality. Some people don't even want to think about an end for them one day.

But everything doesn't have to end—not if you believe in Jesus. You are not limited to the length of your earthly life, because the life that Jesus brings and shares with those who believe in Him is eternal. It is eternal because it is a gift from God, and God is eternal. It has been this way from the beginning. It is part of God's giving of Himself to us.

It is also eternal because it has a divine quality to it. The person who lives "in Christ" doesn't just wander around aimlessly, but is transformed into a child of God and is part of the family of Jesus Christ. Eternal life isn't just an extension of our earthly lives, but the beginning of a better, richer life here and now.

Eternal life is eternal because it doesn't end with death. The grave could not keep Jesus and neither can it keep those who have chosen life through faith in Him. They have received the promise: "Because I live, you also will live" (John 14:19). Those who follow our Savior know that this is undeniably true. Do you know this for sure?

Lord Jesus, I kneel in a prayer of thanksgiving to You for making eternal life available to me. Amen.

Fellowship with God and Christ

We proclaim to you what we have seen and heard, so that you also may have fellowship with us. And our fellowship is with the Father and with His Son, Jesus Christ. (1 John 1:3)

There are many divisions among Christians. The various denominations have different interpretations of Scripture or approaches to church. Some are strictly conservative and others are liberal, which results in them seeing things in different ways.

In the early church the greatest difference was between Christians who had been Jews before their conversion, and the Gentiles. The Jews had strict rules about separating themselves from Gentiles and it was extremely difficult for them to accept Gentiles into the fellowship of believers.

At times it seemed that this problem would divide the church, but wise men saw to it that the church broke new ground and developed instead.

Christ broke down the dividing walls. Christians from different backgrounds were welcomed because in Christ they were one.

The early Christians also supported, taught and instructed one another. In this way both groups grew through the experience of fellowship with believers. We can't have fellowship only with those who share our opinions. The gospel calls us to greater things. Christians grow and enrich themselves through fellowship with each other. This is what Jesus expects from us.

Lord Jesus, grant that I will accept everyone who accepts You as Savior. Amen.

Read 1 John 3:1-10

The Reason for Christ's Coming

You know that He appeared so that He might take away our sins. And in Him is no sin. (1 John 3:5)

William Barclay, the well-known Scottish New Testament interpreter once said, "Christianity begins with a sense of sin. It begins with the sudden realization that life as we are living it will not do. We awake to ourselves and we awake to our need of God."

In the modern Christian world sin is spoken about very cautiously, yet it is one of the central themes of Scripture. People's lives are destroyed by sin. Sin challenges God and separates us from Him. In today's world God is not obeyed and His commandments are broken at random. Even though we try to minimize our guilt, justify our mistakes and focus on our own empowerment, sin remains a horrible reality.

Jesus came, not to make us happy or successful, or clever or prosperous, but to free us from sin. He came to establish peace between man and God and to restore harmony and fellowship with Himself. There was only one way to deal with sin and that was to forgive it. Christ was sent by God to remove our sins. Jesus announced to sinners forgiveness through faith in God. But they had to repent and confess their sins to God first.

You can't handle your sinfulness on your own. You need God's help and that's why He sent Jesus. If being a Christian starts with a consciousness of sin, are you a Christian?

Thank You, Holy Teacher, that You taught me to begin at the beginning: with the realization of my own sinfulness. Amen.

How to Avoid Sin

No one who lives in Him keeps on sinning. (1 John 3:6)

Life would be very different if there was no sin. We all want to be rid of the desire to sin. If it was in our ability we would resist and overcome every temptation to sin. In our better moments we would wish to overcome the weaknesses and vulnerabilities of our sinful nature, which often prevent us from doing good and which lead us down the path of evil.

But the more we love Christ, the more we become convinced of our own sinfulness. Yet the only way to overcome sin is to stay close to Jesus. Only His power and love in our hearts can abate the evil that we are so prone to. This also requires obedience because every time we obey Him, our spiritual strength is built up. Every time we are disobedient to God, we make ourselves a bit more vulnerable to "the sin that so easily entangles" (Heb. 12:1).

Sin in the lives of believers is one of the biggest problems in Christianity. Believers who sin damage the witness of the gospel.

You do not have to carry on living in sin. You can decide to stay close to Jesus. Then you will experience His grace and strength, and the more you get exposed to this influence, the greater your spiritual growth will be.

Master, help those who earnestly fight against sin
and as a result feel that they have disappointed You.
Give them the grace to overcome and live triumphantly. Amen.

Read Galatians 1:1-10

Love Will Triumph

Grace and peace to you from God our Father and the Lord Jesus Christ, who gave Himself for our sins to rescue us from the present evil age, according to the will of our God and Father. (Galatians 1:3-4)

It seems as though evil powers have free reign over the world today. Reports of crime, violence, lawlessness and immorality are delivered daily. People are overwhelmed by these events and many stand by helplessly and wonder what can be done to restore peace and order.

The only way to overcome crime and evil is to follow Jesus' example. In obedience to God's will, Jesus survived the horror of the crucifixion by showering His divine love on the world.

Today this seems like an impossibility to many people. It is often thought that violence needs to be fought with violence, but history shows that this is not the solution. Even though we in no way claim that criminals should escape the law, we must still follow the example of Jesus and pray for the offenders and lovingly care for the victims.

In the same way that Almighty God transformed the horror of Good Friday into the glory of Easter, so He will transform the evil of this moment into His goodness. This requires your obedience to Him. It calls you to pray with Jesus' love for the whole world when it is your turn.

Father God, help me to follow the example of my Savior, Jesus, to love all people in Your name. Amen.

God's Indescribable Gift

Thanks be to God for His indescribable gift! (2 Corinthians 9:15)

Perhaps you have searched for an exceptional gift for a loved one only to discover that you can't afford it. You feel embarrassed and disappointed. When you eventually find something for the person you feel that it's a weak substitute for what you really wanted to give them. You might even apologize to the person receiving the gift. But the receiver might be overjoyed with the gift—perhaps more than he would have been with the original gift you had in mind.

The Bible states that God's gift was "indescribable." This is how much a human life is worth. It is ironic that Judas and the temple authorities of his day set the price of a human life at thirty pieces of silver. Despite this fact, a poor woman used her savings, an amount equivalent to a year's salary, to buy an alabaster jar of perfume to wash Jesus' feet with.

God's love for you is so indescribably great that He poured the gift of His Son out over you. In human terms it was a priceless gift. God did this, not to buy you, but to save you from sin and Satan.

Some gifts enrich the receivers. A gift can equip them to start a new task, give insight into a certain area of knowledge, or a fresh realization of how valuable they are to you. God's gift to you says that you are the most loved person in the entire universe.

God of love, grant me the grace to regard
each gift You give me as valuable. Amen.

Read 2 Corinthians 9:1-15

Indescribable Love

Thanks be to God for His indescribable gift! (2 Corinthians 9:15)

Buying birthday, wedding and Christmas presents is often quite demanding. You have to stay within your budget and make sure that you don't forget anybody important.

In the midst of the hustle and bustle of gift buying it is beneficial to stand still for a moment and consider the gift that stands central to all gifts: Jesus. God's gift to humankind.

Christ is also the Word who became flesh. It was the only form in which God could give Himself to humankind and the only form in which we could receive Him: a human life. Yet this gift of God's Word is indescribable!

It is exciting to receive a gift that is so stunning that it leaves you speechless. We cannot express it in words. This "gift"—the gift of Jesus—leaves us in entirely in awe and speechless with thankfulness, wonder and love.

How can we possibly respond to such a "gift"? You can accept it by opening your heart in the same way you would open your hand to receive a gift from someone. And then thank God for it by living a dedicated and committed life. The amazing thing about this "gift" is that it can't be described in words, yet Jesus filled Paul with words: the message of the gospel.

You too can thank God for this indescribable gift. You can thank Him every day you live through words of testimony and deeds of love.

Savior and Lord, show me each day how
I can thank You more and more. Amen.

When Mirages Become Real

Show me Your ways, O Lord, teach me Your paths. (Psalm 25:4)

It is easy to get lost while traveling to a new place. The thing you need most during this time is a road map or a trusted friend who can give you directions.

Sometimes you can find yourself on the wrong path in life. Or you have to make an important decision but you are unable to do so because your judgment has become clouded. There could also be external forces and opinions that carry a lot of weight and affect your judgment.

Isaiah offers comforting words for exactly this kind of situation, "Whether you turn to the right or to the left, your ears will hear a voice behind you, saying, 'This is the way; walk in it'" (Isa. 30:21). The Christian who constantly follows the path that God shows him will become sensitive to the voice of God.

Subject every decision you make to the approval of God. Wait on Him in silence and in prayer. He will guide you. When you face the world in faith, you will know that you are not doing it alone, because the living Christ is ready to guide you and lead you on the right path.

A personal relationship with Christ is a primary condition for this. It is your road map. It has to apply to all fields of life. Teach yourself to be aware of the Savior's continuous presence in your life. Then the danger of mistaking mirages for something real will disappear and you will be walking in the light and on the right path.

Redeemer and Guide, fill my life to such a degree
that I will clearly understand Your will for my life,
and that I will walk Your path in obedience. Amen.

Read Galatians 4:21-5:1

The Precious Gift of Freedom

It is for freedom that Christ has set us free. Stand firm, then, and do not let yourselves be burdened again by a yoke of slavery. (Galatians 5:1)

The people of Israel knew what a yoke of slavery meant. Their history shows that many times they were defeated and forced into slavery. At the time of Jesus' birth the Israelites were under the rule of the Roman Empire.

They were also bound by slavery in their spiritual lives through the strict and uncharitable pronouncements of the Law of Moses and the interpretation the temple authorities gave to the Law. They laid more emphasis on demonstrating their piousness and holiness than actually living it out.

Jesus' coming brought God's love to the hearts and lives of ordinary people. His sacrifice and death granted them the certainty of forgiveness and salvation. His resurrection then confirmed the promise of eternal life for all who believe. How can we disregard so rich an inheritance?

Joyfully and thankfully accept the promises and sacrifice of Jesus Christ. Believe in His power at all times and resist Satan's attempts to sow seeds of doubt and unbelief in your mind.

Experience the personal and intimate relationship with the living Christ and discover the exultant joy that is a result of salvation from the destructive effects of fear, sin and death.

Savior, Jesus my Lord, thank You that I may know You as the Truth who sets me free. Amen.

Understanding to Understand

We know also that the Son of God has come and has given us understanding, so that we may know Him who is true. And we are in Him who is true—even in His Son Jesus Christ. (1 John 5:20)

People often long to understand something better. You might have a hobby that you just can't get enough of. If something is mentioned about it, you listen attentively.

In a world that was flooded with gods and lords, people hungered for a deeper insight into the nature of religion. In biblical times there was little science as we know it today. There was also no secular teaching. In the time of Jesus, rabbis were school teachers and all education and training was the task of the synagogue. As a result, there were few people who had any understanding of the scientific world. Even religious instruction meant learning what other people knew and had learned.

When people began to convert to Christianity, a great thirst for knowledge existed. Who was Jesus Christ? Where did He come from? Why did He come? Who was the Holy Spirit? What was the relationship between the church and the synagogue?

The apostle John gave the answer, "Because we know who Jesus was, He gives us knowledge about every other aspect of life. We see everything through His eyes and interpret everything in relation to Him." Just as the blind man Jesus healed could see through new eyes, so the Christians of that time began to see and understand God's world in a totally new way.

Lord, my Savior, continue to lead me to new depths and heights of insight in my life with You. Amen.

Read Philippians 4:10-20

Linked to the Source of Power

I can do everything through Him who gives me strength. (Philippians 4:13)

As a child of God you have infinite spiritual reserves at your disposal. Since these reserves cannot be seen or calculated, they are often not appreciated or valued according to their true worth.

Your salvation from sin was completed when you trusted Jesus. At the same time, it's up to you to struggle toward godliness. Of course, you get discouraged and frustrated when your strength fails. Remember that Jesus has sent the Holy Spirit to help you. Seeking the Spirit's help is the first step toward growing in holiness.

A successful Christian life does not involve earning acceptance by God. He has accepted you already in Jesus. Now you must lay claim to your identity as a child of God. You do that by trusting God and relying on the Spirit's help to obey God faithfully each day.

When this glorious truth becomes part of your thinking and your actions, your attitude towards life will radically change. You will no longer expect defeat and failure, but you will live with the conviction that you can be victorious over sin through Christ.

Faith is not what you can do for Christ, but what you allow Christ to do in you through the unlimited power of the Holy Spirit. Only then are there no limits to the possibilities in your life.

Thank You, Lord Jesus, for Your patience with me. I am totally dependent on You. Use me as You wish and to Your glory alone. Amen.

He Comes in the Name of God

Hosanna to the Son of David! Blessed is He who comes in the name of the Lord! Hosanna in the highest! (Matthew 21:9)

Jesus' triumphal entry into Jerusalem is celebrated every year by Christians all over the world. Palm branches are waved and hymns are sung to emphasize the magnitude of the occasion.

The shout of the crowds, "Blessed is He who comes in the name of the Lord!" is worthy of us meditating on. God constantly entered into the lives of individuals like Abraham, Moses, Isaiah, the disciples, Paul and those Jesus healed. But He also entered into the world, demonstrating that He isn't limited to individuals.

Through creation He entered the world and created order from chaos. With the exodus out of Egypt, the birth of Jesus Christ, the calming of the storm on the sea of Galilee and Jesus' crucifixion and resurrection, He entered the world. And He is still to come into this world on Judgment Day. God comes to this world because it belongs to Him.

Never think that the world is out of God's reach, not even with the technological advances of our world today. He comes; if only we will see Him, as those crowds did on Palm Sunday. If only we will honor and worship Him. He is not merely a personal God—He is the King who is coming to reign and receive acclamation from His subjects. Start today to give Him the praise and honor His name deserves.

Holy Jesus, we praise and worship You as the One who came in the name of God. Amen.

February

God's Unconditional Love

Dear friends, let us love one another,
for love comes from God. Everyone
who loves has been born of God and
knows God. Whoever does not love
does not know God, because God is love.

~ 1 John 4:7-8

Eternal God, You are Love!
Teach me to love truly, Father.
You are the source of all lasting and true love,
Teach me then, heavenly source of love:
that there is no problem that enough love cannot solve;
that there is no spiritual disturbance that cannot
be healed by love; that there is no alienation
that enough love cannot overcome;
that there is no misunderstanding that
enough love cannot resolve; that there is no wall
of silence that enough love cannot break down;
that there is no trespass that enough love cannot forgive.
Holy Father, through Your grace we now know:
however hopeless the outlook may seem;
however deep the separation may be;
however shocking the transgression—
genuine godly love can resolve it all!
Teach me, loving Lord, to love as You do—
unconditionally, enduring to the end.
Refine and purify my love, even if
I must go through the fire.
Let my love always burn bright and pure
so that I may be a reflection of Your godly love.
In the name of Jesus who loves His people to the end.
Amen.

Jesus Is Our Perfect Example

All the ways of the Lord are loving and faithful for those who keep the demands of His covenant. (Psalm 25:10)

There are a large number of people who look at the Christian faith in God with a great measure of skepticism. Some people call themselves fatalists and place their trust in their own capabilities. For them faith and trust in God's omnipotence over our lives is of little interest. They have little appreciation for the miraculous works of God's creation and His influence over the destinies of people. When something goes wrong in the life of a Christian, these people are quick to say that Christianity has little value.

No one—especially not Jesus Christ—has ever maintained that the life of a Christian is a euphoric or utopian experience. Surrender to Christ does not mean you are immune to the hardships, difficulties and problems of life. It also doesn't bring you freedom from suffering.

Nevertheless, those who remain faithful to God are assured of God's constant presence and love in every circumstance of life. He will be with you to share in your joys and sorrows, to prevent you from struggling, or to help you when you fall. He will support you and help you along the way.

If you will boldly believe and cherish the conviction in your heart that God is faithful, it will bring you peace of mind and calmness of spirit. You can rest safely in Christ's love.

Dear Lord Jesus, I thank You for Your unfailing love and care in my life. Amen.

Read John 1:1-18

God Truly Loves You

From the fullness of His grace we have all received one blessing after another. (John 1:16)

There is a song that asks the questions, "How deep is the ocean? How high is the sky?" No one can give accurate answers to these questions. Likewise, it is impossible for anyone to measure the extent of God's love for us.

But there are times when we feel lonely; when all our hopes have been shattered; when our best-laid plans go wrong and when nothing comes of our biggest dreams. When these things happen, we run the risk of sinking into self-pity, to lose all hope and fall into despair.

Never lose sight of the miracle of God's love. Study the Scriptures and see how He always cares for His people in every possible situation. Just look around you and you will see the evidence of God's grace where you work and live among His children.

God's endless love for you is proven by the fact that He was willing to sacrifice His own Son for your salvation! There is no greater love than that on earth. Deeper than the deepest ocean; higher than the highest sky; wider than the widest plain—that is the extent of God's love for you.

Thank You, Father God, that Your love for me through Jesus Christ is beyond human understanding. Amen.

An Unforgettable Act of Love

"Greater love has no one than this, that he lay down his life for his friends." (John 15:13)

All around the world, some form of Memorial Day or Remembrance Day is observed. We commemorate the bravery, heroism and self-sacrifice of those men and women who, without consideration of their own safety, have laid down their lives for others for the sake of making the world a better place.

Many centuries before the institution of Remembrance Day as we know it, the lone figure of Jesus Christ signified another valiant sacrifice on the cross at Golgotha. Jesus, who gave His life for the whole of humanity, performed the greatest act of sacrificial love that we have ever known. It was a demonstration of bravery that overshadowed anything humanity had previously witnessed. The Son of God also gave His life to make the world a better place, and a sacrifice of this kind is immeasurable.

One of the best ways to commemorate the sacrifice of Christ is to tell of His coming to others and to live a life that demonstrates the same type of love which the Son of God showed us. His sacrifice is an example of what true love looks like.

In our fallen world, there is no shortage of opportunities to make sacrifices. Let your own acts of remembrance be those moments that you choose to walk the same road as the Lord when the opportunity presents itself.

Living Savior, grant that I may honor You by taking the road that You have ordained for me. Amen.

Read Mark 14:3-9

A Glorious Reality

While Jesus was in Bethany, a woman came with an alabaster jar of very expensive perfume. She broke the jar and poured the perfume on His head. (Mark 14:3)

People have different ways of showing their love. Some will spend as much time as possible with their loved one; some will speak the language of love through poetry; some will come up with pleasant little surprises and some will shower their loved ones with many gifts.

The woman in our Scripture passage for today demonstrated her love for Jesus by giving Him an expensive gift. It is possible that Jesus had done something for her that has not been recorded in the Scriptures and she wanted to show her gratefulness. Therefore, in one impulsive gesture of devotion and thankfulness, she poured out the precious oil over Him. Her conduct was in sharp contrast to the opposition that Jesus was experiencing from the religious authorities. They were intent on killing Him; this woman was intent on showering Him with her love.

In what way do you show your love and thankfulness to Jesus? You can do it with prayer and other religious activities; you can give your energy to a particular ministry in His kingdom; you can spend time in acts of charity—like Mother Teresa. You can tell others of your faith and aim to lead people to Jesus. You can join movements that are trying to stop crime and violence. Do as much good as you can, for as many people as you can, for as long as you can. Make a difference today!

Crucified Lord Jesus, I want to prove my love for You in a specific way. Grant that Your Holy Spirit will help me to do this. Amen.

Love without a Price Tag

"For even the Son of Man did not come to be served, but to serve, and to give His life as a ransom for many." (Mark 10:45)

People are often willing to pay a lot of money for an object that they really want. An affluent Iranian, whose hobby was collecting antique furniture, traveled to London to bid on an extraordinarily beautiful eighteenth-century French wooden table. There were many other bidders and the Iranian had to go much higher than expected. When asked if he did not think he had paid too much, he answered with a smile, "Love has no price tag!"

Jesus saw His crucifixion as the price He needed to pay to save us from the bondage of sin. In the ancient world slaves were bought and sold in the same way as ordinary goods. But a slave could be redeemed from bondage if someone was willing to pay the price (ransom money). Some slaves accumulated savings and paid the ransom themselves. The best thing that could happen to a slave was to be set free, but this didn't happen often as the price was simply too high.

Jesus' love for us is so great that He was willing to pay for our freedom with His own life. He cherishes you in love. You mean more to Jesus than that antique French table meant to the wealthy Iranian. Therefore, repeat Paul's words to yourself, "The life I live in the body, I live by faith in the Son of God, who loved me and gave Himself for me" (Gal. 2:20). Say this over and over to yourself until the miracle of it fills your life with joy.

Lord Jesus, let me live with thankfulness and love for You in return for the freedom that Your death has brought me. Amen.

Read Proverbs 21:21-31

True Riches

He who pursues righteousness and love finds life, prosperity and honor. (Proverbs 21:21)

When people make a success of life by being dishonest and deceitful, we often doubt the old saying that says honesty is the best policy. How often do we find people living in luxury who have made their fortunes unethically, while some honest people with integrity seem to struggle just to make a simple living?

In spite of the modern-day emphasis on luxury, wealth and possessions, the fact remains that integrity, a clean conscience and peace of mind are valuable assets that money cannot buy.

Inevitably you will come across those people who have acquired their wealth at the expense of honesty and integrity, and they will always remain dissatisfied and unfulfilled. Motivated by greed, they are always searching for more wealth. Spurred on by a burning sense of competition, they are always looking to be one better than the opposition and even their own colleagues. They always seem to be greedily striving for more, and as a result they are never satisfied with life.

When you follow the teachings and example of the living Christ, if you place Him first, as your most precious possession, you will experience a life of abundant spiritual wealth that far exceeds any of the riches that this world has to offer. Where does your wealth lie: in earthly luxury or in the riches of Christ's love?

Lord Jesus, for me there is no other name above Yours. In You I find love, life and true joy. Amen.

Fight Fear with Love

Surely God is my salvation; I will trust and not be afraid. (Isaiah 12:2)

In times of great danger our human instincts compel us to focus on survival and self-preservation. Very often our minds become confused when fear takes over and we find it difficult to think clearly. It is in circumstances like these that we run the risk of being overwhelmed by the difficulties that confront us.

It is important to know that God's love is all-embracing and encompasses every facet of your life. He constantly watches over you; He is always ready to listen to your cry of distress, and He is with you at all times. When you do feel that God is far away, it could be that you have distanced yourself from Him in some way—not the other way around.

In spite of anything that may happen to you, always remember that Jesus the living Christ offers you salvation. He died so that you could be saved, and He gave you His Holy Spirit to carry you through all the difficulties and distresses of life—especially those issues that you cannot resolve in your own strength.

When trials are staring you in the face, do not yield to the temptation to give in because of fear. Open your heart to Jesus; He has overcome the evil one. Put your trust in the Lord and remember, "There is no fear in love. But perfect love drives out fear" (1 John 4:18).

Holy Master, I place my complete faith in Your ability to drive out all my fear. Amen.

Read Zechariah 9:1-10

Humility and Love

Rejoice greatly, O Daughter of Zion! See, your King comes to you, righteous and having salvation, gentle and riding on a donkey, on a colt, the foal of a donkey. (Zechariah 9:9)

Many people feel we are living in a time of aggression. There is definitely sufficient evidence to support this viewpoint when we consider the international and national conflict all around us. We can take this even further when we look with concern at the competitive aggression between opponents in the business world and on the sports field. The number of incidents of road rage and aggression amongst motorists is on the increase. There is also elevated interpersonal aggression and all of this contributes to an unsatisfactory state of affairs.

When Jesus entered Jerusalem on the first Palm Sunday, the people were aggressive. They were expecting the promised Messiah to arrive as a great warrior who would lead them in a revolution against their Roman oppressors. Instead they saw someone riding into the city on the back of a donkey—the usual mount for a peace-loving leader of the time.

In that time the Lord Jesus' love won the battle against aggression. Through His followers He must and can achieve the same outcome in this day and age. Ask yourself: Am I contributing to His gentleness and love? Or am I on the side of senseless aggression?

Humble but exalted Savior, thank You that Your Spirit is helping me to be more and more like You. Amen.

The Healing Power of Love (1)

"I will give them a heart to know Me, that I am the LORD. They will be My people, and I will be their God, for they will return to Me with all their heart." (Jeremiah 24:7)

The brain is the part of your body that deals with knowledge. It is the rational organ that absorbs data, stores it, connects the various parts of the body and makes decisions. If you need to increase your knowledge about something, you simply store away the relevant information in your brain and use it whenever needed.

Knowing God is somewhat different. You know Him with your heart. You can take in many facts and ideas about Him in your mind, but it is in your heart that you come to know Him as a Person. God promised that the exiles in Babylon would know Him in a new way after they had repented and confessed, and sought His forgiveness. As a result of their change of heart, deep self-examination and a new yearning for God they would attain a new knowledge of Him.

If your heart is hardened, bitter, or inclined to wrongdoing, you likely don't know God. If you are judgmental, nurse grievances, or are involved in anything that is in direct opposition to the will of God, then your heart will be separated from Him and it will become impossible to know Him. You learn to know Him only when you place Him first in everything. Christ spelt it out for us, "Love the Lord your God with all your heart and with all your soul and with all your mind and with all your strength" (Mark 12:30). Do you love God this way?

Help me, merciful Father, to love You more each day. Amen.

Read Ezekiel 18:14-23

The Healing Power of Love (2)

"If a wicked man turns away from all the sins he has committed and keeps all My decrees and does what is just and right, he will surely live." (Ezekiel 18:21)

The issue of sin and punishment has been a matter of concern over the centuries. There are those who think that evildoers should never be fully forgiven for their transgressions. On the other hand, social reformers plead for forgiveness and rehabilitation. In human relationships people tend to judge and nurse grievances as a result of their reluctance to forgive and forget. This often leads to miserable lives for both the evildoer and the victim.

The glorious miracle of our Christian faith is that, in spite of our fickle nature, our couldn't-care-less attitude and our disobedience, God still loves us with a love that is both forgiving and cleansing. It makes no difference who we are or what we have done; if we are willing to renounce our sins and take refuge in God in true repentance, He will receive us with the loving forgiveness of a Father.

Perhaps you are plagued by remorse and self-recrimination for an action that you feel particularly guilty about. Or maybe you have been hurt and condemned because of someone else's wrong words or actions against you.

Remind yourself once again of the extent of God's forgiving love and take refuge in Him as your source of strength to forgive those who have hurt you. Do this and you will know the freedom of reconciliation in the Lord.

Allow me, O Holy Spirit, to live with You in the love of God. Amen.

Reflect God's Love

Who is a God like You, who forgives the transgression of the remnant of His inheritance? You do not stay angry forever but delight to show mercy. (Micah 7:18)

In your circle of friends, companions and acquaintances, you perhaps know someone who always forgives, regardless of what happened, someone who never holds a grudge or remains angry, who always maintains a loving attitude. Can we honestly say that *we* possess these characteristics?

If we want to be completely honest and sincere, our answer will be "No." We are fallible and our human nature is vulnerable. Consequently we allow our dispositions, feelings and reactions to dominate our thoughts in certain circumstances.

In spite of our weaknesses, however, we can delight ourselves in the knowledge that our God is a God of love, a God who cares and forgives and a Father who loves us with an eternal love.

Such a love can never be paid back, but it can be paid forward through our witness and behavior, and this is our Christian duty. With the help of the Holy Spirit we must allow the love of God and the living Christ to be reflected in our lives in every circumstance, to the glory of the triune God.

Loving Lord Jesus Christ, in whose life I see everything I fail to be, through Your grace let the light of Your love shine in me. Amen.

Read Proverbs 10:20-32

Speak the Truth in Love

The lips of the righteous know what is fitting, but the mouth of the wicked only what is perverse. (Proverbs 10:32)

Some people are careless in their use of words. They do not consider whether it is the right moment to say something or if they might offend or hurt someone. They always boast that they are "straight talkers" while in reality they are just downright rude. These people usually walk a lonely road and wherever possible, are avoided by others.

How you present the truth is always important. Sometimes you have to speak a truth that the recipient would rather not hear. However it is expressed, it will cause pain. When this is the case you need to choose your words extremely carefully. The spirit in which you express yourself is also of great importance. People who understand the impact of words use them to help, encourage, comfort and heal others. Unpleasant things have to be said sometimes, but let them always be expressed firmly, kindly and sympathetically. This will reduce the pain that will inevitably be caused.

When you must speak out directly, as a Christian it is advisable to spend quiet time in the presence of the Lord beforehand and seek the leading of the Holy Spirit. By doing so you can execute your unpleasant task with grace, dignity and love. As a "righteous person" who needs to say "the right thing" in a difficult situation, you can trust in the Holy Spirit to lead you.

Holy Spirit of God, I humbly request that You anoint my tongue and my words when I have to speak out in truth. Amen.

Love Demands a High Standard

Do not gloat when your enemy falls; when he stumbles, do not let your heart rejoice. (Proverbs 24:17)

All too often, people revel in the disasters that befall others. When someone who stands in high repute in the community makes an unfortunate mistake, some people rejoice in his embarrassment and humiliation. When an adversary or enemy suffers a setback, it brings great joy and satisfaction to his rival. How often do people nod their heads sympathetically and smile knowingly when the world of a successful person collapses.

The foundation of the Christian faith is love! You have been commanded by the living Christ to love God first and to love your neighbor as yourself. John puts it very clearly, "If anyone says, 'I love God,' yet hates his brother, he is a liar. For anyone who does not love his brother, whom he has seen, cannot love God, whom he has not seen" (1 John 4:20).

It is not at all easy to love someone you don't like and for whom you have no respect. This is normally far beyond our human capabilities and the requirement is usually too much for us. It is therefore essential to submit and devote ourselves to Christ and invoke the indwelling power and influence of the Holy Spirit.

Allow Him to take control of your thoughts and emotions and lead you so that you will see all people through the eyes of Jesus and be able to love them with a Christian love. When you do this, you will find that your life will take on new meaning.

Holy Lord Jesus, help me to love as You love. Amen.

Read Jeremiah 31:1-9

Everlasting Love

"I have loved you with an everlasting love; I have drawn you with loving-kindness." (Jeremiah 31:3)

Many young people who have been smitten by first love promise to love each other forever. A day or two later there is a small disagreement and it is all over. Soon afterwards they promise the same thing to someone else.

Conflict is one of the characteristics of romantic love, but steadfastness is the benchmark of God's love. He made a covenant on Mount Sinai concerning this. God carried on loving His people. However fickle their love for Him, He never wavered. However weak their faith in Him, His love for them never lessened.

God loves you and me in the same way. He loved your ancestors and He will love your descendants. He loved you when you were ill and when you were glowingly healthy. He loved you in the prime of your youth and He will still love you in your old age. He loves you now and He will love you when you are at death's door. And when this life is over His love will unfold in all its glory.

God will love you when the sun shines and life smiles at you. He will also love you when you bite the dust. He loves you when everyone around you does, and when you are feeling lonely and sad. In Jesus Christ He gave expression to that eternal love in the flesh and blood. God expects you to love in the same way, and the more you do, the better and more complete a person you will become. Keep a watchful eye on the quality of your love; Jesus is your perfect example and your standard.

Lord Jesus, who is love, fill my life with Your love. Amen.

Not Even Death ...

My heart is glad and my tongue rejoices; my body also will rest secure, because You will not abandon me to the grave. (Psalm 16:9-10)

There are three aspects of death that cause people to fear. The first is physical pain and suffering. Some people die in peace, but many do not. We fear that we will be tormented by illness. Our next fear is that we will descend into a bottomless pit where there is only darkness—forever.

Our greatest fear, however, is being separated from our loved ones. The loss of these relationships is too awful to contemplate. Just the thought of the loneliness is unnerving and we cannot even think about being separated from them. They make life on earth worth living.

Christians who follow Jesus Christ do not have to fear this isolation. His resurrection reassures us that He is in control of the life hereafter. The one thing, above all else, that should dominate your thoughts when you think about death is that Jesus will be there. He will never abandon you or forsake you (see Heb. 13:5).

He will ensure that you cope with this period in your life to the best of your ability. He will accompany you through the experience of death. He will keep you safe and love you forever. He will lead you into the glory of the kingdom of the Father, where there is only light and love and where you will be reunited with the ones you loved so much on earth—and who loved you.

Loving Lord Jesus, be with me every step of the way when it is my time to die. Amen.

Read John 6:1-15

A Gift of Love

Here is a boy with five small barley loaves and two small fish, but how far will they go among so many? (John 6:9)

Everyone who prepares food, especially mothers, knows how to make a little go a long way. People develop this art through sheer necessity. Every crumb must be put to good use.

The boy in our Scripture passage for today had a miraculous experience. It was an amazing miracle for everyone, but for him it was a day he would remember for the rest of his life. Each time that the story was told, he most probably said, "Yes, it was my lunch that He used!" He gave what he had to Jesus. Although needy in his own hunger, he nevertheless placed his bread and fish in the Lord's hands.

Bring whatever you have and offer it to Jesus. However trifling your gift may be, give it to Jesus. Bring Him your personal gifts and allow Him to multiply them and use them to bring hope and meaning into the lives of others. Bring your financial resources and allow Him to bless them. Bring your professional skills and knowledge. Bring your abilities, your family relationships, your home, your capacity for caring, your faith, your position in the community, your job, your leadership and influence, your intellect and your enthusiasm—however modest, humble or undeveloped they may be. Put them in the hands of the Master and watch Him go to work.

Are you willing to cooperate?

Holy Spirit of mercy, make my today a blessing to others. Amen.

Humility Is a Fruit of Love

After that, He poured water into a basin and began to wash His disciples' feet, drying them with the towel that was wrapped around Him. (John 13:5)

We will never fully grasp what the atmosphere in the Upper Room must have been like on the eve of Jesus' crucifixion. There were disciples who must have irritated Him endlessly with self-centeredness. Others would flee from Him when He needed their support most. One of them would betray Him to the authorities, opening the door to His barbaric torture and crucifixion.

Jesus knew exactly what was going to happen and He also knew how each disciple was going to react and behave. He knew that He would soon have to endure the bitter hatred of His enemies—completely alone!

It was in the tension of this moment that Jesus taught one of His greatest and most moving lessons on humility and love. He humbled Himself and performed the servile task of washing the disciples' feet. He took on the role of a servant and served these people—one of whom was to betray Him.

There are occasions when you will feel imposed upon, hurt or wrongly judged. When this happens, you should not retaliate with revenge, but rather follow the example of the Master. As it happened in the past, so it will come about again today: Christian love and humility will be triumphant!

Help me, O Spirit of mercy, to follow the example of the Master every day and in all circumstances. Amen.

Read John 14:15-31

Love: The Very Best

"If anyone loves Me, he will obey My teaching. My Father will love him, and We will come to him and make Our home with him." (John 14:23)

Most people want the best out of life, but very few people are prepared to put their best into it. This is not because of selfish motives, but purely because they have never taken the trouble to discover what is best for them. They simply accept what life has to offer.

What you see as the best for yourself is determined by the standards you set, because you will never be able to reach higher than that. If you have a low expectancy, your life will be unproductive. But if you have faith, energy and concentration, you will be blessed and enriched in every way imaginable.

Most people are satisfied with limited objectives because their horizons are limited. They reduce their goals to personal ambition and fail to realize that the person and teachings of Jesus Christ can offer them the best of all—a relationship with God Himself!

When you experience the power of God in your life through the indwelling Christ, you attain the best that life offers. He leads those who are confused, gives strength to the weak, brings comfort to those who are sad, faith to the unsure; and satisfaction in everyday life. He also brings an awareness of eternal life—the perception that the story of human life is not a brief tale but an integral part of God's eternity. When you know God and His love, you have the very best.

Thank You for living in me—I give You all the glory. Amen.

Grow in Christ's Love

*Having loved His own who were in the world,
He now showed them the full extent of His love. (John 13:1)*

It is very easy to lose your self-confidence. Sometimes everything goes well and you feel a rising of faith in what you are able to achieve. In times like these, life is a special experience. But suddenly, for no apparent reason, you begin to lose your self-confidence and start to experience a shattering feeling of incompetence. You convince yourself that you will never again be successful in anything you attempt. To add to your dejection, you start thinking that God doesn't care about you anymore, and that He has given up on you.

One of the amazing truths that Scripture reveals is that, even though Jesus knew that His disciples were going to let Him down, He still loved them and gave them responsibility. Christ saw past their failures and incompetence and knew what they could become through the power and anointing of the Holy Spirit. He persevered in His love for them in spite of their weaknesses and imperfections.

The principle that was laid down then, long ago, remains true and applicable today. God knows you for who you are; nothing can be hidden from Him. But He does not stop loving you and leading you on to a richer and more purposeful life. You may have lost confidence in yourself, but the living Christ will continue to use you as a channel for His love and mercy in the world around you.

*Through my love for You, Lord Jesus,
I grow daily in self-confidence. Amen.*

Read John 14:15-31

Love Breaks Down Barriers

"If you love Me, you will obey what I command." (John 14:15)

Christianity is going through a difficult time. The existence of countless sects that all claim scriptural authority, the rejection in certain regions of the world of Christian thinking, the gospel's transition into an era that is socially and politically correct, the infiltration into the church of forces that aim to bring about its downfall: all these things conspire to confuse disciples who already find it difficult to know what to believe.

Thank the King of the church that in the midst of all the prevailing religious confusion, there is a healthy core of believers who place the living Christ first. They may differ greatly in doctrine and their traditions may be divergent and even irreconcilable, but in their hearts there is a great love for Jesus. It is this love that constitutes the core of the true church of Christ.

Christian love should be expressed in practical ways. The term "social love" is a contradiction, because true Christian love is always concerned with the lonely, the afflicted and the underprivileged. It is an attitude that is inspired by the love of Christ.

If you are in the company of those who sincerely love Christ, you will find you have the ability to rise above differences and you will be more open-minded. You will no longer judge fellow Christians by their dogmatic statements, but by the depth and quality of their love for Christ and others.

Lord of love, let my life be under the control
of the Holy Spirit and Your law of love. Amen.

The Meaning of Love

"Now that I ... have washed your feet, you also should wash one another's feet. I have set you an example that you should do as I have done for you." (John 13:14-15)

Throughout the period of His earthly ministry, Jesus showed people by word and deed how God expected them to live. Each lesson was based on love in the highest sense of the word: love that was willing to make sacrifices to reveal its sincerity.

One of the most exceptional and touching examples of this took place on the evening before Jesus' crucifixion, in the Upper Room where He and His disciples had come together for the Last Supper. On this occasion He took on the role of a servant and performed the humble task of washing the disciples' feet—including Judas, who was to betray Him just a short while later.

Certain people scoffed at this act of the Master as a sign of slavery. On the contrary, however, this humble deed is a demonstration of the gracious charity that is a very real mark of the Christian faith. It ought to be the aim and purpose of every follower of Jesus to imitate Him in this.

Learn from this what the true meaning of love is; follow the example of Jesus and, in so doing, you will be a true ambassador of Christ in a world that desperately needs to understand Christian love.

Grant that by Your example we may live out lives in a manner that reflects your love. Amen.

Read Matthew 27:32-44

Love Will Triumph

Those who passed by hurled insults at him, shaking their heads and saying … "Come down from the cross, if You are the Son of God!" (Matthew 27:39-40)

When we read the story of the first Easter Sunday in the Bible, we are inclined to leave Good Friday and the anxiety it evokes behind us as quickly as we can. We would much rather relive the ecstasy of the Resurrection. By doing this, we often lose sight of the fact that our duty as Christians is to commemorate not only our faith in the Resurrection, but also in the death of Jesus.

Throughout the centuries, since the founding of the church of Jesus Christ, there have always been people intent on sabotaging the work of the Lord by belittling the efforts of those trying to sow the seeds of true faith. Their intention is to create doubt in the minds of those whose faith, for whatever reason, has grown weak.

Those undermining influences are still at work in the church itself. Today, just as much as any other time in the course of history, the Christian faith is under fire through the modern equivalent of passers-by in the streets around Golgotha. They still insult Jesus and shake their heads in disapproval in an effort to drive a wedge between the crucified Christ and His faithful followers.

Our duty is to show the love of God to all people. We follow Jesus who showed us what true love looks like. This is may be difficult, but we will never be put to shame if we faithfully follow our leader.

Holy Spirit of Truth, help me to prove that I am not afraid to confess Jesus and defend His cause by showing true love. Amen.

Read Matthew 24:3-14

Christians Without Love

"Because of the increase of wickedness, the love of most will grow cold." (Matthew 24:12)

The world is full of nice people who call themselves Christians, but they would be just as pleasant if they called themselves something else. They have received the Christian tradition as their heritage and they accept the teachings of Jesus Christ when it is convenient for them. They travel through life on the periphery of faith and contribute little to the work of the Master. They rob themselves of the opportunity for true repentance, the forgiveness of sins and indwelling of the Holy Spirit, as well as the presence of Christ in their lives.

God does not acknowledge "pretend" Christians. Accepting Christ as your Savior means to also embrace Him as your Lord. Faith results in obedience and identifying closely with Him. It is essential in turn to put Him first in your thoughts and deeds, that you allow yourself to be formed and reformed by the gracious influence of His Holy Spirit. Without this surrender and dedication you are just pleasing yourself instead of pleasing God.

The difference between a "pretend" Christian and a true Christian is that the former has not trusted in Christ, and lacks the influence of the Spirit in their life. The Scriptures teach us, "No one can enter the Kingdom of God unless he is born of water and the Spirit" (John 3:5). Everyone who affirms a genuine faith in Christ and confesses it is able to experience the joy and love of being a child of God.

Jesus, at my rebirth I accept You into my life so that I may have a living and sincere faith. Amen.

Read Luke 24:25-35

Love During an Ordinary Meal

He took bread, gave thanks, broke it and began to give it to them. Then their eyes were opened and they recognized Him. (Luke 24:30-31)

It is true that God comes to us at particular times. He comes to some people during a worship service or at a spiritual gathering. He has appeared to many young people at youth camps and claimed their love and service. Others have met Him during adult baptism, or when having Communion.

He came to a house in Emmaus when He was invited one night to stay over. It had been a memorable day and a very long walk home. The stranger led the men into truths they had not known before. After the long walk they were probably hungry, so He spoke the blessing and broke the bread, and suddenly they all knew: It was Jesus! It was just a simple meal. There was nothing special about the food, as they had been away for several days. But it did not matter. Jesus made Himself completely at home in their house! They came to know Him while they were enjoying a very ordinary meal.

God can come to you at any time and at any opportunity. It does not have to be a special time. It does not even have to be a religious or spiritual occasion. God comes to touch your everyday life with His love. He comes to share everything with you: food, conversation, joy and the cross that you bear. He comes to bless your ordinary daily life with love. All you have to do is invite Him in.

Lord of life and love, touch my daily life with Your presence and love. Amen.

Love and the Law (1)

But they rested on the Sabbath in obedience to the commandment. (Luke 23:56)

The crucifixion was over and the threat for the temple leaders had been eliminated. Jesus' body was taken down from the cross, according to the requirements of the Law, while the bodies of the other two men were left as prey for the vultures. All the formalities had been taken into consideration and now, because it was the Sabbath, the people rested according to the demands of the Law and their religious practices. God had commanded that the Sabbath should be a day of rest and in the eyes of the Jewish leaders, nothing could be permitted to break this command, not even love, empathy or mercy.

In their hypocritical approach to life, they found it permissible, however, to disregard all the other commands when they conspired against Jesus to bring about His death. Once again love, empathy and mercy were completely disregarded in their efforts to uphold the Law at the cost of the life of the very One who had come from God to reveal the true meaning of God's Word to humanity.

In your Christian walk it is critical that you do not become enslaved to form and ritual, rules and regulations, foregoing the love of Christ. While order in every area of life is essential, it must always be established in love. This is the way of our living Master and it must also be our way.

Lord Jesus, teach us the art of living in submission to love. Amen.

Read Luke 23:44-56

Love and the Law (2)

But they rested on the Sabbath in obedience to the commandment. (Luke 23:56)

The matter had been dealt with successfully! This Jesus of Nazareth, whose ministry of love, compassion and forgiveness that was such a threat to the religious leaders was now over; He had been crucified with two common criminals. Now He was dead and His body was safely buried in a grave. Their task was complete. Their lifestyle was no longer under threat by this man for whom love had meant a great deal. Now that everything was complete and they had disposed of Christ's body before the arrival of the Sabbath, these so-called religious people could rest "according to the Law."

Every Christian can learn a lesson from the events that followed the crucifixion. While there is a need for rules and regulations to ensure proper order in the affairs of the church, it should never be the case that the love of Jesus Christ is overshadowed or even eliminated.

All too often the letter of the Law takes precedence over compassion, mercy and forgiveness; all too often the rigidity of church law is blindly applied, excluding any spontaneous display of the love of Christ.

Justice should always be tempered by mercy to ensure that the mistakes of the religious leaders in the time of Jesus are never repeated. Then the love that Jesus died for will be freely available to everyone and will never again be relegated to second place in the church of Christ.

Lord Jesus, Your love is greater than the human mind can conceive. Grant that it will never be lost to us. Amen.

Love and the Law (3)

But they rested on the Sabbath in obedience to the commandment. (Luke 23:56)

After the crucifixion, the evil one had taken over the hearts of the people and brought about the death of the one God had sent to earth to demonstrate His love. The threat to their hypocritical way of life was silenced. They were not concerned about the blood on their hands and in their false piety they rested on the Sabbath, as the Law required.

These people, who adhered fanatically to the letter of the Law of Moses, could not (or would not) see that they had disobeyed the true Law of the love that was manifest in Jesus, the living Christ.

The Gospels offer examples of incidents where the temple leaders were critical and strongly judgmental of love, mercy, healing and forgiveness brought about in any way other than the manner in which they had interpreted the scope of the Law.

Christians must learn from this and ensure that nothing is ever allowed, under the guise of religious legalism, to predominate over the compassionate love of God, as demonstrated in the life and ministry of Jesus. Jesus' liberating love can also set us free from the letter of the Law and from empty religious form.

Heavenly Father, grant that nothing will ever cause me to ignore the Law of love. Amen.

Read Proverbs 26:18-28

Let Your Love Do the Talking

Without wood a fire goes out; without gossip a quarrel dies down. (Proverbs 26:20)

Idle words and gossip are probably the main causes of broken relationships. In certain instances these are mean or vindictive, while in others they are just inconsiderate. Whatever the case may be, the end result is always painful. The damage has been done and it is almost impossible to undo.

The Scriptures warn us to be careful about what we say to avoid the consequent difficulty and pain of unguarded statements and assumptions. People often justify their remarks by saying they are innocent, or that they did not mean any harm, but the fact remains that we need to be extremely careful about what we say and the way we say it.

One of the best ways to hold your tongue is to obey Jesus' command to love others as He has loved us. Remember that by hurting your fellow man, you also hurt Christ. If you take His command to love seriously, you will realize that you have been called to share His attitudes in your approach to and behavior towards other people. This leaves no room for anything that can hurt or harm anyone.

Earnestly seek the help of the Holy Spirit in your efforts to conform your life to Christ. Faithfully follow the example of Jesus and become a channel of His love in all your relationships with other people.

Jesus, source of love, grant me the grace to control my tongue by offering myself as a channel of Your love. Amen.

Love Has No Place for the Ego

The Lord said, "You have been concerned about this vine, though you did not tend it or make it grow. … Should I not be concerned about [Nineveh]?" (Jonah 4:10-11)

The Holy Spirit of God is at work in society. There are increasing numbers of people in search of a deeper knowledge of the living Christ. More people are becoming involved in prayer groups, Bible study groups and care groups. People for whom the Christian faith used to mean attending a service on Sundays, are now very involved in mid-week church activities such as Bible schools, conferences, retreats and so on. All of this allows the focus to fall on the Lord.

This kind of zeal is admirable and must definitely be encouraged. However, there is a danger to avoid if you are truly seeking a life of fulfillment in Jesus Christ. The enthusiastic Christian disciple has a tendency to feel sorry for those who are not involved in these kinds of activities. Your duty as a Christian is to go much further than compassion. Discipleship means showing the love of Jesus to all people. Your responsibility is not only to witness Christ through your words and life to unbelievers, but also to help fellow believers grow in their faith.

Draw strength from your meeting with the Master in your group context so that you can go out among other people and extend charity and mercy to them in the midst of the rush of everyday life.

Holy Lord Jesus, grant that I will never be so busy searching for You that I neglect to introduce You to others. Amen.

March

His Path of Love

"For God so loved the world that
He gave His one and only Son, that
whoever believes in Him shall not
perish but have eternal life."

~ John 3:16

Holy Lord Jesus our Savior of love,
We praise and thank You that through
Your coming to our world we have
come to know God as the God of love.
He loved us so much that He sent You so
that we could come to know Him as
the God of everlasting love!
Glorified Savior, through Your life
we know what love truly is.
We know it unshakably through the example
You set for us: no matter
how hopeless the situation might seem,
however irreconcilable the
estrangement might appear,
however horrific the trespass might be—
God-given love can always overcome it.
Teach us, Lord Jesus, to love as You loved—
unconditionally and for all time.
Make our love holy; refine and purify it,
even if it is through fire.
Let our love glow brighter so that we will be a
reflection of Your holy and divine love in our world.
In the name of Him who leads us to love,
Amen.

Rest in God's Love

Come and see what God has done, how awesome His works in man's behalf! (Psalm 66:5)

Human thoughts and emotions can be very inconsistent. A sudden change in emotion can cause you to feel joyful the one moment and sad the next. In a surprisingly short space of time you can change from being hopeful to hopeless, strong to weak, positive and self-assured to uncertain and indecisive. Your whole approach to life can change through events, personal success or crisis—even through weather conditions. It's easy to feel depressed on an overcast day.

Throughout your life and in every conceivable situation you may find yourself in, it is necessary to strive to find and maintain a measure of stability in order to handle each day's demands and challenges. In the face of the uncertainty in the world today, you need to hold on to one or other firm hope so that you can find peace of mind.

To achieve this goal just look around you and take note of the incredible wonder of God's creation. Absorb the beauty of nature, music and art; be amazed at developments in science.

But, above all, remember that God has revealed His love for you through the sacrifice of His Son on the cross at Golgotha. Hold on unflinchingly to this truth and find peace of mind.

Jesus, source of true love, visit us with Your salvation and let us rest in Your love. Amen.

Read Psalm 13:1-6

God Has Been Good to Me

I will sing to the Lord, for He has been good to me. (Psalm 13:6)

A wise person once remarked that most people are as happy as they choose to be. But many people are not happy at all. They complain about the economy, politics, the cost of living, the world's problems and the weather. They even complain about complaining!

Our Scripture reading for today was written by David—and he had first-hand experience of trouble. It came at him from all sides; and some he brought upon himself. He also knew sickness. Despite all the things he could have complained about, he still testified of God's goodness, which was so good that he could sing and rejoice about it.

We also can sing about how good God has been to us. Or we can complain about our problems. You must decide. It is, however, far better to rejoice over God's goodness. View your problems from the right perspective. Behind every problem is a God who lovingly cares for you; who provides for you, redeems you and sincerely loves you.

God was good to David, Paul, Peter and John. He was good to those who were martyred for their faith in Christ. He loves the believer who loves Him. He loves you too. He gave you life and health; He has saved you from dangerous situations, and has continually surrounded you with His love. He has given you hope and salvation. God has been good to you—sing about it!

Give thanks to the Lord, for He is good;
His love endures forever! (Psalm 106:1)

Thankful Prayer

Devote yourselves to prayer, being watchful and thankful. (Colossians 4:2)

People will devote themselves to many things. Some people might dedicate themselves to their jobs or to a particular hobby. Others will devote themselves to their education or a particular way of thinking. While there may be some value in these things, they have limited eternal worth.

The Apostle Paul writes to the church in Colossae, and encourages them to not be devoted to worldly things but to prayer. He instructs them to be disciplined and consistent in coming before the Father, bearing their concerns to their Him. You can benefit greatly from following this instruction. The Lord's door is always open, and He is always ready to hear your every request.

Perhaps you are already consistent in your prayer life, frequently making requests in your private prayers as well as when gathered with God's people in worship. What do you then have to learn from this verse? Notice the manner that Paul prescribes for our prayer—being thankful.

Thankfulness changes our perspective; it will lift our eyes from the worries of this world and direct them to the God who faithfully provides for us. It transforms prayer from a time of laboriously listing requests to an oasis of refreshment. It reminds us that God has been good to us, and He is worthy of all of our praise and thanks.

*Father God, we thank You for Your faithfulness to us.
Thank You for the new mercies we see each and every day.
We are so grateful that Your kindness never fails. Amen.*

Read Colossians 4:1-9

Imprisoned for Christ

Pray for us, too, that God may open a door for our message, so that we may proclaim the mystery of Christ, for which I am in chains. (Colossians 4:3)

Through serving Christ, some people become involved in activities they would never otherwise have pursued. Mother Teresa became world famous by serving the poor and suffering on the streets of Calcutta. Billy Graham became a household name through the massive gatherings he held in the name of Christ. Dietrich Bonhoeffer, a German theologian, became a martyr when his faith led him to become an accomplice in an attempt to assassinate Hitler.

The apostle Paul was a zealous Pharisee who became a missionary for Christ, which landed him in prison. He then used his time in prison to write letters with instructions and encouragement to the churches he had planted. The gospel he spread brought freedom to thousands, but caused the loss of his own freedom. And yet, out of that prison cell came incredible teachings.

You never know where discipleship to Christ might lead you. It takes some people to the ends of the earth. For some it leads to great accomplishments in music, prayer, writing and teaching. But you can't prescribe to Christ where He must lead you. You must open yourself up to Him. His calling may not lead you to fame—more often it will lead to isolation, poverty and loneliness. The key is always obedience to Him—even if your obedience leads you to a prison cell!

Savior and Master, help me to obey You, despite the cost. Amen.

The Comforting Love of God

Keep yourselves in God's love as you wait for the mercy of our Lord Jesus Christ to bring you to eternal life. (Jude 21)

Even though the Christian believer has the glorious promise of eternal life, the death of a loved one leaves a painful wound in your heart when you have to get over the shock and work through the reality of the loss. Even though you can rejoice in the fact that those who have died in the faith have gone on to receive their reward in God's eternal kingdom, what do you do with the loneliness in your life in the meantime?

When the Master prepared His disciples for His return to His Father, He poured His peace over them. At the same time He gave His comforting Holy Spirit so that God's all-encompassing love could fill their lives on earth, until His love would lift them up into God's kingdom in heaven.

This same peace and love is Christ's wonderful gift to you. Trust Him and open your life and heart to Him; allow Him to show you where to serve; offer your love and compassion to others so that the living Christ can work in and through you for the good of His people. In this way you will remain in the never-ending embrace of God's love. He will lead you through your disappointments until you enjoy God's glory in eternity.

"Breathe, O breathe Thy loving Spirit into every troubled breast! Let us all in Thee inherit, let us find the promised rest." Amen.

Read Colossians 3:5-17

Thankfulness

Be thankful. (Colossians 3:15)

There are people who find it very difficult to show their gratitude. They also find it difficult to *feel* grateful. They fear that they will then be obligated to acknowledge that they owe the person they are grateful to.

Many of our Christian experiences are born out of the gratitude we feel toward God for what He has done for us. The Christians in Colossae were encouraged to be thankful. By hearing the gospel and believing in Jesus, God led them out of heathenism and idolatry into a healthy, living and loving way of life. They were also placed in a loving, truthful and forgiving Christian fellowship. In short: they received salvation through Christ and were filled with God's Holy Spirit. There was so much for them to be grateful for.

We also have so much to thank God for. He provides for our daily needs, however meager it is at times. Thank God for your health and safety, for your family and faithful friends and all the other good things that God has provided for you. Be especially thankful for the salvation through Jesus Christ that you now experience. Thank Him for your Bible, your church, and your pastor. Be thankful for all the help God gave you when you were in trouble, or when you were upset or depressed.

Thank God that He has forgiven your sins. Be thankful that you can look forward to renewal on the other side of this life in the Father's house with Jesus Christ.

Gracious Father God, besides all the other gifts You grant me, please grant me the gift of a thankful heart. Amen.

One Path to Wealth

Let the word of Christ dwell in you richly. (Colossians 3:16)

Many people are obsessed with money. They think about it day and night. Everything they do is measured against what it will cost them or how much they will gain. They haven't mastered money; money has mastered them.

There are many forms of wealth. In Charles Dickens' famous *A Christmas Carol* the miser, Scrooge, had a lot of money, but was miserable and nasty to others. His clerk, Bob Cratchit, who could barely make a living, had a loving family that he valued far above all Scrooge's treasures. He was by far the richer of the two.

Paul considered his new life in Christ as his greatest asset. He often wrote about the "riches in Christ." When you hear about Christ and He speaks to you it is a source of wealth that you can draw on and cherish. If you regularly meditate on God's Word you are connected to an immeasurable source of wealth. If that same Word remains in you, it will enrich you more than any gold mine can. Spiritual wealth does not erode through inflation. Unlike a gold mine, it doesn't have a limited lifespan.

As a believer in Christ it is important to realize the different forms of wealth you have access to. Knowledge, wisdom and health are all valuable. So are your family, friends and fellow believers. Let Christ's words lead you in determining which type of wealth you regard most.

Holy Savior, help me to appreciate spiritual riches so that I will not desire things of no eternal value. Amen.

Read John 9:24-34

Does God Listen to You?

We know that God does not listen to sinners. He listens to the godly man who does His will. (John 9:31)

A Jewish man went to the Wailing Wall every day for twenty years to pray to God. Someone noticed this and asked how it felt to always pray there. He replied, "It feels like I'm praying to a wall." It's possible that sometimes your prayers to God also feel like this.

The early Israelites believed that the only way to get to God was through living a good and God-honoring life. "God doesn't listen to sinners" was the common wisdom of those days.

Jesus proved that this is not true. God does listen to sinners! Every person is a sinner and God does listen to prayers, so He listens exclusively to sinners. He listens especially to those who know that they are sinners and who bow before Him in repentance and humility. Righteous people, good people and strong people don't have more of a hold on God than anyone else.

The fact is that God longs to hear your prayer, whether you are a hero of the faith or a sinner, young or old, well educated or uneducated. He rejoices in hearing your prayers, whether you pray with confidence or find it difficult to put a sentence together. God does not prefer the eloquence of those with a gift for speaking. God rejoices in receiving your prayers, even if they are blundering and simple utterances that are confused and mixed up. Whatever your situation, "pray without ceasing."

Lord Jesus, teach me to pray! Amen.

No Condemnation: Only Love!

Therefore, there is now no condemnation for those who are in Christ Jesus. (Romans 8:1)

It is surprising how many people live their whole lives terrified of God's condemnation. They live under a cloud of despondency and are convinced that God is waiting to punish them for every little faux pas.

To maintain such a view of God makes your religion a burden. It creates a destructive attitude toward life because you can't appreciate what is good and beautiful if you are scared of the One who created all beautiful things.

It is love, not fear that brings out the best in you. This is one of the things Jesus demonstrated and taught. If you live in fear of condemnation, you can't possibly give your best or grow to spiritual maturity. Fear might prevent you from doing certain destructive things, but it is only love that will remove the desire to do them. In this context Christ no longer condemns you, but He requires your faithfulness through the dynamic power of love.

When you have been freed from deadly fear through Christ's love and mercy, your view of life expands. You realize what you can become while, through the power of Jesus, you undergo a deepening of your love for Him. You are gloriously freed from all destructive fear of condemnation.

Thank You, Lord Jesus, for freeing me from all destructive fear and for the gift of Your indescribable love. Amen.

Read Acts 16:25-34

And After Death?

Believe in the Lord Jesus, and you will be saved—you and your household. (Acts 16:31)

Throughout the history of humankind there have been those who have had little or no idea of what awaited them after their physical death. There have been some who pretended not to care about the future, while others have vehemently denied that there is any future after death. Most people are confused and unsure and as a result of their uncertainty, they are afraid.

For Christians, the glorious truth of eternal life was confirmed when Jesus rose from the dead after His crucifixion. Through His victory over death He brought redemption and eternal life for all who believe in Him and accept Him as Lord of their lives. The empty tomb forever confirms the power of God's love over the grave—a love that brought hope to those for whom Jesus died.

If you are looking for reassurance that God is in your life, believe in His promises. Accept Jesus Christ as your Savior and Redeemer; open your heart and life to Him so that His Holy Spirit can live in you.

Dedicate yourself to Him anew and be assured that the Risen Savior will banish all fear and uncertainty. Your inheritance will then be eternal life in His kingdom.

Savior who grants eternal life, without You I cannot live; without You I dare not die. Amen.

No Other Name

Salvation is found in no one else, for there is no other name under heaven given to men by which we must be saved. (Acts 4:12)

There is no creature on earth that can escape sin. All of God's creation is calling out for salvation. All those who live, yearn for freedom, salvation and holiness. Not everyone wears their problems on their sleeves. Every heart knows its own bitterness, even if you do not show it to other people.

In your life, too, there are times when anxiety rise within your soul and you long to open your heart to a friend. Your inner sanctuary is the place where you can go to pour out your heart before God.

Be assured of this: only the unfailing love of God has an answer for the cry of desperation of a suffering soul. Because He, the One who is in Himself Almighty, brought about an eternal solution for us.

For us, He gave His eternal love—the image of the Father's glory! And from us nothing more is required than to bow before the name above all names, Jesus the living Christ, our Redeemer and Savior. He delivers us out of every problem, even the greatest need of the soul.

He delivers us from every curse, including the curse of sin. Have you bowed and accepted Him as Your Savior and Redeemer?

I praise and thank You, Lord Jesus, that You gained mercy for me from God through Your reconciling blood. Amen.

Read Ephesians 5:1-5

Is it Love or Sentiment?

Live a life of love, just as Christ loved us and gave Himself up for us as a fragrant offering and sacrifice to God. (Ephesians 5:2)

There is a world of difference between sentiment and Christian love. Sentiment depends on human feelings or the mood we are in at the time. Christian love is born from the indwelling Holy Spirit who is our source of eternal life and godly love.

Sentimental feelings vary from person to person. They fluctuate and are easily affected by time, attitudes, special occasions, music and a whole range of other influences. In contrast to this, genuine Christian love is deep-rooted and lasting because it comes from Christ who is always the same, yesterday, today, tomorrow and for eternity.

Christ's love does not depend on circumstances or people's feelings, because it has its foundation in the sacrifice that Jesus made for you and me on the cross: a sacrifice that undoubtedly proved the extent of God's love for us.

When you learn about the love that Christ has for you, you will find your own love growing—a love for God and for others. Meditate on the patience, kindness, generosity, care that He has shown to you, and pray that the Spirit will cultivate these same expressions of love with you.

Most loving source of love, let me never wander away from Your love and give myself over to sentiment. Amen.

Jesus' Influence

If anyone is in Christ, he is a new creation; the old has gone, the new has come! (2 Corinthians 5:17)

Religion is like a magnet for people who like to argue. They can quote a Scripture verse out of context and waste precious time by giving it a meaning it was never intended to have. Religion can become so philosophical that it loses its significance for the average person.

A meaningful religious faith must always lead to practical results. It is of little value to tell people to love God if you do not demonstrate it through your love for others. To emphasize the therapeutic benefits of forgiveness is certainly not enough. It is essential that you reach beyond the theory and apply forgiveness in practice.

You might be a dedicated follower of Jesus Christ, but if you are selfish and easily offended your faith counts for very little. It is when you abide in Christ that you reflect something of His merciful and radiant character, and then you bless those you come into contact with. They will sense that you walk with Jesus by seeing that He has truly changed you."

No one can effectively argue against a positive and living faith. When dishonest people become honest, when lives are transformed through Christ's love, when homes that were horrific become heavens, there can be no argument against the influence of the living Christ on people's lives.

Savior and Lord, grant that the greatest argument I can give for my faith will be the quality of my daily life. Amen.

Read 1 John 3:18-24

Dynamic Love

Dear children, let us not love with words or tongue but with actions and in truth. (1 John 3:18)

It is often said, "Talk is cheap." It is sad that one of the most beautiful and meaningful words in human language is so often misused, interpreted incorrectly, or misunderstood, to the point that it has become cheap and unimportant in the eyes of so many people. The word I am talking about is "love!" It has been watered down to such an extent that its true meaning has in fact been lost.

Love must come to expression in tangible and visible ways. This may be by financial support, spiritual guidance, emotional consolation, wise advice and many other ways. All of these actions cost the giver something. It could mean spending money or giving up valuable time. True love always demands a sacrifice from the giver.

The greatest example of truly sacrificial love was demonstrated at Golgotha where Jesus took on the burden of our sins and was crucified so that we could receive forgiveness and salvation. Christian love means giving of yourself for the sake of others. It is an action that pleases God. Anything else is only lip-service.

Teach me Your way, dear Lord, that You demonstrated at Golgotha, to serve others through acts of love. Amen.

To Truly Know Jesus

"Yes, you know Me, and you know where I am from. I am not here on My own, but He who sent Me is true. You do not know Him." (John 7:28)

The old saying, "familiarity breeds contempt," was proved to be true by the crowds in the temple. They asked if Jesus was the Messiah and then answered their own question with an air of finality. "We all know where this Man comes from and can anything good come out of Nazareth?" This reminds us of another saying, "A prophet is not honored in his hometown."

There are many people who have made an intensive study of the life of Jesus Christ. They are very familiar with the prophecies that predicted His coming; they have, in spirit, traveled with Him along the roads of Palestine. With a certain amount of justification they can say that they know something about Him.

But in spite of all the knowledge that you can gather about Jesus Christ, it will not lead you to a more sincere and deeper understanding of the divine nature of Christ unless you personally accept Him as your Savior and Redeemer.

It is the act of personal surrender and commitment that makes Jesus a living reality in your thoughts and emotions. There is no established formula for the act of surrender, but when you, figuratively speaking, place your hands in His nail-scarred hands, you become one with Him and only then can you truly get to know Him.

Lord Jesus, through faith I have accepted You as Savior and Redeemer. You are the Lord of my life. Amen.

Read Romans 1:1-7

The Human Savior

The Good News is about His Son. In His earthly life He was born into King David's family line. (Romans 1:3 NLT)

Through the centuries there have been many great men of God. Some of them were prophets and others were martyrs. Some were very dedicated and others sacrificed themselves in God's name. There were great teachers among them.

These were all people who were sent by God. In other words, they were ordinary people who God used in extraordinary ways. Jesus was also fully human. He had the same physical form as all the others. He ate and drank, worked and slept. He sometimes got tired and searched for the rejuvenation of solitude. He prayed and received strength from God.

In biblical times a person's identity was confirmed, through the naming of his parents, not by a number or reference in a central register. This could be extended by naming the great-grandparents. Jesus is described as being "born into King David's family line."

Only a person who was fully human could save us. He had to experience our fears, temptations, loneliness and sorrow so that He could give us life in all its fullness (John 10:10). By becoming fully human, Jesus fulfilled God's Law perfectly. By living a sinless life, He showed us everything that man was created to be. And our hope is that by trusting in Jesus, that God will continually help us look more and more like His Son.

God of mercy, help me to be
more and more like Jesus. Amen.

Son of God!

He was shown to be the Son of God when He was raised from the dead by the power of the Holy Spirit. He is Jesus Christ our Lord. (Romans 1:4 NLT)

You might sometimes ponder and marvel at the fact that the life of a Galilean carpenter, who lived more than two thousand years ago, still receives the admiration and worship of millions of His followers. What was it about Jesus that drew people to Him? Why were so many lives changed by the impact of His life and teachings?

Jesus was far more than an ordinary person. He was not only fully human, but fully and perfectly God. He was more than a man called and empowered by God because many prophets were called by God in this way. Jesus was the Son of God. He came from God and He was God. When He rose from the grave it was the final confirmation that it was God who had come to earth. It confirmed His dominion over the forces of evil. It proved that He triumphed over death!

The gospel of God, the gospel of Jesus Christ, and the gospel of the Bible is always the good news of the resurrection. Because Jesus rose and triumphed you can also triumph over temptations. Through Jesus' resurrection we have the hope that life is stronger than death. Because He lives you can know joy instead of sorrow, hope instead of despair, peace instead of confusion. They come to you as God's gift through His triumphant Son—Jesus Christ!

Savior and Master, fill my whole life with Your resurrection power. Amen.

Read 1 John 2:1-11

A Sacrifice of Reconciliation

He is the atoning sacrifice for our sins, and not only for ours but also for the sins of the whole world. (1 John 2:2)

From time to time we all do things that are completely wrong and then we feel really bad about them. You would feel very embarrassed and ashamed if someone were to find out. Perhaps you are afraid that you will be hauled into the spotlight and people will laugh at you.

It is a particularly painful experience to feel guilty toward God. When the consequences of your actions are of such a nature that things cannot be rectified, you feel compelled to pay for your mistake in some way or other. People long ago "paid" in the form of offering some kind of sacrifice—usually an animal—to God. Animals or other produce from farming were the sacrifice used for payment in those days. To slaughter an animal and place it on an altar before God was the acceptable way to say, "I'm sorry" to God. It said, "Please accept this offering. Restore me to my normal relationship with You." The sacrifice had to be proportionate to the trespass for which it was being offered.

Christians believe that the death of Jesus Christ is a sacrifice that Jesus made for all of us. It paid for all of our sins. It was no longer necessary to slaughter animals.

Because Jesus died, you and I have once again been placed in the right relationship with God. You no longer need to feel guilty. Christ has reconciled you to God.

Crucified Lord Jesus, thank You that You sacrificed Yourself for my sins. Amen.

Strength Comes from God

We have not stopped praying for you and asking God to fill you with the knowledge of His will through all spiritual wisdom and understanding. (Colossians 1:9)

There are many different kinds of power. A balanced diet will give you the energy to be able to work and play and it will build up your body properly. But you also need mental strength, which has everything to do with a positive self-image, motivation to succeed and the ability to persevere to see things through to the end.

Paul, the author of our Scripture reading for today, knew the necessity of also having spiritual strength. He found out in his own life that Christ alone can provide that power. He had tried in his own strength to satisfy God and fell hopelessly short. But Christ provided what he did not have, both for himself and for the whole church. That is what he meant by the body.

We all need spiritual strength—no matter how strong we are physically or mentally. Christ is the only one who can give you that strength. First acknowledge your absolute weakness in this area. Then accept Christ's offer of redemption and the strength that He promises you. Exercise your faith and let Him prove Himself to you.

Acknowledge that God's strength is not your strength, and realize your dependence on Him. Feed your faith by remaining in the presence of God and acknowledge the rulership of Christ. Go to the source of spiritual strength, Jesus Christ and renew your strength every day.

In my weakness I come to You, Lord Jesus,
to draw from Your strength. Amen.

 Read 1 Peter 2:1-10

The Living Stone

As you come to Him, the living Stone—rejected by men but chosen by God and precious to Him—you also, like living stones, are being built into a spiritual house. (1 Peter 2:4-5)

These days buildings are built on concrete foundations. Before cement was invented, early builders used to lay a foundation using large rocks. The builder had to measure and fit to see which stones would suit the layout and appearance of the house. Once they were firmly in their place they carried out a valuable function, and it could be said that they became a stone of honor.

In the Bible, the people of Israel considered themselves to be a nation that was rejected by the world but who had been chosen by God to be His people. And so it was with Jesus too. He was the foundation stone for a new building—the church. As the Rock on which the Christian community was built, He was a living stone.

The world still rejects Christ. They think that His values are too idealistic, His way of loving too weak, His power limited to substandard areas of life, and His importance confined because it is only one choice out of a whole row of religious convictions.

But He is still the Rock on which God chooses to build His community. From Him comes the grace that grows and strengthens the church that bears His name. He is the source of the Spirit who empowers His disciples. At the end they will see that God will reign forever and ever (see Rev. 11:15).

Merciful God, help me to build on the foundation that is Christ. Amen.

Powerful in All Things

"Are you only a visitor to Jerusalem and do not know the things that have happened there in these days?" (Luke 24:18)

There are not many people who are considered powerful in all things. Some possess power because of the position they hold but they are not particularly strong people. Some hold a position of power but do so only because of their strength in a particular field. Some people are powerful in the business world because of their wealth and skill but they have weaknesses in other areas.

The disciples on the road to Emmaus described Jesus as a prophet who was mighty in word and deed before God and the whole nation. He showed His strength in His teachings—He revealed His power in the healing of the sick. He attracted people to Himself like a magnet.

He challenged the spiritual leaders and brought their offences into the light in the temple. But suddenly His strength dissipated and He was crucified. There were rumors that He had risen from the dead. Was He or was He not as powerful as He had claimed to be? They would soon know the truth!

His power is the strength of love, the power of God Himself. It is the power to place ordinary people on the heights. It is the power to give hope where despair is taking hold; joy instead of tears; and love instead of hate.

His power is the strength to build up rather than break down. It is the power to create and not to destroy. This strength can be at work in you. The choice is yours.

Victorious Jesus, fill my life with strength from on high. Amen.

Read Ephesians 3:14-21

Knowledge vs. Living Faith

May you experience the love of Christ, though it is too great to understand fully. Then you will be made complete with all the fullness of life and power that comes from God. (Ephesians 3:19 NLT)

It is a proven fact that many Christians are dissatisfied with their faith. It is not that they have become antagonistic or aggressive toward holy things, but rather dissatisfied with changing circumstances and unfavorable attitudes toward their spiritual lives. Christianity has progressively lost its attraction and they no longer acknowledge Christ's reign in their lives.

How is it possible that a once pulsating Christian faith can fade away until it eventually becomes a mockery of its initial glory? There could be many reasons for this: neglecting fellowship and worship; the inability to develop a constant prayer life; superficial Bible reading and study; and the challenge of peer pressure. These are just a few things that can lead to spiritual numbness.

A famous philosopher once stated that it is possible to know what Christianity is about without being a Christian. There are many people who study the content of the faith, who know all the church's dogmas and who can passionately debate a theological issue, but whose lives reflect nothing of the beauty of the living Christ.

To experience the fullness of a living and positive faith, you need to consecrate yourself to Christ. Then you can rise above all the theories of religion.

Savior, grant that my knowledge of You will lead me to a deeper appreciation of Your divine character. Amen.

Rich in All Things

I always thank God for you because of His grace given you in Christ Jesus. For in Him you have been enriched in every way—in all your speaking and in all your knowledge. (1 Corinthians 1:4-5)

There are different ways in which a person can become rich. Most people strive for material wealth and some see this as the sole purpose in life. Others dedicate themselves to acquiring academic knowledge and attain degree after degree. Some of them become authorities in their chosen field of study. There are people who become rich in friendships and they build an extensive circle of friends whom they can depend on at all times. Then there are people who become rich in "treasures," things they collect that have artistic or historical value.

The Corinthian converts were rich in a completely different way. They possessed spiritual wealth—they had many spiritual gifts, like prophecy, healing, speaking in tongues, wisdom and miracles. The Holy Spirit worked in them in these dramatic ways, not for their own glorification, but so that the church as a whole could be enriched. Paul had much to say to this specific group of Christians about their disunity and boasting. And yet, they were spiritually rich.

You can also be blessed by God, despite your shortcomings. He makes you rich in love, faith and hope. Don't envy other people's worldly riches. Cherish the true riches God has graciously blessed you with.

Lord Jesus, with Your love in my heart I am extremely rich. And for this I praise and thank You. Amen.

Read 1 John 5:1-12

Do You Have This Life?

He who has the Son has life; he who does not have the Son of God does not have life. (1 John 5:12)

What is true life really all about? For some it is about satisfying their desire to own things: cars, houses and other material objects. For others, life is mostly about money: the more money, the better the life. For many it is a life of pleasure while others look for prestige, power or self-fulfillment.

The message of the Bible is simple and direct: life is about Jesus. If you have Jesus, you have life—if you do not have Him, then you do not have life. To know Jesus might possibly bring you prosperity, but it might not.

When Jesus walks into your life, He brings fulfillment. He sets priorities for you that you would never have thought of, and yet they are nourishing and healthy and sometimes even exciting. By forgiving your sins He grants you peace of mind and serenity; a sense that you can live peacefully with your God. The poet John Masefield has said, "The deep peace burnt my 'me' alive." If you will invite Jesus into your life He will open your eyes. You will see yourself as you really are; you will see God as He really is; and you will see the world around you as it really is. You gain a perspective on every aspect of life and existence.

These things happen when you have Jesus. In John 10:10 God said, "I have come that they may have life, and have it to the full."

Lord of Life, I have only one short life to live. Make it the best that I am capable of through Your grace. Amen.

Christ Is All That Matters

Here there is no Greek or Jew, circumcised or uncircumcised, barbarian, Scythian, slave or free, but Christ is all, and is in all. (Colossians 3:11)

Differences of nationality, economic standing, social position, academic achievement and cultural background are all things that influence our evaluation of ourselves and of one another. We often judge other people in a favorable or unfavorable light.

The early church was people from various backgrounds. Some were Greeks who came from a more intellectual background. Others were Jews who were aware that God had called them to be His chosen people. Many were former slaves and others came from so-called heathen countries where the people were hard-headed and barbaric.

Paul was clear about one thing: if they had accepted Christ and had learned to know Him, background counted for nothing. They were all one in Christ. To put aside the old self meant putting aside all the privileges of culture, nationality, social status and economic position. Christ was greater than all these human distinctions.

In the church of Jesus Christ today we are part of a multicultural and multinational body. The world's way of determining status falls away when you are in Christ. Christ is all that matters! And hear this: Christ might come to you in the embodiment of another culture, color or race. Are you ready to talk to that person about Jesus?

Jesus, help me through the Holy Spirit not to look down on my fellow Christians. Amen.

Read 2 Corinthians 5:11-21

Christian Love Is Not Selective

He died for all, that those who live should no longer live for themselves but for Him who died for them and was raised again. (2 Corinthians 5:15)

Self-centeredness of any kind has no place in the Christian faith. We often hear of Christian organizations, institutions and communities that are involved in many good works, but they limit these works to their own people.

Adopting an attitude like this means a complete denial of the whole purpose of the birth, life, suffering, death and resurrection of Jesus Christ—disregarding His great command that we should love one another.

As a Christian, your mission is to bring the love of Christ to all people in all circumstances. It was never God's intention that you should operate only within your intimate circle of friends, or your brotherhood. Jesus paid attention to the needs of everyone who came to Him. The Holy Spirit commands us to do the same.

To ensure that your witness is effective, you need to put your trust in the Master. He will give you the opportunity and the ability to serve not only those whom you know and feel comfortable with, but all people—no matter what their needs or circumstances may be.

It is your duty, because remember, Jesus died for everyone!

Merciful Lord Jesus, grant that in my service to You, I will never withhold Your love from anyone. Amen.

Get Your Priorities Straight

He died for all, that those who live should no longer live for themselves but for Him who died for them and was raised again. (2 Corinthians 5:15)

The Christian faith requires absolute obedience to God, but how often is this requirement faithfully kept? Everything we have, even life itself, belongs to the Lord who has graciously entrusted it to us. We must practice good and faithful stewardship over what He has given us. But do we acknowledge Christ's sovereignty over every aspect of our lives?

True stewardship involves all our material possessions, our time, our entire being. What you undertake must be done in the name of God if you want to be faithful to your high calling in Jesus Christ.

You are indebted to Him for everything you have and everything you are, and as a result, He must enjoy priority over your life and daily activities. This means that you must first satisfy God before you think about yourself—however difficult this might seem. He has redeemed you, and through your acceptance of Jesus Christ, He has not only become your Father and Friend, but also your Savior and Redeemer.

If you call on the help of the Holy Spirit and allow Him to guide your thoughts on your journey through life, you will have the desire to subject yourself to God's will. Then He will become more real to you.

Savior and Redeemer, in thankfulness I consecrate myself anew to You and accept Your rulership over my life with absolute obedience. Amen.

Read 1 John 3:1-10

Jesus, Our Role Model

Dear friends, now we are children of God, and what we will be has not yet been made known. But we know that when He appears, we shall be like Him, for we shall see Him as He is. (1 John 3:2)

It is human nature to copy other people. A teenager will try to copy the facial expressions of an older person. A child will laugh because an adult laughs, even though he doesn't understand the joke. We dress like our sports heroes and celebrities and copy their hairstyles. Even in adulthood, some people take on a leading figure in their profession as their role model.

Jesus is the only role model for Christians. The Spirit works His fruit into our lives, "love, joy, peace, patience, kindness, goodness, gentleness, faithfulness and self-control" (Gal. 5:22-23). All these qualities are found in Christ. Those who excel in these qualities are more Christlike than those who don't have them. But these qualities don't all come at once or in equal measure, sometimes it takes years for the Spirit to bring them all to maturity.

Even a young believer who has trusted in Christ is growing in Christlikeness. Becoming more Christlike doesn't mean becoming less you-like. While sanctification involves growing in holiness and obedience, God created you unique and that wasn't by mistake. We are never told that Christians must all look the same or that growing in holiness means giving up our personality. Rather, Jesus is our role model and as we grow as Christians, we demonstrate the same qualities that characterized Jesus.

Lord, help me to be more like Jesus. Amen.

Strong to the End

He will keep you strong to the end, so that you will be blameless on the day of our Lord Jesus Christ. (1 Corinthians 1:8)

The Christian's earthly journey is a marathon and some people make it to the end. Others fall by the wayside. To journey with Jesus requires grace and perseverance.

For most of His disciples it means a bumpy ride rather than a smooth, uninterrupted progression. If you have given up or are considering it, our reading today is especially for you.

It was difficult for the early Christians to believe. They were surrounded by strange beliefs. They were continually spurred on to deny their faith and return to their old ways. It was impossible for the Christians to worship the Roman Caesar, but it was demanded from them. At times they were even persecuted. They always feared that they would backslide.

On the other hand these Christians lived with the strong expectation that Jesus would return in their lifetime. Paul encouraged the believers in Corinth to trust that Christ would grant them the strength and ability to persevere. Had they depended on their own strength, many of them would never have survived.

Just as the disciples needed Jesus to stay on course, so we still need Him today. If the bumps in the road have slowed you down or even derailed you, turn to Jesus and trust Him. He's glad to let you travel at His side!

Savior on our journey through life, we pray that today You will grant Your power and grace to those who are battling to persevere until the end. Amen.

Read Isaiah 65:17-25

Face the Future with Hope

"Behold, I will create new heavens and a new earth.
The former things will not be remembered,
nor will they come to mind." (Isaiah 65:17)

It is helpful to meditate on the way in which our faith directs us to view the world. You might have good reason to be optimistic or pessimistic. This will probably depend on your plans for the future or disappointments you experienced in the past. But try not to focus on your own circumstances and instead think about God—the God of the Bible and the Father of our Lord Jesus Christ.

We have hope for the future because He is the God of unlimited resources and incredible initiative; He is the God of renewal and recreation. His work of creation continues endlessly, even if you are caught in the past. He is the God of the future because He comes to us in the future He continually creates anew. His actions were breathtaking in the past, and He is still busy planning a new heaven and a new earth.

Revelation ends with a glorious vision of God's great future and even there He creates a new heaven and a new earth. God is never finished and He continually creates new things. He creates new generations; He makes people new creations. Out of the destruction and decay of the past, He creates new things and new people. Look for God's creativity in the world around you every day.

Holy Spirit of God, grant that I will
always face the future with hope. Amen.

Jesus Is Coming!

"Behold, I am coming soon! Blessed is he who keeps the words of the prophecy in this book." (Revelation 22:7)

People have tried to predict Jesus' Second Coming for many centuries. Much publicity has been given and much preparation has been done, but the end result of all of these predictions has been anti-climax, disappointment, disillusionment—and unbelief. Even followers of the resurrected Jesus tried to find an answer, only to find that God alone knows when that day will come.

In several cases the predictions about Jesus' Second Coming have forced people to get their lives in order. They keep themselves busy with this and try to overcome their transgressions and shortcomings in the hope that they will meet the great Master. This is commendable, but when the predicted date comes and goes without anything happening, people relax because they think the urgency is no longer there.

Because Jesus said that no one except the Father knows the date, it is essential that you live in such a way that you are always ready and willing to receive Him. There are constant opportunities to improve your life. Make a habit out of living according to God's commandments, live close to Christ, and make sure that when He comes again, you will be ready to receive Him with thanksgiving and worship.

Savior, following Your example, I will live in such a way that I will be ready to welcome You with thanksgiving when You come again. Amen.

April

Father, Son and Holy Spirit

Hope does not disappoint us,
because God has poured out His love
into our hearts by the Holy Spirit,
whom He has given us.
~ Romans 5:5

Loving God,
we call to mind the descent of the Holy Spirit.
As always You have kept Your covenant:
You have sent us the other Comforter
to comfort us in our deepest sorrow,
to be our leader when we are unsure of
the road that we must travel,
to be our teacher who reveals Your will to us,
who teaches us how to love You truly and
how to serve our fellow human beings in love.
Send Your Spirit as a flame,
to cleanse and purify me of all false
motives, all envy, all unforgiveness and hate,
all pride and self-exaltation.
Send Your Spirit as a wind,
to rush through my life and bring
new life and growth.
Send Your Spirit as a dove,
to confer on me the peace of God
that transcends all human understanding.
Send Your Spirit as water,
to wash me whiter than snow
and to allow me to grow spiritually so that I
may bear the fruit that befits my conversion.
Send Your Spirit as the dew,
to refresh me and nourish me with heavenly strength.
Recreate, O Spirit, let live, O Spirit.
Let the kingdom come in glory.
Amen.

Confidence for the Future

The way of the Lord is a refuge for the righteous. (Proverbs 10:29)

To be forewarned should mean to be equipped to cope with every life situation. Unfortunately many people disregard warnings and then they are surprised and hurt with the consequences of their actions.

The Bible is full of warnings. Some have already been fulfilled, but others refer to prophecies that have not yet been fulfilled. It would seem as if current world events are inexorably moving towards a climax. The times in which we live are unparalleled in human history, and intelligent people justifiably wonder what the future holds.

People who believe that mankind is not controlled by fate but by a loving Creator can draw comfort from the knowledge that, despite how much things may appear to the contrary, there is a divine plan at work in man's life.

This faith creates trust and provides hope; it conquers fear and gives the Christian disciple the ability to step into the future with confidence and in the certain conviction that God is still in control. To possess this kind of faith God must stand at the center of your life. If this is the case you will see world events in the light of the eternal design of God and you will be equipped to meet the future with confidence.

Almighty God, I believe with conviction that
You are still completely in control of Your creation
as well as of the world events of our time.
Once more I place my trust fully in You. Amen.

Read 1 Timothy 3:8-16

Faith Is the Answer

The mystery of godliness is great: He appeared in a body, was vindicated by the Spirit, was seen by angels, was preached among the nations, was believed on in the world, was taken up in glory. (1 Timothy 3:16)

However contradictory this statement may appear to you, it remains an indisputable fact of the Christian faith, in all its simultaneous complexity and simplicity. Where else would you find God assuming a human form or a King living as a simple town carpenter? Kings live in palaces, and yet the Prince of Peace had no place to rest His head. Jesus stood His ground against the scholars of His time and overwhelmed them with His knowledge and intellectual abilities. And yet simple people understood Him when He explained profound truths in the form of parables.

Your circumstances might confuse and trouble you, and sometimes you are unable to understand a particular situation. Your peace of mind can be disturbed by fear, illness, death and other negative things. You might even start questioning God's love.

This is the time to rely on God. He arranges everything for the benefit of those who love Him. For the faithful, good is born from evil. From the evil of Golgotha the victory of the resurrection emerged. God has a sacred purpose with everything that happens to you, and when the time is right this purpose will be revealed to you.

I praise and thank You, Lord my God, that I may faithfully accept Your every act in my life because I know that everything works for the good of those who love You. Amen.

God's Benevolence

"How I long for the months gone by, for the days when God watched over me, when His lamp shone upon my head and by His light I walked through darkness!" (Job 29:2-3)

There is nothing strange about people occasionally losing their spiritual way. It can easily happen after the ecstasy of a dramatic conversion has abated and you start living your life according to your accustomed ways again, with old temptations creeping up.

Or perhaps you are suffering from depression and despondency as a result of sorrow or illness, anxiety or fear, or setbacks and failures. It is in these circumstances that feelings of helplessness and despair may easily overwhelm you.

In times like these you need to hold on to your faith and place your trust in Christ who has promised never to forsake or abandon you. Think of the goodness of God and constantly remind yourself of the path along which He has guided you up to now, how He has protected you and looked after you in the past.

Jesus never changes. As He has done in the past He now waits for you to turn to Him in your times of crises. Lay all your fears and worries before Him. True to His promises, His perfect love will drive away all fear and you will be enveloped in His love.

Be still my soul, the Lord is on your side. In this knowledge I will struggle through all my disappointments, sorrow and grief, because You grant me the strength to do so. For this I praise and thank You. Amen.

Read Psalm 25:11-22

Share Your Problems with Jesus

The troubles of my heart have multiplied;
free me from my anguish. (Psalm 25:17)

Worrying about problems might feel natural, but it can harm your well-being in spiritual, emotional, and even physical ways. It is not unusual for someone to worry so much, that it becomes impossible for them to think straight. As a result, they might just become a physical and spiritual wreck.

When Jesus called those who are weary and overburdened to Him He did not guarantee them complete exemption from problems, nor did He promise that all their problems would disappear. Instead, He offered to share your burden and also to teach you how to cope with it so that you may find peace of mind.

You can never predict setbacks in life, nor can you foresee how serious these incidents will be. What is of crucial importance is that you prepare yourself to handle these problems when they appear. To be unprepared for these eventualities may have devastating results.

To maintain a healthy balance and harmony in your mind, it is essential to develop a healthy personal relationship with the living Christ. Remain near to Jesus through faithful prayer and contemplation. If you do this, you will find that when problems strike, He will be with you to help you conquer them with peace in your heart.

Faithful Lord Jesus, thank You that I may come to
You with all my problems and worries in the certainty
that I will find peace and rest in You. Amen.

God's Way

Good and upright is the Lord; therefore He instructs sinners in His ways. (Psalm 25:8)

In today's world it is very easy to lose one's spiritual way. The pressure exerted by the sinful world is felt by young as much as old; temptations are countless and offered on a silver platter; the variety of detours makes it extremely difficult to follow the right path. In an era that constantly questions standards and morality there is always a fundamental danger that our principles may be compromised, however innocent and harmless the first step may seem at the time.

There is only one way to live your life and that is to keep to God's ways. In His commandments He set out the basic rules for a pious and devout life. In addition to this Christ became a living example that demonstrated to us how such a life ought to be lived.

Even though centuries have passed, nothing has changed with regard to the way of life that is acceptable and pleasing to God. Christ is still the way, the truth and the life, and the path of righteousness is still that of obedience to God in all things.

If you open your heart and life to the immanent Holy Spirit, you will become increasingly aware of His influence. Follow His guidance and you will know that the path you are following is God's way.

Search me, O God, and know my heart; test me and know my anxious thoughts. See if there is any offensive way in me, and lead me in the way everlasting (Ps. 139:23-24). Amen.

Read 2 Corinthians 2:12-17

Too Much?

And who is equal to such a task? (2 Corinthians 2:16)

We all go through times when things threaten to overwhelm us and our faith appears to be an inadequate defense. It seems as if our circumstances are continually worsening, our relationships suffer grievous blows and everything appears unmanageable.

What is actually happening is that your fear of your circumstances has become greater than your trust in God. The demands of life have not shown that your God isn't enough, but rather that your trust in Him is insufficient. When you feel that you've reached a breaking point, remind yourself that your God is sufficient and that He will never abandon you. This will help you regain your footing in life.

It is definitely not God's intention to place you under so much pressure that you reach breaking point. A faith that sees God correctly is a stabilizing influence under the most confusing circumstances. Possessing such a faith is not a spiritual luxury, but an urgent necessity if you wish to deal with the demands of life successfully.

Realizing the necessity of faith is the first step to possessing it. If you are unaware of your need, how will you be able to fulfill it? When you tell the Lord that you need His help and trust Him unconditionally you will know that He will carry you through, because you love and trust in Him.

Lord Jesus, through Your wisdom and strength
I am able to cope with all the demands of life.
Keep me close to Your heart at all times. Amen.

Bolster Your Self-Confidence

*The Lord is my light and my salvation—
whom shall I fear? The Lord is the stronghold of
my life—of whom shall I be afraid? (Psalm 27:1)*

There are times when everything appears dismal and uncertain. Your thoughts are bewildered, with the result that your life loses its sense of direction. You've lost all confidence and hopelessness sinks in. When this happens you inevitably become unsure of God, your faith falters and your life starts losing meaning and significance.

A tried and proven way of restoring your faith in life so that you can live a life free from feelings of inferiority, is to be absolutely sure that God is all-sufficient. This all-sufficiency is not something that is forced upon you from an almighty being, but is rather the effect of the merciful Spirit of God in your own spirit. It is the knowledge that God lives and works in you daily. This tremendous truth gives you the self-confidence to face the demands of every day.

When you invite the Spirit of God into your life, all detrimental fear is defeated and eventually vanishes because you know that God is busy actualizing His plan with your life. Because His presence is a reality to you, the future will unfold before you in all its joy, peace and self-confidence.

*Thank You, Almighty God, that destructive fear is
removed from my life by the ministry of the Holy Spirit,
and instead replaced with quiet confidence. Amen.*

Read Romans 12:9-21

An Exercise in Prayer

Be joyful in hope, patient in affliction,
faithful in prayer. (Romans 12:12)

Is your prayer life everything that you would like it to be? And everything that Christ would like it to be? You may regard this as a rather presumptuous question, but you are the only one who needs to know the answer. However, your answer can make the difference between an ineffective prayer life or one that is filled with an awareness of the presence of God.

While you are praying you undoubtedly think of your family and friends. They probably form part of your normal prayer pattern. And yet the whole world is pleading for prayer. If you doubt this statement, all you need to do is take a look at your newspaper. Every newspaper is a prayer manual in itself. You can pray for the editors and those who form the public opinion; you can pray for those who grieve, who are the victims of violence, and even for those who committed the acts of violence.

When you move out of your everyday world you will find innumerable opportunities for prayer. Rejoice together with those who are happy and thank God for their happiness. You never have to search for a reason to pray.

The great advantage of expanding your prayer base is the fact that it intensifies your own quiet time with God. While you are praying for others you will find a more intimate communion with the living Christ.

Lord Jesus, I want to plead: Teach me to pray! Amen.

Beware! Pitfalls Ahead!

They mingled with the nations and adopted their customs. They worshiped their idols, which became a snare to them. (Psalm 106:35-36)

People attach much value to material things and the pleasures that life offers. This often becomes the dominating factor of everyday life and eventually life in its totality begins to revolve around materialism and pleasure, so that people become completely dependent on it. This dependence may be work or leisure; it may even include some kind of addiction. Whatever it may be, it becomes the controlling factor in the life of the particular person.

Regardless of what it may be, when it relegates God to a lesser position in your life, it becomes an idol. And whether people like it or not, or whether they are willing to admit it or not, he who makes himself guilty of this becomes an idolater.

Any form of addiction, be it work, pleasure or habit, leads to a road that is riddled with pitfalls. Obsession, addiction and uncontrolled desires are but a few forms of fixation that, if left unchecked, will inevitably lead to disastrous and grim consequences for those involved.

Beware of anything in your life that runs counter to your relationship with Jesus. If it clashes with His life, example and principles, abandon it. Follow Christ and enjoy a life of peace and fulfillment.

I know, my Redeemer and Savior, that I will only be happy and prosperous in this world if I follow Your example meticulously. Please let Your Holy Spirit assist and help me in this. Amen.

Read Romans 8:1-17

Spiritual Maturity

You are controlled not by the sinful nature but by the Spirit. (Romans 8:9)

When you see how majestic God truly is, and respond by worshiping Him accordingly, you are able to keep all of life's problems in a healthy perspective.

When you cannot rise above the pain inflicted upon you by the thoughtless tongue of a flippant person, when it seems as if your life is restricted by a lack of opportunities and undesirable circumstances, when you have fallen into a rut from which you just can't escape—these are the times when you should start questioning the basic reason for your existence.

The direction you are traveling in life is a clear reflection of the priorities that are guiding you. If you seek financial success or social prestige to the exclusion of more important things in life, you may reach your destination but also lose much.

Because God has created you to be a spiritual being, your spiritual life can never be satisfied by material matters. The world can offer you a variety of trials and temptations, but letting these control our lives will never bring lasting joy or satisfaction. Rather, trusting in Jesus and living according to the Spirit will bring about lasting and encouraging spiritual growth.

Holy Father, grant me a profound awareness of the importance of spiritual growth. Amen.

Prove to God that You Love Him

If anyone obeys His word, God's love is truly made complete in Him. (1 John 2:5)

There are times where some people might be concerned about emotionalism in the Christian life. As a reaction—or perhaps an overreaction—some have tried to eradicate emotions entirely from Christianity. This is not only misguided, but also deeply unhealthy.

Telling God how much you love Him may create an impression of cheap sentimentality, and yet it is one of the most inspiring things that you can do. It fortifies your inner spirit, focuses your thoughts on eternal realities and confirms the convictions that you have always held but seldom expressed.

To tell God you love Him is much more than a noble sentiment, because love without constructive action is useless. Love demands deeds that uplift and inspire. James asks, "What good is it if a man claims to have faith but has no deeds?" (see James 2:14). How genuine can your love for God truly be if you are aware of a serious need and do nothing to alleviate it?

When you tell God that you love Him without any intellectual or spiritual reservations, you are offering your very best to Him and expressing your willingness to serve Him in any sphere where He wishes to use you. Love that does not practically manifest itself becomes an emotional gimmick that lacks the essence of dynamic spirituality.

Beloved Father, I want to tell You repeatedly and with complete conviction: I love You with all my heart, O Lord! Amen.

Read John 13:18-21

Betraying the Master?

"I tell you the truth, one of you is going to betray Me." (John 13:21)

The name of Judas Iscariot has a place in the annals of history that will never be erased. His betrayal is known to everyone who has ever heard the name of Jesus Christ.

Nonetheless, is he really the only person to have betrayed Jesus? Whatever the motive for his betrayal, it must already have been developing in his mind while he enjoyed the intimate companionship of Jesus and his fellow disciples. He was one of the chosen twelve. However, the motives that drive people are known only to themselves and God. Judas was probably frequently excited when Jesus spoke of the kingdom of God. Unfortunately his idea of the kingdom of God differed radically from that of Christ. Judas tried to force Jesus' principles into his own thought patterns.

We must guard against trying to force Christ and His powerful principles into our own preconceived ideas and doctrines. If you are trying to force Christ into your thought patterns you are betraying Him because you are attempting to limit Him. What is of fundamental importance in your relationship with Christ is not what you try to do with Him, but rather what you are willing to allow Him to do with you. Having the mind of Christ entails submitting our thoughts to His thoughts. Then you will never betray Him.

Pull me ever closer to You, dear Lord, so that I may better understand Your purpose with my life and never betray You for the sake of things that are of lesser importance. Amen.

Something to Live For

"Before long, the world will not see Me anymore, but you will see Me. Because I live, you also will live." (John 14:19)

In these ominous times there are many people who wonder whether it is worthwhile to be alive. They harbor doubt about an unknown future and as a result they lapse into pessimism and dejection. Regardless of this we have to remember that life is extremely precious, and the most despairing person knows this when his life is threatened.

Despite how hopeless the future may appear, it is of the utmost importance to admit and accept the fact that both your life and your future are in the hands of God. The Christian's life is not ruled by a blind fate. God is in control of every situation in which you find yourself. He knows your needs and is prepared to provide for you through the wealth and abundance of Jesus Christ.

As your faith grows and becomes stronger, and as you start trusting Him more, you will also begin to realize how great the joy of a life in Christ is and how trustworthy God is. He is the Rock upon which you can build your entire life and future in the knowledge that His grace is enough to get you through each day.

Through His death and resurrection Jesus not only gave you life, but also a reason to live. Through His Holy Spirit He provides you with the ability to live life to the fullest. Seize this life and live it in the abundance of Jesus.

*Throughout all the changing circumstances
of life, beloved Lord, in joy as well as sorrow,
my heart will sing Your praise. Amen.*

Read Galatians 3:21-29

A Part of God's Family

You are all sons of God through faith in Christ Jesus. (Galatians 3:26)

No one is alone in this world. This hope is from God. There are many people who feel that they have no one to turn to, and there are others who claim that they have no family. Neither they nor you are alone in this world, because through Jesus you can be part of the most privileged family on earth: the family of God.

Your surrender to the Lord Jesus can open the door to the love and concern of the Almighty God who is also your heavenly Father. Before the coming of Jesus, the Almighty was worshiped primarily by Israelites, but Jesus came as evidence of God's love for all of humanity.

Through Christ you too are invited to become a child of God, and as such to enjoy the ultimate loving relationship that exists between parent and child. This is a constant relationship, because the Lord will be with you always and will never to forsake you (see Heb. 23:5).

If you remember to turn to Jesus in all circumstances and place your trust in Him completely, you will experience the protective love of God that will grant you the peace that transcends all understanding. And then you will never again feel alone in life.

Great and holy God, it is beyond my understanding how You can condescend to be my Father and Friend. My life is too brief to thank You sufficiently for this. Amen.

Worship God

My message and my preaching were not with wise and persuasive words, but with a demonstration of the Spirit's power. (1 Corinthians 2:4)

There is a great danger present in our churches today, namely, the number of people who attend services to hear the speaker rather than the Word. This kind of attitude may easily lead to church attendance for the sake of entertainment rather than for the sake of worshiping God and sharing communion with the faithful.

In the establishment of the first church Christ predominantly used simple and uneducated people. Throughout the ages many of the great pillars of the church possessed little or no learning, and yet hundreds of thousands were converted by their preaching. God has often chosen people who would by conventional standards fail a preaching test to be His instruments.

This serves to prove that it is the Holy Spirit, and not people's competence, that moves people to surrender their lives to Jesus. In all preaching the emphasis should be on the glory of God, and Christ should not be an incidental part of the sermon but its main content.

In your worship you should always seek the guidance of the Holy Spirit. If the message impels you to dedicate your life to Jesus Christ, you will know for sure that you worship God in spirit and in truth.

Help me, O Lord, to worship only You as the triune God: Father, Son and Holy Spirit. Amen.

 Read 1 Corinthians 2:6-16

Your Invisible Support

For who among men knows the thoughts of a man except the man's spirit within him? In the same way no one knows the thoughts of God except the Spirit of God. (1 Corinthians 2:11)

Beggars have no social support structure. These unfortunate people have no money and are dependent on the generosity and charity of their fellow human beings. They live in truly dismal circumstances.

In the spiritual life many people live in similar circumstances. These are the people who manage their pilgrimage towards eternity only by being carried along by the faith of their parents or by a religious tradition. They pride themselves on a religious inheritance, but when tension and pressure start taking their toll, the absence of their faith is revealed and their entire lives collapse. They too have no apparent support structure.

As a Christian the inner support of your spirit cannot be calculated in worldly terms. Paul writes, "God has revealed it to us by His Spirit. The Spirit searches all things, even the deep things of God" (1 Cor. 2:10). Only when you have surrendered yourself to the living Christ and have felt His love and strength, can you know the force that supports your inner spirit. Then you no longer need artificial and external support structures.

Without a personal experience of Jesus the qualities that are necessary for a living faith are absent from your inner life. It is Christ in your spirit that is your invisible support structure.

Holy Lord Jesus, I praise and thank You for giving me inner power and strength. Amen.

Aspire to that Which Is Noble

Finally, brothers, whatever is true, whatever is noble, whatever is right, whatever is pure, whatever is lovely, whatever is admirable—if anything is excellent or praiseworthy—think about such things. (Philippians 4:8)

Life can be an unpleasant or an exquisite experience, depending on your attitude towards it. It is unfortunately true that when you are confronted with the cruelty of life it is all too easy to allow it to become ingrained in you. Because we live in a world where the accepted norms are not the standards of God, it is dangerously easy to set your spiritual goals lower in order to conform to popular opinion. When this happens life loses its beauty and you no longer experience the joy and strength of Christ.

It requires spiritual sensitivity to appreciate the beauty of life. To believe in God as the origin and Creator of all things that are beautiful and noble you should start by seeing Him in unexpected places: in the smile of a friend, the innocence of a child, the unobtrusive deed of love, the ultimate success of someone who has struggled for a long time—In ways that are too many to mention you will begin to see the wonder and beauty of life.

The greatest gift of all is, with the grace of God, to develop the ability to distinguish between that which is offensive and that which is noble, and to accept the responsibility for making the right choice. In choosing Christ you open your life to beauty, nobility and truth.

I bring You my humble thanks, O Savior, that through the awareness of Your immanent Spirit I have the ability to appreciate the beauty and grandeur of life. Amen.

Read 1 John 5:1-12

Conquer Boredom

His commands are not burdensome, for everyone born of God overcomes the world. (1 John 5:3-4)

It is astounding to see how many people are bored with life. Boredom is not limited to a particular group or social. Young people who ought to be enjoying life complain that they have nothing to do.

Many of the elderly who are no longer active find life tedious because they have lost all interest in it. Boredom deprives life of its beauty and creativity. However, those who find life boring have only themselves to blame.

God has placed you in a wonderful world filled with fascinating people. If you are bored, you have simply become detached from the wonders of God's creation. It is also an indication that your faith is insufficient to satisfy your spiritual needs and therefore you experience a serious deficiency within yourself.

If you are filled with the love of God it will be manifested in your love for people, your appreciation of life and your enthusiasm for everything worthwhile happening around you.

When you begin a new day, believe that it will be the best day ever, and live it to the fullest. Resolve to be enthusiastic and joyful. Allow God's purpose with your life to unfold while you live purposefully for Him. Your enthusiasm and joy will flow to others and life will prosper. There will be no time to be bored.

Heavenly Father, because Your Holy Spirit is my inspiration and guide I can never be bored with life. I stand before You in grateful awe. Amen.

True Religion

Now to each one the manifestation of the Spirit is given for the common good. (1 Corinthians 12:7)

There are many people who refuse to identify themselves with any form of religion. They point out the failings of religion and the hypocritical behavior of religious people or the apparent conflict between science and religion.

Arguments such as these have existed from the earliest days of Christianity and are still with us today. The main objection is not against the Christian faith as such, but against what its followers have made of it and the way in which it is presented. The quality of many of these followers' lives seldom achieves the high standard set by Christ. Their pronouncements and confessions of their faith are not confirmed by their lives, and this causes disappointment and even aggression.

God is close to His people. He has created us and supports us by His strength. When your Christianity is only keeping tradtions and following rules, it is possible to know nothing about God. But when you have put your faith in Him, you begin to know God on a personal level. God has revealed Himself to man through His Son, Jesus Christ.

Numbers of people have reacted to His summons to become vessels that His Holy Spirit may fill and use. True religion is God at work through your life as a dedicated disciple.

Holy Spirit of God, teach me to be a willing instrument in Your hands, so that I may reflect Your image in the world. Amen.

Read Luke 6:6-11

Let Christ Remain Central

They were furious and began to discuss with one another what they might do to Jesus. (Luke 6:11)

It is so easy to allow your values to become jumbled. When this happens unimportant things become extremely important and essential matters are treated as trifling. This confusion of priorities happens in all spheres of life, but when it occurs on the spiritual level the consequences can be disastrous.

Confessions and dogmas are valuable as tools to clarify what the Bible teaches about various topics. But if these become more important to us than loving Christ, the result can be pettiness, bitterness and even hate. Convictions about theology may differ, but we may never be indifferent about Christ being central in our lives. Christ is the center of your religion; He is your motivation to live differently and His Spirit enables you to now live a life that reflects your Lord.

All of our spiritual privileges are not due to our own moral or spiritual achievements. But rather, they are due to the mercy and grace of Christ who paid for our sins. If we know Him and His Spirit is working in our hearts, then suddenly pettiness, bitterness and hate begin to lose their foothold. If we have been united to Christ through faith, than the all disparaging and disobedient characteristics slowly become replaced with a more constructive attitude—an attitude that desires God's will to be done in our lives.

Come and fill my life with Your Spirit, Lord Jesus,
so that there will be no room in my life
for bitterness, jealousy and hate. Amen.

God Is with You

When Jacob awoke from his sleep, he thought, "Surely the LORD is in this place, and I was not aware of it." (Genesis 28:16)

Through the ages the practice or convention developed for people to attend services of worship to enter into communion with God. It is true that many search for Him in their quiet time through private prayer, Bible study and contemplation. But in many cases there is still the feeling that you can only really encounter God during the communal worship of a church service.

However, God is omnipresent. While it is undoubtedly true that you are in the presence of God during church worship, you should remember that He is present in every situation in life.

When you stand in awe before the beauty of a sunset or are astonished by the wonder of a sunrise, when birdsong fills you with excitement or the laughter of playing children gladdens your heart, when you look with reverence at the grandeur of the mountains or the splendor of the restless ocean; when you admire nature's wealth of flowers: be assured of God's presence!

When you enter a sick-room or provide help to an aged person, when you assist someone in need or offer loving sympathy to someone who is grieving, when you rejoice with someone who is happy or help carry someone else's burden: then too will you become aware of the presence of God. Look around: God is everywhere.

Omnipresent God, when I put myself in Your service, I realize once again the wonder of Your love and I know that You are with me. Amen.

Read John 6:22-31

Prepare Yourself for Eternity

"Do not work for food that spoils, but for food that endures to eternal life, which the Son of Man will give you." (John 6:27)

It is amazing how many people have limited patterns of thought. Some live from day to day without any thought of tomorrow. Others, who carry certain responsibilities, plan their matters carefully, but refuse to think about the certainty of death.

It is astonishing that intelligent people are serious as they develop of their earthly plans, but pay no attention to the time when they will leave this world and step into eternity. Only a fool ignores this certainty. To plan for greater profits and to neglect planning for death is to be spiritually short-sighted; they try and avoid something that you have to face at some point or another.

To say that one cannot plan for something that you cannot determine is also not an appropriate response, because the Scriptures teach us the truth about the spiritual world. Jesus spoke of the life after death in realistic terms and His words ought to be sufficient for anyone thinking seriously about the matter.

To survey life with a sense of eternity is to give new perspective to your daily life. You ought to perform your daily task to the honor of God and should live your entire life so that it is acceptable to Him. To stand in the doorway of the spiritual life and place your hands with love in the hand of God, is the soul-enriching culmination of this life.

Risen Savior, I place my life and welfare in Your faithful care and step into the unknown future with confidence. Amen.

Jesus: Truly Human

Many deceivers, who do not acknowledge Jesus Christ as coming in the flesh, have gone out into the world. Any such person is the deceiver and the antichrist. (2 John 1:7)

It is fundamental to the Christian faith that Jesus Christ was born as a human being and lived, died and was buried as such, and that He was resurrected from death and ascended into heaven.

By becoming human, Jesus is able to sympathize with all of our weaknesses by experience as well as knowledge. Contrary to every other religion, the God of Christianity is one who wants to be near His people and has paid the price to draw them near.

God, in His infinite wisdom and love for His people, assumed human form and came to live amongst humans. He shared in their joy and sorrow and suffered the same pain and emotions as they did. Therefore, this Jesus understands people and life—the good as well as the bad. This places an extremely strong emphasis on the importance of Christian love. If God had not assumed human form we would never have known the dynamic impact of Jesus Christ on mankind.

It is now your duty as a disciple to show Jesus to the world in the way that you live your life. His Holy Spirit enables you to be a follower of Jesus and your task is made easier by the knowledge that Jesus understands because He has walked this path as you are doing now.

Lord Jesus, You left the glory of heaven and laid down Your royal crown to come to this world for the sake of people like me. For this I thank and praise You. Amen.

Read Ephesians 5:6-19

Spiritual Lethargy

"Wake up, O sleeper, rise from the dead, and Christ will shine on you." (Ephesians 5:14)

Abnormal sleepiness is also called lethargy. The dictionary defines this word as "apathy; lack of interest and energy." This drowsiness can sneak up on you unexpectedly and when it takes hold of your spiritual life it spells disaster for you as well as your church.

No one wishes to be a lukewarm Christian, but when your standards are compromised your spiritual life will inevitably be affected. It is simply a matter of time before these second-class standards drive out the dynamic principles of the Master. And then they become a pleasant, gentle-sounding philosophy that no longer challenges you to a life of quality and excellence.

To keep your faith alive you need to work at it constantly. It is fatal to rest on your spiritual laurels, because in the love to which God has called you there can be no vanity. How does one then sustain a living and dynamic faith? A continually deeper prayer life, an inspired and intelligent study of the Bible and participation in the fellowship of the faithful are essential factors for spiritual growth. You know all these things; the question is whether you apply them.

If every believer would wake up spiritually, the church would be on fire for Christ. Materialism and pride would be diminished, and the gospel would change lives in pews and in nations.

Holy Master, through the inspiration of Your Holy Spirit I plan to be a resolute Christian, all to Your honor. Amen.

Can People See Jesus in You?

If Timothy comes, see to it that he has nothing to fear while he is with you, for he is carrying on the work of the Lord. (1 Corinthians 16:10)

So many of people's problems originate from their inability to communicate. Interpersonal relationships are of the utmost importance for our social well-being, and yet it is a sad fact that we often pay little attention to this important aspect of our lifestyle.

This is especially true of the relationship between employer and employee, because it is a relationship in which social status plays an important role. In the same way someone who asks a favor of us may be refused, and this can inflict severe emotional scars.

Jesus commanded us to love one another, and Christian love can basically be defined as doing good. It follows necessarily that when we do something for someone else we should do it in such a way that the presence of Jesus is evident. Treating someone with contempt or creating the impression that they are a nuisance is in direct conflict with everything that the Master taught and did, and everything that He expects of you and me.

In order to create good relationships among people it is essential to follow Jesus' example. Seek the help of the Holy Spirit and ask Him to take control of your life so that you may act with love, peace, joy, patience, compassion, faithfulness and self-control. This will be your contribution to making the world a better place.

Holy Spirit, please help me to act towards all people in the spirit of Jesus Christ. Amen.

Read 2 Timothy 2:14-26

In the Service of God

Do your best to present yourself to God as one approved, a workman who does not need to be ashamed and who correctly handles the word of truth. (2 Timothy 2:15)

God has many workers who are active in His service. Their involvement becomes apparent in various ways. They often attend church meetings, persevere in doing good deeds, and seldom have idle time on their hands. Some of them tend to move in a clique that forbids interaction with anyone whose feelings and beliefs are different from theirs. But their mental and spiritual views are very limited.

This can have dismal consequences. You can become so involved in God's work that you lose your vision of what God wants you to do. Then you are diligently working for God without working with Him. You may nevertheless be industriously busy and other Christians may be impressed with what you are doing for the kingdom of God. You may even delude yourself into thinking that you are doing extremely important work.

And one day, when it is too late, something suddenly dries up in your soul, and you snap. You cease your Christian activities because of a nervous breakdown.

The most important duty of any Christian worker is to maintain and strengthen his relationship with God every day. If you are too busy to spend time with Him in daily prayer, you are simply too busy to serve Him.

Loving Master, I humbly ask that You will inspire and strengthen me for the service that I offer to You in gratitude for my redemption. Amen.

Light in the Darkness

To those who have been called, who are loved by God the Father and kept by Jesus Christ: Mercy, peace and love be yours in abundance. (Jude 1-2)

For as long as one can recall it has seemed as if the world was in a state of chaos. Apart from dozens of lesser confrontations between nations and people, humanity has also experienced two world wars in the past century. Lawlessness and violence have lately been increasing steadily. The cost of living continues to climb and people live lives of fear and insecurity. What is the solution to this sad state of affairs?

There can be only one answer and this is to fearlessly place your faith and trust in Jesus Christ. He has conquered a dark and hostile world and replaced fear with love. He has restored hope where circumstances appeared to be hopeless. To those who believe in Him, He has given the blessing of His peace that transcends all understanding.

This is your answer to the dismal confusion and fear of our time. Believe in Jesus Christ and His promises; place your trust in Him unconditionally and He will lead you from the darkness into the light of His unfathomable love for mankind. If you do this you will no longer worry about the future because you will always be protected by the peace of God.

Thank You, Lord my God, that You grant perfect peace to Your children in this dark world. Thank You that I may experience this inner peace because I trust in You. Amen.

Read Colossians 3:5-17

What Do We Owe One Another?

Bear with each other and forgive whatever grievances you may have ... Forgive as the Lord forgave you. And over all these virtues put on love, which binds them all together. (Colossians 3:13-14)

Courtesy is not so much an outward act as the expression of an inner spiritual experience. If Christ lives in you, you will be kind and patient towards your neighbor. This is what courtesy is all about: to take others and their feelings into consideration.

In some social circles courtesy is cultivated only to impress those gullible people who are easily deceived by appearances. A person who is truly courteous is humble and never tries to impress others. His attitude is the same regardless of whether he is talking to his equals or his subordinates. He treats everyone alike, regardless of race, color or religious creed. This attitude is the consequence of regular contact with God.

It is impossible to say that you love and serve God while at the same time treating your neighbor with contempt and disrespect. If you choose the people you want to treat with respect you expose the superficiality of your spiritual experience. Courtesy is not something that you can switch on and off. It is either an inherent part of you, or an act of hypocrisy.

When the Holy Spirit lives in you, you reflect the qualities of Christ in your life. Love and courtesy are basic characteristics of the Christian life, and good manners are the product of true Christianity.

Favor me, Lord Jesus, with the gift of courtesy that springs from a heart that is in harmony with You. Amen.

The Scourge of Discouragement

Though he stumble, he will not fall, for the Lord upholds him with His hand. (Psalm 37:24)

Feeling discouraged is an experience that is all too familiar to most people. It usually occurs when disappointment or failure destroys a long-cherished dream, or when lofty ideals and plans collapse like a house of cards. If discouragement takes hold of your spirit your life becomes bitter and you may find it difficult to recover your vision or ideals.

If you find yourself discouraged by a setback, carefully analyze why this setback was so challenging. If you're discouraged because it harmed your personal ambitions, perhaps this is a good time to reevaluate the motives behind your feelings. It is so easy for our eyes to move away from the Lord's priorities to our own. Then we become overly invested in things with minimal eternal value.

If you find yourself fixating on your own ambitions, bring them before the Lord. Ask Him to align your goals with his goals. Doing this will remove the sting when you face personal setbacks. Seeking God will ensure that your heart is set on His priorities, and our God is never confounded.

The application of Christ's teachings and the guidance of His immanent Spirit form the foundation upon which your decision rests to fight discouragement as something fleeting, so that you may achieve the goal that burns brightly in your heart.

I praise You, Lord my God and Father, that I am able to combat discouragement successfully with Your help. Amen.

Read Lamentations 3:31-42

God Calls Each One of Us

Let us examine our ways and test them, and let us return to the Lord. (Lamentations 3:40)

One of the wonderful facts of the Christian life is that the Lord knows us, and yet still loves us. Sometimes His challenges to us are so direct that we want to avoid them, but at other times He calls us to Him with a tenderness from which we cannot turn away.

No one can say how God will work within a particular person, or in which way He will choose to call someone to His service. He has His own methods of doing this, and a wise disciple will never try to force his own will on another person. Instead, he will always be sensitive to how the Master directs other people's lives.

To know that the living Christ works in different ways with different people deepens our understanding, expands our view, improves our sympathy and enriches our communion with the Master. If your heart is filled with love towards your neighbor, there is no room for the meanness that embitters your spirit and deprives it of the wealth and beauty of God's grace. By realizing that God uses different methods for different people you will intensify your understanding of the Master and add to your love for Him in a marvelous manner.

Be continually mindful of the way in which the Lord handles people. This will not only strengthen your faith, but also make life interesting and exciting.

Lord Jesus, grant me an immeasurable love for my neighbors and their unique personalities so that I may serve them more effectively. Amen.

May

The Holy Spirit

"I will ask the Father, and he will give you another advocate to help you and be with you forever—the Spirit of truth."

~ John 14:16-17

Holy Spirit of God,
who through repentance and sorrow has led us
out of sin, back to the heart of God,
who through Jesus Christ gives us new life:
We worship You as the Spirit of Truth.
We praise and thank You that
You are still at work in our lives
and abide in us, that through You,
Jesus Christ abides in us and we in Him.
We worship You as the source of our lives.
Thank You that You are the
Teacher who helps us to understand
the difference between right and wrong.
You make us, as Christians, part of one another
because we all have the same Spirit.
You enlighten our minds with Your gifts.
You give us rest and send us out to proclaim the gospel.
We praise Your name because You have opened up
the Holy Word for us so that we can learn
to know and obey the will of God.
Through You, O Spirit, God is present
in our hearts and that is why we live!
Touch our spirits with the fruits of love,
joy, peace, patience, kindness, goodness,
faithfulness, gentleness and self-control.
We thank You, O Spirit, that You have helped us
to become mature in our prayers and that You
make it possible for us to speak to the Father and
to listen to Him. We praise You for the wisdom that
You give us and that You enrich our lives so lavishly.
In the name of Jesus who sent You to us we pray.
Amen.

Waiting for God's Gift

"Do not leave Jerusalem, but wait for the gift My Father promised, which you have heard Me speak about." (Acts 1:4)

People can be so impatient! Sometimes this can be a good thing. Many of the marvelous inventions we have today are because men and women got up and took action, eager to find ways of making things work. Such people know that life is short and it is very easy to put things off for a better day. Sometimes that better day never arrives.

There are times when we need to wait on God. The disciples had to learn this after the ascension of Jesus. They needed to wait for the gift which God had promised them. The gift was of course the coming of the Holy Spirit. Undoubtedly, they were eager to go out and declare the joyful tidings that Jesus had risen from the dead. But they had been commanded to wait.

It was the work of God that they were going out to do; it was the message of God that they had to proclaim; and it could only be done in God's time and in God's strength. They had to wait in Jerusalem: the place where their hope had been completely destroyed and then wonderfully revived.

Sometimes when God wants to do something important, you also need to wait for His gift. You cannot force God's hand; you dare not turn His clock forward, because without the gift you will be ineffective and without guidance. With the gift of His Holy Spirit you are empowered. Stay focused and be filled with God.

Holy Spirit of God, fill me with power and help me to wait patiently for the Father's leading and direction. Amen.

Read John 3:1-8

Only Through the Spirit

"Flesh gives birth to flesh, but the Spirit gives birth to spirit." (John 3:6)

There are many things that you can do to change certain aspects of yourself. You can follow a strict diet to lose weight, change your appearance and improve your health. By studying long and hard you can equip yourself for a better career with more benefits. By learning a foreign language you can increase your circle of acquaintances and improve your ability to communicate. By planning your finances, you can manage your assets better.

But if you want to become a born-again Christian, it cannot be achieved through any process or discipline, exercise or action. God alone can do it. Only when the Spirit of God comes and lives in you and changes you, can a spiritual birth take place in your life. Your spiritual birth is from God.

When God gives you new life, He changes you from self-centered to Christ-centered. He changes you. He takes your anger and bitterness away and helps you to become compassionate and to care for other people. Instead of being interested in trivial things, your whole being is now consumed by things of God. Instead of your living on the surface, He teaches you what life is really all about.

This can only happen if you allow the Holy Spirit to come into your life. Are you willing to take the risk?

Through Your Holy Spirit, make me Your child, O Lord, and let me live for Your glory. Amen.

Be Filled with the Spirit

Be filled with the Spirit. (Ephesians 5:18)

In our Scripture reading today, Paul states that it is better to be filled with the Spirit than to get drunk on wine. Being drunk may give you happiness for a while, but only being filled with the Holy Spirit brings lasting joy.

After Jesus had risen from the dead and ascended to heaven, the disciples waited in Jerusalem for the coming of the Holy Spirit. While they had witnessed the Resurrection power of Jesus, they still needed to be empowered by the Spirit before they could proclaim this good news to the nations.

God empowers you, through His Spirit, to grow in Christlikeness. He helps remove the evil intentions of your heart and replace them with good things. Then day by day He helps you conform more and more to the image of Christ. When you meet someone who makes you think of Christ, you can be sure that that person is filled with the Spirit of God.

When the Spirit fills you, He empowers you to love and serve others just as Jesus did. You might do so simply by caring, by testifying of Jesus, or by bringing joy, hope and peace to those who have none.

You will work actively to build up the body of Christ, the church. Only God, if you open your life to Him, can fill your life with the Holy Spirit.

Come to me, Spirit of God. Come into my heart and fill me with love for Jesus and for other people. Amen.

Read John 1:29-34

Baptized with the Spirit

"The man on whom you see the Spirit come down and remain is He who will baptize with the Holy Spirit." (John 1:33)

Often our faith is weak and we seem to backslide because we are trusting in our own strength. When Jesus was baptized, the Holy Spirit descended upon Him and His work of ministry was empowered by the Holy Spirit. He taught, served and testified as the expression of His Father's work of salvation. Just as the Spirit was at work in the ministry of Jesus and His disciples, so He is at work in our own lives and ministries.

Sometimes people talk as if they own the Holy Spirit, but that is far from the truth. Rather, the Spirit influences us and teaches us to give up our own ambitions and serve God rather than ourselves. Its not about harnessing some supernatural power to accomplish our ambitions, having the Spirit entails learning to submit our plans to God's plans. This also means that your power comes from the Spirit. You cannot serve Christ in your own strength, following your own ideas, motivations or human ability. But the Spirit enables you, helping you to serve Christ.

Lastly, being baptized in the Spirit means that you need to go out into the world and serve others. You are not baptized with the Holy Spirit to glorify yourself. You allow the Spirit to come into your life and to show you what ministry He has chosen for you.

Your faith and spiritual growth are meant to be strong. Are you ready to obey the Holy Spirit and let Him work in your life?

Savior and Redeemer, empower me with the Holy Spirit to do Your will here where You have placed me. Amen.

The Best Is Yet to Come

"I will pour out My Spirit on all people. Your sons and daughters will prophesy, your old men will dream dreams, your young men will see visions." (Joel 2:28)

We may often use the expression, "You haven't heard the half of it!" When something dramatic happens we tend to predict, "Wait, this isn't the end of it."

God was in the process of saying something of the same kind through Joel to the children of Israel, "You will praise the name of the Lord your God, who has worked wonders for you" (Joel 2:26). But there is much more to it than that. God said that in the distant future He would lead all the people of Israel in prophesy. Before this time only certain people were called to be prophets.

But one day He would come in such overwhelming power that everyone would belong to Him. They would all be moved to declare His message. It would indeed be a mighty outpouring of the Spirit. After the spiritual drought, God would demonstrate His almighty power in a dramatic way and make His presence known to all.

At Pentecost He poured out His Spirit on an even greater crowd. God has the power to bring about renewal. He has even more good things in store for you than what you could ever dream of. How the disciples of Jesus could have dreamed, on that Good Friday when they turned home defeated, that He would rise from the dead and that the Resurrection would be followed by Pentecost. God has not yet finished His work.

Pour out Your Spirit once again,
O God, and start Your work in me. Amen.

Read Ezekiel 37:1-14

The Life-Giving Spirit

*"I will put My Spirit in you and you will live,
and I will settle you in your own land." (Ezekiel 37:14)*

One of the sad things of the Christian faith is the fact that people who regularly attend worship services—who get involved in the opportunities for service within the congregation—confess that there is something missing in their spiritual lives.

The danger of this is that they will go through life as lukewarm Christians, or even worse, they might become so disillusioned that their faith dies and they completely lose all hope and drift away from the church.

The church of Christ is living and active and the Lord whom you worship is the living Christ. It therefore goes without saying that you too can taste this abundance, the fullness of life for which Jesus Christ came to this world (see John 10:10). This is the powerful life that Christ demonstrated in His earthly ministry.

The place to start is to trust the Lord and to obey Him. As we are faithful in seeking Him, He will always be faithful in giving wisdom, guiding our way, and causing our work to be fruitful—even if it is in ways we didn't expect. A dynamic Christian life does not come from dramatic gestures or emotions, but from faithfully serving the Lord.

*Come down, Spirit of the living God, and fill
my soul. Make me zealous to serve You. Amen.*

God's Overshadowing Power

"The Holy Spirit will come upon you, and the power of the Most High will overshadow you." (Luke 1:35)

The scientific achievements of mankind during the last few centuries have been so amazing that we have begun to think that we can accomplish just about anything. We have reached the point where we think of ourselves as "masters of the universe" in spite of the many things at which we fail. Even in the realm of religion and faith we tend to think, *How can I make this happen?*

When the angel announced to Mary that she was going to be the mother of Jesus, she did not ask what she needed to do. It was completely a work of God. The Holy Spirit overshadowed her—that was all.

God decided to create mankind and so He acted. God decided to call Abraham and He instructed him to leave his country and to move away to the Promised Land. God decided to set His people free from slavery and so He parted the waters of the Red Sea. In the same way, He overshadowed Mary—and Jesus was born! He raised Jesus from the dead. He knew that His disciples were weak and that is why He overshadowed them with the Holy Spirit at Pentecost.

God is an awesome God: He works with overshadowing power through His Spirit. Do not let your ego stand in the way when God wants to overshadow you with the power of the Most High. Amazing things happen when that takes place.

Lord my God, come with Your overpowering might and touch each one of us. Amen.

Read John 3:22-36

Absolute Power

The one whom God has sent speaks the words of God, for God gives the Spirit without limit. (John 3:34)

How weak and ineffective faith and religion sometimes appear! For those who do not believe, they seem to be some kind of gimmick, a clever rouse that misleads weaklings who believe anything.

And yet they have the power to change people's lives; to motivate them; to inspire them to sacrifice, and fills the despairing with a burning hope. God is at work here. Through Jesus Christ, God came to us in human form and experienced human emotions and thoughts.

This message, the actual words of God, was written on people's hearts and filled them with understanding and spurred them on to good deeds. The Spirit of God did just the same with Jesus, in whom the Spirit lived in all His fullness. Jesus was by no means just exclusively set aside for God—He was Himself God! Not only did the Holy Spirit walk with Jesus and live in Him, He went ahead and began to extend the work that Jesus had begun on earth by empowering His followers.

The same Spirit is at work in you if you're trusting in Christ, giving you the strength to do the work that the Lord has laid ahead of you. As you grow in Christlikeness, you will become a more noble person; you will abound in love, hope and joy as the fruit of the Spirit take root in your heart.

Father God, so often I feel weak and helpless. Give me Your empowering Spirit and build me up in Christ. Amen.

Do Not Be Misled

Dear friends, do not believe every spirit, but test the spirits to see whether they are from God, because many false prophets have gone out into the world. (1 John 4:1)

One of the reasons why you must be certain of what you believe about God is so that you can be on your guard against people who might try to deceive you with false teachings.

When our Scripture verse for today was written there was no New Testament against which believers could measure the things that they heard. Even the most senior teachers of the day had less of the Word than we do today. People were left to the mercy of deceivers.

There were isolated small Christian communities who needed the guidance of men and women of the Spirit. From time to time they would receive a visit from an apostle and he spent his time helping them, teaching them and encouraging them.

But those early congregations never knew if an apostle was really a sincere believer and teacher or whether he was a false prophet. The false prophets caused a lot of damage and often undermined the faith of the people. They fed on their ignorance. They threatened Christianity.

False prophets are still a threat to our congregations today. They can even be found in the established church. They are particularly active where people are ignorant and easily deceived. Be alert and test the spirit.

Lord, help me through Your Spirit to discern between truth and lies. Amen.

Read 1 John 5:1-12

The Spirit of Truth

It is the Spirit who testifies, because the Spirit is the truth. (1 John 5:6)

You have probably heard the expression, "There are three sides to every story: My side, your side and the truth." To arrive at the truth can be a very complicated process. The Bible teaches that everything that comes from God is the truth. It is not an academic discussion—it is a spiritual matter. God is truth; Jesus Christ is the Truth and the Holy Spirit teaches us to know the truth and He is a witness to the truth because He points us toward Jesus.

The Spirit guides us into the truth about Jesus. Therefore, no matter how complicated and confusing it might sound to assert that Christ is truly God, it is also a simple truth that can be accepted and believed by any believer who is aware of his own sins and accepts that his sins have been forgiven.

When you get confused about a Christian teaching or interpretation, first seek the guidance of the Holy Spirit. To do so is not a weak excuse for intellectual laziness. It is your duty to think and sometimes you need to think very seriously. When doubts arise, choose the answer that is the closest to the inward whispering of the Holy Spirit. Just be careful that you do not insist that the Spirit supports you in a particular opinion.

Always remember that the Spirit points to Jesus as the Truth and therefore a simple test will be to ask: Is this in agreement with the thoughts of Christ?

God, guide my thoughts so that I can discover Your truth. Amen.

The Spirit of Christ

The Spirit of Christ in them was pointing when He predicted the sufferings of Christ and the glories that would follow. (1 Peter 1:11)

A young woman who was training to be a nurse had problems with her transportation to and from the hospital. The hospital was quite a distance from her house and the road was uphill, and so it was difficult for her to ride her bicycle to work.

Someone then suggested that she buy a small engine. The engine was attached to the back wheel of the bike. Soon she was riding up and down the hills to hospital without a worry.

For many Christian believers their Christian walk is also an uphill battle. But the Holy Spirit is available to accompany them on their life's journey. He empowered the prophets to take the message of God to the people and He gives believers the power to do things that they can't do themselves. This is because He is the Spirit of Christ. He comes from God the Father and from Christ our Savior and He reforms you and forms Christ in you. He is God's agent who works in your innermost being to free your heart and your mind. He renews your spirit and transforms you into a self-assured, joyful, mature and loving person.

The Holy Spirit molds you with tenderness, faith and self-control. He leads you every day to become more like Christ. Invite the Spirit today to work in you.

Spirit of the Living God, fill and empower me once again in the service of the Master. Amen.

Read 1 Peter 1:10-16

The Power of the Holy Spirit

It was revealed to them that they were not serving themselves but you. (1 Peter 1:12)

How can insignificant, ordinary people take it upon themselves to bring the message from God? Is it not supreme arrogance on their side to think that they can say anything that reflects the thoughts or will of God? The Bible shows us that God uses insignificant human beings in His way. He chooses ordinary people to be His messengers: fishermen, tax collectors, tentmakers, bakers, farmers and cabinet-makers. Then He empowers them with His Holy Spirit.

God is with His people through His Spirit, showing that they are His own. Through the power of the Spirit, they are able to serve both God and others with a power beyond they own capabilities.

When He enters into the hearts of people and forms Christ in them, He empowers all those who possess Him to offer some or other kind of ministry to others. Some will preach, while others will show mercy, encourage and build people up for the Kingdom. Others will use their gifts for administration or healing.

The prophets did not bring their own message but the message of God. They did not speak out of their own strength but through the power of the Holy Spirit.

No matter what kind of service you might be involved in—whether preaching, intercession, caring, healing or encouragement—never try to do it in your own strength. Earnestly seek the empowerment of the Holy Spirit. He will use you mightily.

Lord, fill Your people with the power of the Holy Spirit. Amen.

Spiritual Maturity

As for you, the anointing you received from Him remains in you, and you do not need anyone to teach you. (1 John 2:27)

When you went to school you were taught by teachers who had been trained at a university or college. You followed a curriculum. Eventually you learned everything that school could offer you. Then you continued with higher education, or you went to offer your services on the open market where you learned more about the kind of work you had chosen to do. People have an amazing ability to learn and to grow.

The same procedure can be applied to spiritual growth. Here the teaching is brought by human instructors such as a minister, priest or pastor. But the inner growth that takes place is the exclusive work of the Holy Spirit whose coming we celebrate every year at Pentecost.

He instructs you in two ways. First He guides you to live a holy life. A hymn by Harriet Auber that is dedicated to the Holy Spirit states: "And every virtue we possess, and every victory won, and every thought of Holiness is His alone."

You become a better, more dedicated and more loving person because the Holy Spirit sanctifies you.

He teaches you the truths of Christianity. This happens through reading the Bible, studying of your daily readings and worshiping together with other Christians. The Spirit gives you the insight to discern between the truth and a lie. The Holy Spirit is working in you.

Lord, give me grace to learn and to grow until I reach spiritual maturity. Amen.

Read 2 Peter 3:8-18

The Responsibility Is Yours

Grow in the grace and knowledge of our Lord and Savior Jesus Christ. (2 Peter 3:18)

If you want to take your spiritual life seriously you need to have a clear goal that you want to achieve. Failure regarding your goals means that you are drifting and that you are lacking the motivating strength to go further on the path of God. Either you go forward in your spiritual life or you become careless and lose the initiative that brings you closer to your heavenly Father.

If you have accepted the living Christ as your Savior and Redeemer, it is your responsibility to make progress along the chosen path. There are so many disciples who pity themselves and say, "Oh, if only I had more faith!"—and yet they neglect to exercise the little faith that they do have.

Many serious and committed disciples plead with the Lord for a deeper and more serious faith and prayer life, but forget that the development of a blessed prayer life is something that God really wants them to have. He actually gave them the privilege and the responsibility to develop this spiritual gem.

True spiritual maturity is not brought about in a flash of inspiration but is a process that progresses over many years. Spiritual growth will always occur under the guidance of the Holy Spirit but it requires constant prayer.

Always remember that the final responsibility to develop spiritual awareness and growth lies with you.

Holy Lord, help me to remain aware of my personal responsibility for my spiritual growth. Amen.

When Your Heart Is Troubled

O my Comforter in sorrow, my heart is faint within me. (Jeremiah 8:18)

There are many things that can upset you and get you down. Family conflicts are a primary cause of sorrow and depression. Difficulties at work are another. Employers can sometimes be very demanding and unreasonable and work colleagues can be a pain in the neck.

Money and finances are all too often the source of problems and difficulties: debt can gnaw at you mercilessly. Rulers and people in authority can make life unbearable. A continual barrage of accidents or adversity can break you, just as tiredness and over-working can get you down.

Jeremiah preached his heart out but the people rejected the message that he brought to them, and that broke him. He was frustrated and uncertain. He was worried about the imminent punishment from God and that it would destroy the land and its people. Just the thought of the sin of his nation and their rejection by God made him feel sick. Sorrowful and confused he turned to the only help that he knew—to God! "Is the Lord not in Zion? Is her King no longer there?" (Jer. 8:19). He was honest before God—Jeremiah did not put on a brave face before God to try and hide the true situation.

You too, through the Holy Spirit, can pour out your heart before God. If God is your sunshine when the day is fine, He is also your candle at midnight. When your heart is troubled, allow the Holy Spirit to comfort you.

Holy God, I know that You care for me because You sent the Holy Spirit as my Comforter. Amen.

Read Proverbs 17:14-28

The Spirit of Self-Control

Starting a quarrel is like breaching a dam; so drop the matter before a dispute breaks out. (Proverbs 17:14)

It does not take much to start an argument, and once it has begun it can easily get out of control and lead to great unhappiness and grief. Often a remark that just seemed to be an innocent difference of opinion becomes an offensive and hurtful comment or a derogatory remark that cuts to the soul. As a result, the argument stirs up feelings of bitterness and rage and a feeling of hostility develops between the persons involved.

The tragedy of the whole situation is that it is all so unnecessary. It is a fact of life that there will be differences of opinion. The world would be a very boring place if it were not so. People need to develop the ability to differ from one another without allowing bitterness to creep in and obscure the whole issue.

Jesus commanded us to love one another, just as He loves us. This of course does not mean that we need to agree with everything that is said or done; just as Christ did not agree with everything. Instead we should follow the example of the Lord and make sure that love is the dominant factor in all our interactions with other people.

The Holy Spirit offers you the wisdom, tenderness and self-control that are needed in all circumstances. Accept His loving offer and live in love, peace and joy with all people.

Grant us, O Holy Spirit,
the self-control to differ in love. Amen.

To Know the Truth

You have an anointing from the Holy One,
and all of you know the truth. (1 John 2:20)

Understanding some of the doctrines of the Christian faith might be difficult. You maybe think that others who are better equipped intellectually understand it and that you will just have to trust them.

You do not need to be intellectually sharp to be a Christian or to understand the deeper truths of the Christian faith. Jesus sent us the Holy Spirit to lead us into all truth (see John 16:13). To know the truth is more about allowing the Holy Spirit into your life to enlighten you, to teach you and to show you the direction you need to take, rather than simply gathering knowledge.

Jesus Himself is the Truth and through knowing Him you are placed in direct contact with the truth. This kind of truth has much more to do with a powerful life that is lived in faith, humility and love than overloading your mind with useless facts. A simple believer can know more of the truth (as it is reflected in Jesus) than a professor who does not know Jesus.

If you have trusted Jesus and are seeking to obey His Word, then the Holy Spirit will continue to grow your understanding. The Spirit will protect you from false teachings and from speculative guesswork about God. He will broaden your insight, strengthen your integrity and deepen your ability to show compassion, love and care.

Holy Spirit of God, lead me still deeper
into the truth about Jesus. Amen.

Read 1 John 4:1-6

Acknowledge the Spirit of Truth

This is how you can recognize the Spirit of God: Every spirit that acknowledges that Jesus Christ has come in the flesh is from God. (1 John 4:2)

How can a person possibly distinguish between true and false doctrines? Many theories exist in this regard; many ideas have been tested; many philosophies are floating around. Many of them sound feasible; some of them refer to God; others recommend spiritual disciplines; still others promise prosperity.

The most important question always remains: Who do they say Jesus Christ is? What they teach about Jesus Christ determines whether their teachings are true or false. When our Scripture reading for today was written there were false prophets who taught that Jesus only pretended to be the Son of God. They argued that He could not really take on human form because human flesh is basically evil. John wrote this letter to show how wrong they were.

Later the church declared: Jesus was completely God and completely a sinless human, and nothing else. He was not a good man who was sent by God. He was not half-God and half-human.

Many of these old ideas have regained popularity in certain sects and cults today. You can still apply this test today: Do they say that God came to us as completely God and completely man through Jesus Christ? If not, have nothing to do with them.

God of righteousness, let true and pure teachings about You flourish. Amen.

God Is Spirit

"God is Spirit, and His worshipers must worship in spirit and in truth." (John 4:24)

People bow in worship before various gods. The ancient Egyptians took a bird or animal and made a god out of it. There are people who worship the sun; others create an idol and bow before it. There are those who worship their ancestors. The heroes of modern music, sports and culture can also take on the form of gods. These are all man-made gods and false representations of the one and only true God. The fact that there are so many of them proves how easy it is to worship the wrong god.

When it comes to God there is just one way to get it right. That is to submit yourself to the guidance of the Holy Spirit of God. One of the functions of the Holy Spirit is to point people to Jesus. The Spirit came from God the Father and from Jesus.

When we worship God we do so with the help and inspiration of the Spirit. If we don't we will quickly lose our way. This means that we are not just worshiping some kind of higher power. We seek and respond to the One who comes to us with the name of Jesus. It is only His Spirit who will help us to succeed in worshiping God properly and to worship Him for who He really is.

Worship is far more than what we do each Sunday. The whole of our lives, our prayers, and our work must be undertaken with the help of the Holy Spirit: then it will be worship of the true God in the true sense of the word.

Spirit of the living God, help my worship to You to be pure and right. Amen.

Read Philippians 2:12-18

The Spirit Who Preserves

Continue to work out your salvation with fear and trembling, for it is God who works in you to will and to act according to His good purpose. (Philippians 2:12-13)

There might have been a time in your life when you felt absolutely overwhelmed by the burden of responsibility that had been placed on you as a Christian. There might have been those moments when you felt completely inadequate and incapable of fulfilling the requirements that Christ established for those who want to be His disciples—requirements that are impossible for an ordinary person to fulfill because the degree of surrender that this requires is just too much.

If this has been your experience, or if it still is, do not become discouraged about it; do not give in to the temptation to let your faith disintegrate as a result of the high level of requirements demanded.

In this situation rather turn to the Lord Jesus Christ and open yourself to be filled by the Holy Spirit. Allow Him to be part of your daily life by making yourself available to serve Him. Spend some quiet time in His presence so that you can tune in and understand His holy will for your life. Ask Him to make you sensitive to the movements of the Holy Spirit within you.

You will quickly experience an overwhelming desire and determination to serve Him in everything you do. The power of the Holy Spirit will take control and He will bring direction and purpose to your life.

Father God, through Your Spirit I will serve You and glorify Your name. Amen.

God Lives in You

The Most High does not live in houses made by men. (Acts 7:48)

The fact that church attendance in the modern world has reached an all-time low is a matter of great concern for the church leaders of our day. There are regular reports about diminishing numbers in congregations where previously many people were drawn to worship.

There might be various reasons for this—some even feasible. One of the primary reasons for the death of a congregation is because many people try to limit God to the place of worship.

The God whom we worship is a living God. We serve the risen Christ. You meet Him during your worship in your congregation; when you read the Bible and when you sing His praises. But you cannot lock Him behind church doors and limit Him to the pages of your hymn book. If this is your practice, the light of your faith will soon begin to fade and eventually be extinguished altogether.

You are the temple of God and in order for you to grow in grace and taste the fullness of joy of a life in Christ, you must, when you meet with Christ in your quiet time, prepare yourself to learn to know Him through worship. Once you have done this, you must then allow Him to come in and take control of your whole life.

In this way the living Christ will fill your whole life in every aspect. You will reflect His glory in all that you do—and you will learn to know life in all its richness and fullness.

Father of grace, let my life be a display of Your love. Amen.

Read 1 Peter 1:1-9

The Spirit Is at Work in You

To God's elect, strangers in the world … who have been chosen according to the foreknowledge of God the Father, through the sanctifying work of the Spirit, for obedience to Jesus Christ and sprinkling by His blood. (1 Peter 1:1-2)

There are many influences at work in and over you. Some of them are good and others are bad. If you have a solid family background or grew up in a Christian environment that influenced you for the good, then you are fortunate. If you mix with those who reject religion and who find their joy in debunking God, it will be much harder for you.

One of the best influences in your life is that of the Holy Spirit. His purpose is to cause Christ to live in you. He, and He alone, can create the love in you that Christ so desires to see. He teaches you to know the peace that is beyond all understanding. If you wrestle with temptations the Holy Spirit can help you.

The Holy Spirit fulfills two main functions. He empowers you to work for Jesus, and He works in you to make you more and more like Christ.

Every good thought that you have the Holy Spirit gives to you. Every good thing that you do, is under His incentive. Every time you overcome doubt through faith, He is there to encourage and support you. When people in need call out to you for support and help, the Spirit moves in you with compassion. He makes you like Christ. He leads you to holiness.

Holy Spirit of God, make me more and more like Jesus Christ. Amen.

Filled with the Holy Spirit

I baptize you with water, but He will baptize you with the Holy Spirit. (Mark 1:8)

Many people feel threatened when you talk of the Holy Spirit. They know that they love Jesus and that He loves them. But they are somewhat afraid that if they do not experience some or other dramatic manifestation, they are not true Christians.

The Holy Spirit is God's gift to Christians. If you feel that your circumstances are too difficult for you to manage, then take a moment and remember that God is with you through His Spirit. If you are depressed and discouraged and feel that you are good for nothing, then the Holy Spirit will uplift you. He will help you to overcome your problems.

If you have been broken down by bad luck, accidents, disasters or failure, then the Holy Spirit is for you. He will show you how you can pick up the broken pieces of your life and put them back together again. He will be the glue that restores your brokenness.

If you feel that you are on the road to nowhere, then the Holy Spirit is there for you. He will quicken your spiritual footsteps, sharpen your focus on the purpose for your life and give you strength.

You are not expected to do anything extraordinary to learn to know the Holy Spirit. Trust in God, seek His will through His Word, and ask Him to open your eyes to the work that is being done in and around you through the power of His Spirit

Lord Jesus, fill my emptiness, strengthen me in my weakness and heal my brokenness through Your Spirit. Amen.

 Read 1 Thessalonians 1:1-10

Welcome the Message

You became imitators of us and of the Lord; in spite of severe suffering, you welcomed the message with the joy given by the Holy Spirit. (1 Thessalonians 1:6)

For Christians Sunday is our day of rest and Easter Sunday is the time we celebrate the Resurrection of Christ. Unfortunately some people just view Sunday as a day to take a break from their routine. Some people think that one day is just the same as all the others.

It is good to remember that Easter Sunday is the day on which the message of the empty tomb is proclaimed across the whole world. Some people will despise it, while others will mock or ignore it. For Christians, it is welcomed with joy because it is an encouraging message, a word of hope, of trust and of anticipation.

It gives courage to those who suffer; it brings comfort to those who mourn; it brings the expectation of victory to those struggling with temptation. It promises strength to the weak; it strengthens the faith of those who doubt; to the lonely it brings the words of Christ, "I am with you always, to the very end of the age" (Matt. 28:20).

That is why every Sunday, Christians should pray that the Holy Spirit will give them the message of joy, carefully tuning our hearts to God's Word. They will remember that they are part of a worldwide community across the whole planet of which each one without exception has need of the message.

Let Your light and Your truth shine over the whole world, Lord Jesus. Drive away the darkness and despair and bring joy and blessing wherever it is heard. Amen.

Keep on Growing

We ought always to thank God for you, brothers, and rightly so, because your faith is growing more and more, and the love every one of you has for each other is increasing. (2 Thessalonians 1:3)

Of necessity there comes a time when you stop growing physically, but that does not mean that you have to stop developing intellectually and spiritually. Even when the body has reached adulthood, you still possess an inquiring and investigative mind that causes your horizons to broaden. There are unfortunately too many people who are satisfied to let the whys and hows of life remain unanswered.

With the passing years, growth in understanding should be revealed in emotional maturity. Petty attitudes and accusations from other people no longer irritate or unsettle you. You can develop in this way so that the attitudes of thoughtless people no longer hurt you.

Some people believe in God in a vague way but their lukewarmness prevents them from investigating the mysteries of God. There was a time when they prayed their childish prayers that were comforting and inspiring at that time in their lives. But now those prayers—if they are indeed still prayed—have little meaning and purpose.

As you grow intellectually, you should also grow spiritually so that you can become a dynamic, vital and growing personality and so that Jesus Christ can become a living reality to you. The Holy Spirit is the motivating power for growth in your life and faith.

Loving Lord, give me the desire and the wisdom to continue growing in my spiritual life. Amen.

Read Psalm 143:1-12

On Level Ground

Teach me to do Your will, for You are my God; may Your good Spirit lead me on level ground. (Psalm 143:10)

A wheelchair-bound man who suffered from muscular dystrophy said, "I fight a battle with the terrain. I need to live on even ground. It is impossible for me to go up and down stairs." Uneven ground has fought its way into our everyday vocabulary. We refer to a difficult task as an uphill battle. We refer to a person whose health is deteriorating as someone who is going downhill. Level ground is necessary for farming, construction and to move around on.

It has never been easy to carry out the will of God. David lived close to God and wrote beautiful poems about his relationship with God. But sometimes he did not succeed in carrying out the will of God. He discovered, as no doubt you have too, that he could not carry out God's will in his own strength. God needed to teach him what His will was and how he was to obey it.

Here we are anticipating the New Testament understanding of the Holy Spirit. You cannot get far by trying to obey God in your own strength. God empowered you with the Holy Spirit to walk close to Him.

Through the empowering of the Spirit life is no longer an uphill struggle. You are then on level ground because the Spirit shares something of His strength with you.

Gracious God, give Your Spirit to all those who attempt to walk the road of discipleship. Amen.

Actions Speak Louder Than Words

In everything set them an example by doing what is good. In your teaching show integrity, seriousness and soundness of speech that cannot be condemned. (Titus 2:7-8)

It is a sobering thought that people judge the lordship of Christ, His true value as well as His teachings, through the quality of your life and actions as a Christian. If you are a Christian, unbelievers will look for the qualities of Christ in your life. This is also true of your interactions with others. To fail in this means far more than simply disappointing yourself; it also causes a weakening of your witness concerning all that Christ means to you.

The true Christian experience is not some set of rules dictated to us, robbing life us its natural fun and beauty. And yet, if you take note of the way in which most Christians act, you would tend to think that the Christian faith is forced on to people to rob them of all joy. True Christianity exists in the hearts and lives of those who are in harmony with God. That is why it is something far more than a self-imposed and wretched discipline.

True Christianity is the living out of the living Christ in and through your life. To allow the Spirit of Christ to work in your life is not a burden but a joyful privilege. Other people no longer see your weaknesses and failures—even though they are still present—but they understand something of the redeeming love of Christ. He continues to love you in spite of who you are.

I open my life to Your Spirit, Holy Lord Jesus, and willingly allow Your love to flow through my life. Amen.

Read Luke 9:1-9

You Can Do It!

*When Jesus had called the Twelve together,
He gave them power and authority to drive
out all demons and to cure diseases. (Luke 9:1)*

There is an innumerable number of people whose desire to serve the Lord leads to nothing simply because they are afraid to take the risk of making an effort. These are people whose talents are lost because they rely on themselves and on inadequate resources.

The result is that they not only disappoint the Lord, but on top of that they rob themselves of the opportunity to taste the joy that comes from serving God.

If you read the Old and New Testaments diligently, you will discover something from beginning to end. Not one of the men or women who were called by God had the training or the ability to undertake the task that had been allotted to them in their own strength. From the earliest times the giants of faith of the Old Testament as well as the disciples who followed Jesus were ordinary people who were willing to serve.

In their own strength they had nothing to offer, but through the Spirit of God they became powerful and effective witnesses. The Lord called; they responded, and He gave them the strength to serve Him.

Jesus has a task for you. If you would submit yourself to Him and seek His guidance through prayer, He will not only show you what you should do, but He will also through the Holy Spirit give you the ability to undertake it in His name.

Holy Spirit, fill my life with Your Spirit. Amen.

Good News!

Timothy has just now come to us from you and has brought good news about your faith and love. (1 Thessalonians 3:6)

Sometimes, when we have heard nothing about someone for a while, we say, "No news is good news!" It is of course much better if good news is conveyed to us: the graduate who tells you that he has found a job—a young man who rejoices because he is getting married. Family achievements and success are always good news. As too are economic progress, political agreements and social justice.

There are also spiritual happenings that are good news. When someone who has never prayed seeks the face of God in prayer, then that is good news. When a young person accepts Christ as his Savior and Redeemer, it is good news. When adults who have long been estranged from one another are reconciled, then that is good news.

When someone who has lived in enmity with God and has wasted many years in a life of unbelief comes to repentance and conversion through bowing in humility before Christ—then that is the best news. Jesus said, "In the same way there will be more rejoicing in heaven over one sinner who repents than over ninety-nine righteous persons who do not need to repent" (Luke 15:7). It is good news when a believer in Christ is changed by the Holy Spirit and becomes an effective servant for Christ.

The ultimate good news is that Jesus Christ sacrificed His life so that we can have eternal life.

Lord Jesus, help me to come to a place where I can spread the Good News. Amen.

Read Isaiah 35:1-10

The Highway of Holiness

A highway will be there; it will be called the Way of Holiness. (Isaiah 35:8)

It is always exciting to drive down a brand-new road. It is straighter, smoother, shorter and more pleasant than the old road. Usually it also has a better surface. As expensive as it is to build them, modern highways are one of the greatest achievements of the modern world.

You might never have thought of God as an engineer before, but the prophet of old did! He saw how God performed all kinds of miracles that made human life richer and more beautiful. One of them was a road—and it would also be a safe road. It would be the road to Zion, or Jerusalem, and the redeemed and the elect would return to God along it and enter Zion with rejoicing. "The ransomed of the Lord will return. They will enter Zion with singing; everlasting joy will crown their heads. Gladness and joy will overtake them, and sorrow and sighing will flee away" (Isa. 35:10).

If you have given your life to Jesus Christ, then you are one of the redeemed for whom God has prepared this sacred road.

As the Spirit of God forms Christ in you, you begin your journey along that road. And those who also believed and went ahead of you wait for you at the final destination.

We pray for all those who are traveling on the roads today, Lord our God, that You will protect them and will bring them safely to their destination. Amen.

Spirit of Love

Hope does not disappoint us, because God has poured out His love into our hearts by the Holy Spirit, whom He has given us. (Romans 5:5)

People all over the world can testify of their love for Jesus Christ. These people differ in nationality, tradition and culture. Nevertheless, they bear witness to the love and faith in Jesus Christ who died on the cross 2,000 years ago. They are convinced that He is still alive today. How is this possible? They've never seen Him.

The secret of His unique attraction does not lie in some theological formula or religious organization—regardless of how important these things may be in the right context. But Jesus promised to grant His Spirit to everyone who accepts Him and confesses that He reigns over the earth.

Through the ages He has kept His promises. He said that His Spirit would live in every person who loves Him and serves Him. We see that this promise is true today as God continually works in and through the lives of His followers by His Spirit.

If you want to stand on the sideline, remember that Christ can convert your life. When your sins are forgiven through trusting in Jesus, you experience hope and strength that can only come from Him God's Spirit will enable you to do the things that please Him and will reassure you of Christ's life-changing presence in your life.

If you have the Spirit of Christ in you, you will know the reality of His holy presence. Love for Him will radiate from your heart and life.

I praise You, Lord, that I can experience the power of Your living Presence through the work of the Holy Spirit. Amen.

June

God and Us

As they talked and discussed
these things with each other,
Jesus Himself came up and
walked along with them.
~ Luke 24:15

Lord Jesus, our Savior:
You became what we are,
so that we can become what You are.
In our pain and suffering, You are the Great Physician;
in our confusion and darkness, You are the Light;
when we wander and get lost, You are the Way;
in this world of corruption and lies, You are the Truth;
when we are dead in sin, You are Life;
in our spiritual hunger, You are the Bread of Life;
in our thirst for God, You are the Living Water;
in our brokenness and sorrow,
You are the Balm of Gilead;
in You, Lord Jesus, heaven and earth come together
so that You can create a heaven on earth for us.
You fulfill our every spiritual desire.
We worship You as our Incarnate God
and praise Your name for eternity.
Amen.

As Predicted by the Prophets (1)

Beginning with Moses and all the Prophets,
He explained to them what was said in all
the Scriptures concerning Himself. (Luke 24:27)

Pastor James Hayes presents this Scripture verse as follows:

In Genesis He is the Seed of the woman; in Exodus the Lamb for sinners slain; in Deuteronomy He is the Great Rock; in Ruth our Redeemer; in 1 Samuel He is seen as the Great Judge; in 2 Samuel He is the Princely King; in 2 Kings as the Holiest of all; in 1 Chronicles as the King by birth.

In 2 Chronicles as King by judgment; in Ezra He is seen as Lord of Heaven and Earth; in Nehemiah as the Builder; in Job our Risen Returning Redeemer.

In Psalms the Son of God and the Good Shepherd; in Proverbs our Wisdom; in Ecclesiastes as the One Above the Sun; in Isaiah He is the Suffering and Glorified Servant; in Jeremiah the Lord Our Righteousness; in Ezekiel the Glorious God.

In Daniel the Smithing Stone and the Messiah; in Hosea He is the Risen Son of God; in Joel the Out-Pourer of the Spirit; in Amos the Eternal Christ; in Nahum He is the one who brings the Good Tidings; in Zephaniah the Merciful Christ.

Lord Jesus, we thank and praise You that
in all things You are for all people. Amen.

 Read Luke 24:25-35

As Predicted by the Prophets (2)

Beginning with Moses and all the Prophets, He explained to them what was said in all the Scriptures concerning Himself. (Luke 24:27)

Pastor James Hayes continues his presentation:

In Matthew He [Jesus] is the King of the Jews; in Mark He is the Servant; in Luke He is the Son of Man, in John He is the Son of God; in Acts He is the Risen Savior; in Romans He is our Righteousness; in 1 Corinthians He is the Resurrection; in 2 Corinthians He is our Comforter.

In Galatians He is the End of the Law; in Ephesians He is the Head of the Church; in Philippians He meets our every need; in Colossians He is the Fullness of the Deity.

In 1 Thessalonians He comes for His Church; in 2 Thessalonians He comes with His Church; in 1 Timothy He is the Mediator, in 2 Timothy He hands out crowns; in Titus He is our Great God and Savior; in Philemon He is our Intercessor.

In Hebrews He is the Rest of Believers and the Defender of Persons; in James He is the Coming Christ; in 1 Peter He is the Savior; in 2 Peter He is the Lord of Glory; in 1 John He is the Way, in 2 John He is the Truth; in 3 John He is the Life; in Jude He is our Security.

In Revelation He is the Lion of Judah; the Lamb of God, the Bright Morning Star, the King of kings and the Lord of lords.

Thank You, mighty Lord, for all that You encompass. You are truly everything. Amen.

Jesus' Miracles in People's Lives

"Neither this man nor his parents sinned," said Jesus, "but this happened so that the work of God might be displayed in his life." (John 9:3)

It has been said, "Man's disappointment is God's appointment." Although it is difficult for us to deal with vulnerability, weakness and adversity, God can perform miracles in such circumstances.

Jesus' disciples met a man who was born blind and they wanted to know whether this man or his parents had sinned. The disciples had grown up with the belief that any form of hardship was the punishment for sin. Jesus answered that it isn't always so simple. Instead of blaming someone, rather look at how God can demonstrate His omnipotence through the man's problem.

When we are insufficient, God is all sufficient. If you are experiencing a crisis, don't panic or lose hope; ask God to work through it and to glorify Himself. Stand aside and allow God to demonstrate His omnipotence. It is more likely that God will perform a miracle when you are at your weakest than when you are riding the crest of a wave.

In your disappointment, turn to the Savior and allow Him to turn your darkness into light, your blindness into sight, and your defeat into victory. He will carry you through. In the darkness of your loss He might perform a miracle that not only demonstrates His omnipotence, but that will also be beneficial to your faith.

Jesus, Almighty Savior, let the world see
Your omnipotence at work in my life. Amen.

Read John 9:1-12

God of No Limitations

Having said this, He spit on the ground, made some mud with the saliva, and put it on the man's eyes. "Go," He told him, "wash in the Pool of Siloam." (John 9:6-7)

There seems to be no limitations to the ways in which God can work. Sometimes He uses known and typical methods, at other times He uses unknown methods. Jesus used a well-known method of healing with the man who was born blind: the combination of saliva and mud to form a mixture. In those days it was believed that saliva had certain healing qualities. There are also other documented cases where this method was used.

Jesus can open your spiritual eyes by using known methods. Although dramatic conversions do take place and God is glorified through them, most people come to know Christ in ordinary ways like attending worship services, reading the Bible, and attending Bible studies. Because our God is almighty and loving, He can come to you at any time, on any day and in any way He chooses.

He may come to a family member or friend in a remarkable way, but may not open your eyes in the same way. Trust Him—He knows best which method to use at the right time. Don't look for dramatic events or astonishing signs just because this is the way He came to other Christians.

It's unnecessary to envy those who have more exciting stories to tell. Just be sincerely thankful that He has opened your spiritual eyes and that you can see Him in all His glory. That is a miracle in itself.

Light of the World, thank You for opening my eyes. Amen.

Sent by God

"Go," He told him, "wash in the Pool of Siloam" (this word means Sent). (John 9:7)

We always try to provide ordinary solutions for extraordinary events. If we can't find any solution, then we think that someone is holding back a part of the story.

There are people who try to find common solutions to Jesus' miracles. "Saliva *does* have healing qualities," they claim. This explains how Jesus could make the blind man see.

John suggests another way of interpreting and understanding this story. Jesus told the man to wash himself in the Pool of Siloam. This bath was built to provide Jerusalem with an external supply of water when they were under siege. The water was "sent" from the outside and therefore the bath was called "Sent!"

For John it was clear that Jesus was "sent" to heal the blind man. His healing came from God. It is pointless to try to explain how Jesus healed people. All Jesus' healings were "sent by God"—just as Jesus Himself was sent by God. The man wasn't really healed by the mud that was mixed with saliva, or by the water in the pool, but by Almighty God!

Expect God to work in your life in the same way. Seek your own growth, progress in skill, wisdom and maturity. But open yourself and your life completely to the healing of Jesus Christ—the One sent by God! Be prepared to be sent to open the eyes of others.

Here I am, Lord. Send me. Amen.

Read John 9:13-23

Get Your Priorities Straight

They brought to the Pharisees the man who had been blind. Now the day on which Jesus had made the mud and opened the man's eyes was a Sabbath. (John 9:13-14)

Religions tend to develop strange ideas about faith and behavior. Different groups choose different lifestyles which they think are the essential choice for true faith.

The Jewish religion in Jesus' day made a great deal about keeping the Sabbath day holy, which was of course on Saturday. Healing was considered work and should not be performed on the Sabbath. Because Jesus healed the blind man on the Sabbath, He received the disapproval of those who strictly conformed to the Jewish laws.

Jesus, however, had His priorities straight. God's compassion and omnipotence were available on the Sabbath, just as on every other day of the week. Jesus knew that He would probably not meet the blind man again because He was continually on the move. He considered the law about healing on the Sabbath a trifling matter that stood in the way of God's Kingdom acts.

We must try our best to get our priorities straight. What is it about? Compassion, love, acts of grace and faith, healing, the work of the Holy Spirit, evangelism and reaching areas where Christ is unknown—this is what Christ focused on. To maintain traditions and keep to the letter of the law as prescribed by denominations and academic debates, is not unimportant, but it is *less* important. Follow the Savior and hold on to the basics.

Lord Jesus, help me to see and do the greater and more important things. Amen.

How Can You Tell?

Others asked, "How can a sinner do such miraculous signs?" (John 9:16)

It is often difficult to know whether someone is a true servant of Christ or a deceiver. If a person is pleasant he is usually accepted as being sincere. But it is more difficult to identify a false person from a sincere one.

The Pharisees didn't want to accept that Jesus was sent from God. Their criterion was whether He obeyed the letter of their laws Only a few—of which the Pharisees' were most important—could keep their regulations fully. Jesus regarded love for God and people as more important than keeping laws. Therefore, He was a sinner in the Pharisees' eyes and He could not have come from God.

Jesus taught that you should be able to tell whether a person has been sent by God by what he *does* rather than by what he *says*. He performed the kind of deeds that was said the Messiah would do, the kind of deeds people in trouble needed to live strong and healthy lives. The people could see that His actions supported His teachings. They could gather that He was sent by God from what He *did*.

To be an effective witness for Christ, you need to do things that a person sent by God would do. Simple, honest godliness speaks louder than many sermons. Acts of compassion, support in times of crisis, love and care all speak of Jesus. Pray that it will happen in your life that people will know you have been sent by God.

Good Master, grant that my actions will support my words. Amen.

Read John 9:13-23

Making the Blind See

Finally they turned again to the blind man, "What have you to say about Him? It was your eyes He opened." (John 9:17)

We don't change our opinions easily. To discover the truth is a step-by-step process that often takes years.

The man who was born blind was healed in two quick steps. Firstly Jesus put mud on his eyes, then he had to wash it off and he could see again. As John's story unfolds we see how God gradually restores the man's inner vision.

At first the man referred to Jesus simply as "the man they call Jesus" (John 9:11). At this stage Jesus was only a man to him. Later on the unbelieving leaders questioned the man and we see that he has reached a new level of insight about Jesus as he declares, "He is a prophet!" (John 9:17)

A prophet is a servant or messenger from God. Later the man also declares that Jesus has been sent from God (see John 9:33). As his spiritual eyes opened, the man came to full faith in Jesus and also worshiped Him.

You might also be traveling the difficult road from unbelief to true faith. God is leading you gradually to the next step of faith, as you become ready to take it. Your spiritual eyes are continually opening. On this side of eternity you will continue to move toward greater faith and deeper devotion. Someday, when you are with God, you will find yourself drawn fully into praise and worship for Him as your Savior and Redeemer.

Savior and Redeemer, lead me daily into deeper insights of faith and love. Amen.

Undeniable Facts!

He replied, "Whether He is a sinner or not, I don't know. One thing I do know. I was blind but now I see!" (John 9:25)

Some people like to argue about religion. They grab hold of any incident in Scripture and question whether it really could have happened.

The religious leaders again questioned the man who was born blind. They tried to force him to say that Jesus didn't heal him because He was not a prophet. The man replied that he couldn't judge the situation, but that there was one all-important undeniable fact that could not be argued away, "I was blind but now I see."

All believers who have come to know Christ's power and love in their lives and who have been irrevocably changed, base their understanding on their own experiences. Some can't understand how Jesus calmed the storm on the Sea of Galilee, yet they experienced that He has calmed the passions and hate in their own hearts. They might not understand how He changed water into wine, but they know that He filled the emptiness in their own lives with purpose, love and hope.

They know that He has forgiven their sins, healed their sinful and hurting hearts, restored their broken marriages and reunited them with people they had become estranged from. They have hard, undeniable facts on which they firmly base their faith. I trust that this is also true in your own life—or that God, through Jesus, will make it true to you.

Holy Lord Jesus, please guard against my faith ever wavering through the unbelief of others. Amen.

Read John 9:24-34

Testify Again and Again!

He answered, "I have told you already and you did not listen. Why do you want to hear it again? Do you want to become His disciples, too?" (John 9:27)

Many people resist the message of Jesus. They hear Him, but they don't listen carefully to the message. Some people develop a resistant layer that makes them incapable of reacting. Their hearts have been hardened to the gospel message.

The religious leaders in Jesus' time didn't want to know anything about Him. They stubbornly refused to listen to anything that had to do with Jesus. They asked the man who was born blind to repeat his story in the hope of trapping him and making him say something negative about Jesus. The man refused to repeat his story and quite sarcastically asked them whether they wanted to become disciples of Jesus too.

What was once said in sarcasm actually contains more than just a bit of truth. People need the story of Jesus to be told to them again and again, until it touches them. Disciples of Jesus also need to hear it often because it strengthens us and causes us to grow in faith.

We need to hear it again and again—when you are consumed with doubt or despair, and even when you are strong and confident in your faith. You benefit from good times, but also from bad ones. You need to hear the Good News because the impact it makes grows stronger the more you hear it.

Heavenly Teacher, grant that I may still discover new truths in the Gospel message. Amen.

The First Time

Nobody has ever heard of opening the eyes of a man born blind. (John 9:32)

When something unique happens or we do something new, someone usually says, "There's always a first time for everything!" It's exciting when a new invention is tried out for the first time. "Firsts" are important milestones that emphasize humankind's progress—whether it is climbing Mount Everest, setting a sports record or finding a cure for a deadly disease.

Jesus was the first to heal a man born blind. This was because Jesus performed a new act from God that had never been done before. God is always original. He breaks into our circumstances with surprises, miracles, new creations, and new words of direction. He works with His people in a new way and leads them to the final destination of the world according to His sovereign will in a way that people have never expected. We often don't recognize these acts, like His deeds in those days. Only when we look back can we identify that they were acts of Almighty God.

Always look for the new things that God is busy doing. He still has surprises in His treasure chamber that He wants to reveal. There are glorious possibilities ahead. He might lead scientists to a cure for cancer, reveal ways for communities to overcome poverty and starvation, or even lead nations to live together in peace. There is always a first time for everything.

Holy Spirit of God, help me not to limit God's innovative powers through unbelief. Amen.

Read John 9:24-34

God Can Work Through You!

If this man were not from God, He could do nothing. (John 9:33)

Despite the tremendous progress that has taken place over the last two hundred years, there are still things that seem impossible to us. We can't live in peace with each other; we can't share natural resources in such a way that everyone gets the opportunity to live a good life; we can't prevent millions around the world from dying of AIDS, malaria and tuberculosis; and we can't provide each child the security that he will grow up in love and trust.

The man who was born blind and whom Jesus healed had more insight into God and Jesus than all the learned leaders, even though he was just a beggar. He could not only see Jesus, but could see *into* Him. The awesome power that Jesus revealed proved to the blind man that God was at work in Jesus.

Is God at work in you? He performs mighty deeds through some people and is surely waiting to do it through you. He might be waiting for you to humble yourself and acknowledge your emptiness and failures, because you have probably tried to perform deeds in your own limited strength. Likewise, He might expect you to discover your strengths, gifts, and potential and grant them willingly to His service. He expects you to be obedient and to envision what you can do for Him and for others. You probably have abilities you have never even dreamed of—and Jesus wants to work through you.

Lord Jesus, guide me to discover my full potential in Your service. Amen.

Spiritual Blindness

Jesus heard that they had thrown him out, and when He found him, He said, "Do you believe in the Son of Man?" (John 9:35)

There are many well-meaning people, including some who call themselves Christians, who are not sure what they believe. They know that one should have faith in God and that Jesus and the Holy Spirit are involved somehow—but they aren't exactly sure about it. They prefer to leave the details to the teachers, theologians and pastors.

Jesus is the object of our faith. He healed the blind man, and the man became an active partner in the miracle. When the man could see and become part of the community, Jesus invited and challenged the man to believe in Him as the Son of God. There is no doubt that the man believed in God before, but believing in Jesus as God was a totally new step of faith for him.

Jesus also stands before us. He will find you, wherever you are in your wanderings and battle to believe, or how far you have wandered off. He finds you, not only to help you, comfort you and make it easier for you—He challenges you to move beyond the vague notion of "God that is up there somewhere" and to put your trust in Him as the object of your faith!

Regardless of your past problems with faith, focus on Jesus, the Man from Nazareth, the Son of God, and the crucified and resurrected Lord who ascended to heaven. He is the only Redeemer, Savior, and hope for humankind. Make Him your God and your King!

Savior, broaden my faith and deepen my love for You and my fellow man. Amen.

Read John 9:35-41

Who Is He?

"Who is He, sir?" the man asked. "Tell me so that I may believe in Him." (John 9:36)

Even though two thousand years have passed since Jesus walked the streets of Jerusalem, people still find it difficult to determine who He really is.

For some He is a "prophet from long ago." For others He is "a good man who performed acts of love." Some see Him as a teacher who spoke beautiful words. Others see Him as the rebel leader of His time and even call Him a revolutionary.

The miracle that happened in the blind man's life plunged him into a series of amazing experiences and discussions that must have confused him. Suddenly he was not blind anymore—he could see! Then the religious leaders tried to argue that his experience never happened. They cast him out of the synagogue where Jesus found him and spoke to him about faith. No wonder the poor man wanted to know, "The Son of Man, who is He, Sir?"

However strong, weak, confused or full of self-confidence your faith might be, you will benefit from knowing exactly who Jesus Christ is. He is the God who became Man to open your spiritual eyes, to expose you to God's light, and to become your Friend and Savior. Through the ages He comes to find you anew, to lead and accompany you through life and death, and to show you the future that He has prepared for you. No matter how confusing life might be, learn to know Jesus more and more every day.

Teacher and Savior, teach me more about You every day. Amen.

Please Tell Me!

"Who is He, Sir?" the man asked. "Tell me so that I may believe in Him." (John 9:36)

Some people believe everything they hear, no matter how far-fetched it sounds. Other people will only believe something if it is told by a person they trust or who has authority. And some don't believe anything and they go through life suspicious and distrusting.

Jesus healed a man who had been born blind. Undoubtedly the man would have great respect for the person who performed this miracle. But when Jesus challenged him to believe, he was still trying to figure out who Jesus really was, even though he accepted that Jesus came from God. "Who is He, Sir?" he asks. He had to be told. His faith alone was not enough. He needed help to get to the point where he could place his faith in Jesus.

But we have to be told, shown, guided, helped and sometimes spurred on to surrender ourselves. Faith is never our own accomplishment. We need to be coached by someone with greater faith than our own. We have to hear it from others because the small flame of faith in our hearts is often ignited by the fire of faith in another person's heart. We are constantly needing to receive from external resources. It is made alive in us through the power of the Holy Spirit. Maybe someone will ask you today, "Tell me so that I may believe in Him."

Lord my God, thank You for those who told me about You and who irrevocably changed my life. Amen.

Read John 9:35-41

Now You See Him

Jesus said, "You have now seen Him; in fact, He is the one speaking with you." (John 9:37)

We sometimes look at people and things without really seeing them. We watch a variety of sports events on TV, but it's only when there is an action replay, or when the commentator explains the details, that we really see and understand what happened.

Countless people met Jesus, but few really saw Him. When Jesus found the man who had been born blind and healed him, the man had not had much time to see many people. Even so, he saw Jesus better than those who saw Him often. In answer to the man's question, Jesus revealed Himself as the Son of God, "You have now seen Him." This was the culminating point in Jesus' self-revelation and the greatest moment in the man's life.

Jesus, the Savior, seeks to guide you to the point where you can see Him as He really is. He wants to be your Friend and Master. You have possibly read about Him, heard about Him and discussed Him for years already, but He stands before you now, as you read this page, and He says to you, "I am the Light of the World, the strength you need for your specific task and your guide for your journey through life. Open your eyes and see Me in a new light, then you will see things around you differently." He challenges you with a decision: to see Him spiritually or to live in spiritual darkness forever. The choice is yours.

Savior and Light of my life, grant that I may never miss an opportunity to see You. Amen.

"I Stand at the Door and Knock!"

When Jesus reached the spot, He looked up and said to him, "Zacchaeus, come down immediately. I must stay at your house today." (Luke 19:5)

We all enjoy receiving guests—at least most of the time! Jesus Christ enjoyed visiting people. The Bible is full of incidents where God unexpectedly paid people a visit. He visited Abraham, Jacob, Moses, Samuel, Amos, Isaiah and Jeremiah in this way. Most of the New Testament instances where Jesus met people tell how He came to them first.

Jesus' visit to Jericho was not just a casual or random visit. He went straight to Zacchaeus's house, into his heart and into those things that were closest to Zacchaeus—his possessions! This was very important because Zacchaeus's possessions owned him. That is exactly where Jesus touched him—in the sanctuary of Zacchaeus's true self. As a tax collector for the Roman authorities, Zacchaeus was a social outcast.

Zacchaeus opened his home and heart to Jesus. Jesus entered and took possession of the rich man's possessions. Christ is only truly in you when He takes possession of those things that own you. It might be your house, business, career, sport, abilities, or even your failures. You might be addicted to your sins, your fears, or your problems. Let Jesus come in. He made a difference in Zacchaeus's life and He can make a difference in your life too.

Redeemer, come into my life and take full possession of my inner being. Amen.

Read Luke 19:1-10

How Big Is Your Heart?

But Zacchaeus stood up and said to the Lord, "Look, Lord! Here and now I give half of my possessions to the poor, and if I have cheated anybody out of anything, I will pay back four times the amount." (Luke 19:8)

When Jesus enters your life and your heart, your hands reach out to a world in need. Mother Teresa knew Jesus and she reached out to the poor of Calcutta. When Jesus broke down the stumbling blocks in Paul's thinking, his heart went out to the heathens with the gospel message. When Jesus entered Zacchaeus's heart, he compassionately reached out to the poor. In the past he didn't care about the poor because he was too busy making money.

When the love of Jesus reached him deep inside, the smallest man in Jericho obtained the biggest heart on earth. This stingy little man reached out to others with grace that could only come from Jesus.

When Jesus Christ comes into Christians' hearts, they reach out to others. Some reach out with money, like Zacchaeus did. Others reach out with prayer, the gospel message, good deeds of compassion, the gift of healing, the joy of music or by simply caring for and encouraging others. You can determine the depth to which Jesus has entered a person's life by how they reach out to others.

If your faith focuses exclusively on yourself and what you can get out of God and religion, then it's time to seriously consider what it's all about. Faith in Jesus requires us to live like Jesus—pouring ourselves out for the sake of others.

Spirit of God, show me the place where Jesus expects me to reach out to others in love. Amen.

A Bubbling Spring

"Those who drink the water I give will never be thirsty again. It becomes a fresh, bubbling spring within them, giving them eternal life." (John 4:14 NLT)

Water is a source of life. Some streams and rivers are permanently full while others fill up with rain and then eventually dry up. People often depend on this temporary water supply and collect it in dams or containers to keep their animals alive or to water their crops.

The Israelites knew about temporary and disrupted water supply. But they also knew about the much greater value of a permanent water supply. Flowing water was also much better than stagnant water. They spoke of flowing water as "living water." Jesus used this image to describe the spiritual life that was possible through His Spirit and love. This water not only flowed, it bubbled up. Jesus spoke about a vibrant flow of water and the spiritual dynamic it brings, which leads to eternal life—just like a living spring supports plant and animal life on a continuous basis.

The spring freely shares its valuable, life-giving water with the surrounding landscape all the way down to the sea. Therefore, the eternal life that you receive from Jesus is not something you can keep to yourself. It gives you life as you give hope, joy and love to the people around you. It can never remain static. It must always bubble up and flow over to others to really be living water.

Lord and Master, make my life a fountain of living water that bubbles up and gives eternal life. Amen.

Read John 4:11-26

Give Me This Water!

The woman said to Him, "Sir, give me this water so that I won't get thirsty and have to keep coming here to draw water." (John 4:15)

Most of us know how to ask for things that we want. When we were children we nagged for sweets. As we grew older we asked for love and success. In a way these things are selfish, but a normal part of being human.

The woman at the well came to fetch her daily supply of water, just like many others in rural areas do. This woman came with a basic need of life. Even when Jesus spoke of the "living water" she thought of what she could get out of it. She would "never thirst again," in a region that was very hot and dry. She would never have to carry the water can all the way to the well and back home again. She was only aware of the short-term benefits she would get.

It is okay to come to Jesus to ask for something. You might be yearning for security, peace of mind, or healing from a serious illness. You might be battling with bitterness, depression or loneliness. You might feel that it is dishonorable to come to the Master with an apparently selfish need. No, come as you are in your weakness and need. Jesus will accept you, help you and make you whole. Then you can spend the rest of your life in praise to and worship of the Savior.

Holy Lord Jesus, transform my demands and needs into joy and thanksgiving. Amen.

Our Steadfast Rock

*Jesus Christ is the same yesterday
and today and forever. (Hebrews 13:8)*

It is only natural that our image of Jesus Christ would be of someone with a Palestinian background from the Roman golden age. It was at that time that God chose to reveal Himself to the world and ever since people have thought of Christ in terms of the idiom, costume and customs of that time. Because we imagine Him in that time, we easily lose sight of the eternal Christ.

If Jesus was merely a historic figure, we might wonder if He is of limited value to us. But this is not the Jesus of Christianity. We believe in a Jesus who is as alive today as He was two-thousand years ago. Because He is eternal, He is with us today.

As He taught, guided and blessed His first disciples, He wants to do the same for you. Unfortunately our perspective on His ability to help and bless us is clouded by the problems and confusion of our modern society.

You may think that you are living in a unique period of time, and in a certain sense this is true. But the basic problems of the world today are still the same as when Jesus was on earth. Greed, lust, self-centeredness, pettiness, hatred and bitterness are still powerful influences.

The living Christ can deal with these deviations and illness of man's spirit and intellect, just as He could centuries ago, because He is eternal and unchanging. On this steadfast Rock we can build our lives.

*Holy Master, I gain peace of mind from knowing that You
are eternal and steadfast in this ever-changing world. Amen.*

Read John 13:1-17

Our Example of Love

"Now that I, your Lord and Teacher, have washed your feet, you also should wash one another's feet. I have set you an example that you should do as I have done for you." (John 13:14-15)

Throughout Christ's earthly ministry He demonstrated through word and deed the kind of life God wanted people to live. Every lesson was based on love in the truest sense of the word—love that was willing to make sacrifices to prove its truth and trustworthiness.

One of the most moving and striking examples of this was on the evening before the crucifixion and glorification of Christ, when the Son of God took on the form of a servant and performed the humble task of washing His disciples' feet—including Judas Iscariot who would soon betray Him.

Some consider this act of Christ as menial and inappropriate. On the contrary, this humble act revealed the gracious charitableness that characterizes the Christian faith which every Christian should strive toward.

Let us learn from this and follow Jesus' example. In this way we will become true and trustworthy ambassadors for Christ in a world that desperately cries out for Christian love.

Gracious Lord, make us worthy to follow Your guidance and become servants and ambassadors for Your kingdom. Amen.

Another Lesson in Humility

He was in Bethany, reclining at the table of a man known as Simon the Leper. (Mark 14:3)

Jesus knew exactly what was going to happen to Him. With divine knowledge and insight He was fully aware of the plot to kill Him, the methods His enemies would use, and the cruel way in which He would die through the crucifixion.

But at the same time He knew, in the fulfillment of God's plan of redemption, that He would gloriously triumph over death, rise from the dead and rule with God for all eternity.

When we know that we are going to be honored at a particular occasion, most of us bask in expectancy about the coming exaltation. We enjoy the attention we get before and after the event. It is human nature for us to seek this kind of attention.

Jesus, however, sought the quiet loneliness of Simon the Leper—away from the crowds and out of the spotlight. Because lepers were banned and rejected from society, Jesus was sure that He would not be accompanied by a cheering crowd. This indicates the humility of the Son of God and is the example He sets for all Christians. Let us follow in His footsteps.

Lord Jesus, teach me each day to follow Your example and walk the road of humility. Amen.

Read Mark 14:3-9

A Good Deed

"Leave her alone," said Jesus. "Why are you bothering her? She has done a beautiful thing to Me." (Mark 14:6)

After Malcolm Muggeridge visited Mother Teresa to find out more about her work, he wrote a book entitled, *Something Beautiful for God*. She cared for the sick, fed the hungry, and prayed for the people on the streets of Calcutta. She knew that Christ was present in those people and she wanted to do it out of love for the Lord and compassion for them.

People often do beautiful things for God for different reasons. In his last will and testament, one affluent believer bequeathed an amount to a Bible school. In a colorless city a church is surrounded by a garden with the most beautiful flowers. Passersby stop just to admire the beautiful flowers. An elderly member of the congregation who lives in an apartment building took over the care of the garden and used his "green fingers" to demonstrate his love for God. One person might demonstrate love through music or singing, another through encouraging words and another through serving the community.

As a Christian you may think that you do your duty when you have your quiet time, attend church and tithe. The woman in today's reading went further than mere duty. Jesus approved of what she did because He understood the nature of love. He saw that her expression of overflowing love far exceeded duty. May this inspire us to do something beautiful for God and for people.

Faithful Savior, help me to perform my duties and to look for opportunities to perform beautiful deeds of love. Amen.

Help for the Poor

"The poor you will always have with you,
and you can help them any time you want.
But you will not always have Me." (Mark 14:7)

Poverty is a huge problem all over the world and this global crisis is worsening. Half of the six billion people on earth survive on less than $2 a day. While most Christians feel powerless in the face of this overwhelming challenge, we can't simply turn a blind eye.

Jesus was very serious when He said that we would always have the poor with us. But He didn't say that we should not do anything about it. In fact, He said that we should *always* do something to help them. Jesus moved among the poor, the outcasts of society and the mentally ill. He said that God was present in them and in their need.

One way in which we can help the poor is through personal gifts. Some of them live in such dire conditions that an item of clothing or a proper meal would be of great help. You could also offer them a job, even if it is temporary or for a small wage. To reward their work also allows them to feel worthy and have self-respect.

Another way of helping is by supporting organizations that specialize in assisting the poor. You can also encourage movements that attempt to better conditions and social economic practices. In any of these ways we can follow Jesus' example and act in love.

Master, deepen my empathy and
understanding of poverty. Amen.

Read Mark 14:12-26

An Extraordinary Meal

While they were eating, Jesus took bread, and when He had given thanks, He broke it and gave it to His disciples, saying, "Take it; this is My body." (Mark 14:22)

Sharing a meal is a way to build relationships. Through countless millennia, sharing food with others has been a sign of hospitality and an invitation to a deeper relationship. There is no doubt that families who meet at the dinner table each evening develop a special bond. Likewise, couples will often go out for a meal in hopes of seeing their relationship blossom.

When Jesus shared this meal with His disciples, it was clear that they had become uniquely close to the Lord. Yet rather than focus on social relationships, Jesus draws attention to a spiritual relationship. Just as people tend to grow closer to each other through breaking bread, Jesus teaches all His followers that through His broken body, we can grow close to God Himself.

While fellowship with others is undoubtedly important, the heart of the Christian faith is that Jesus' death makes a relationship with God possible. Jesus bore the judgment for our sin; He experienced the consequences of our sin and shame, and in Him we have forgiveness.

If you trust in Jesus and follow Him—knowing that His death was sufficient—then you are invited into the presence of the Father, not on the basis of physical bread, but on the grounds of the all-sufficient sacrifice of Jesus.

Thank You Jesus, that You made friendship with God possible. Thank You for the promise of salvation and that I can one day feast with You in heaven. Amen.

Is Your Heart Burning within You?

They asked each other, "Were not our hearts burning within us while He talked with us on the road and opened the Scriptures to us?" (Luke 24:32)

There are various and diverse forms of touch. The doctor touches you on the spot where the pain is and you say, "Yes, there!" The parent touches the crying child and kisses the pain away. If your spouse falls asleep during the Sunday service you nudge him with your elbow to wake him up.

Whenever God touches people, He awakens hidden senses. When Jesus touched the two friends on the road to Emmaus, He ignited a flame within them. They were sad, disillusioned and felt that they had been let down. Their thoughts were clouded by confusion, but Christ enlightened their thinking. His questions directed them to what really mattered and His love set their hearts on fire. When they recognized Him and He disappeared from before them, they were wide awake and speedily traveled back to Jerusalem to share the good news with the others.

When the risen Christ touches your heart it fills you with passion, warmth and conviction. He gives energy to your soul and motivates you like never before. When you understand Christ, then you will love Him and be filled with His love, which will reach others through you. May Christ our Savior ignite that flame in your life today.

Lord Jesus, may You ignite the holy fire in my life and purge away all wayward and evil desires. Amen.

Read John 5:1-17

Get Up and Walk!

Jesus said to him, "Get up!
Pick up your mat and walk." (John 5:8)

It's easy to fall into a rut. Some people dig ruts for themselves that are so deep they can't see anything else. Someone once said that the only difference between a rut and a grave is the depth. The routine of everyday life and the necessity of reliability can easily turn into monotony and a resistance to change. Sometimes it takes a kick-start or a disaster to get us out of the comfortable rut in which we live.

Jesus summed up the sick man who lay beside the pool at Bethesda for thirty-eight years, waiting for someone to help him. He thought that he needed a helping hand. Jesus must have surprised him when He said, "Come on, don't just sit there—get up and walk! Start to really live for a change!" Jesus said it with love, but also forcefully. It challenged the man to leave his comfort zone. It created the possibility of walking instead of just waiting, of moving instead of keeping still, of reaching out instead of being closed within himself.

Jesus commands you and me to also get out of our rut. A better and greater life awaits us. There are no limits to the possibilities that stretch out before us. You can explore, "How wide and long and high and deep is the love of Christ" (Eph. 3:18). Our spiritual journey doesn't begin when we die. It begins now—the minute you stand up and walk! With Jesus as your Savior.

Savior and Redeemer, help me to move
towards the place You are sending me. Amen.

Immediate Action

At once the man was cured;
he picked up his mat and walked. (John 5:9)

Many things in this life can lead to our downfall. Habits ensure that we get stuck in a rut. Fear prevents us from moving in a new direction. Doubt continually gnaws away at our faith and trust, both in God and ourselves. Failures of the past haunt us. Many things in the world around us, as well as within us, threaten to destroy us.

But it doesn't have to be like this. The man at the pool of Bethesda was a failure for thirty-eight years. He was ruled by sickness and self-pity. Then a word from Jesus transformed him from failure to faith, from sickness to health, from self-pity to radiant confidence in God.

Two things happened to lift this man out of his depressing condition. The one was a command from Jesus, and the other was the man's faithful obedience to Jesus. At Jesus' word, and apparently also His gaze, the man believed that he could be healed—and it happened.

Jesus does not want you to continue to wallow in the mud of self-pity forever. No matter how long you have battled with your doubt, defeat or failures, when you trust in Jesus you know that your future is always more hopeful than your past. We are never promised success as the world views success, but as we faithfully obey the Lord, we know that we are given strength beyond ourselves. Are you willing to leave self-pity behind and take your first steps of obedience?

Lord my God, forgive me for allowing negative things
to rule my life. Help me to make a new start now. Amen.

Read Mark 1:32-39

The Great Physician

The whole town gathered at the door, and Jesus healed many who had various diseases. He also drove out many demons. (Mark 1:33-34)

In a radio interview a pastor was asked what percentage of people who went for healing was really healed and he replied, "About one out of three." The advert for the campaign marketed the gathering as an opportunity for "miraculous healing." The pastor admitted that no follow-ups were done to see whether the healings lasted.

In Jesus' time, before technology and science, sickness was a far greater threat than it is today. There were many false healers on the scene. Many healers claimed that they could perform miracles. The lack of adequate medicine increased the popularity of faith healers.

When the Israelites dreamed of God's coming Messianic age, it included healing (see Isa. 35:3-6). They knew that it had to come from God. Through Jesus Christ it did happen. Health and wholeness are a blessing from God, and Christians thank God for the many ways in which healing takes place.

One form of healing is divine healing. Jesus often healed people in sudden, dramatic, and miraculous ways. He might also use the quiet road of prayer, or even the laying on of hands. God also uses the medical profession and its advancements to aid healing. Many won't receive the healing they desire in this life, but we know that when Christ returns, our bodies will be transformed, and all impairments and disease will be gone forever.

Lord Jesus, we pray for all who are involved in medical research and for those who make healing their calling. Amen.

July

Soli Deo Gloria

If Your Presence does not go with us,
do not send us up from here.

~ Exodus 33:15

Almighty, all-knowing,
all-seeing and omnipresent God:
How could we attempt to enter
this new month without You?
To know You is to choose life! To turn away from
You is to miss the purpose of our lives.
Take hold of my hand, O Lord,
and lead me along Your path.
If You go with us we will stand firm and succeed,
but if we turn away from You and deny You,
we will stumble and fall.
We ask for Your support and love
which we need every day.
Your protection for every uncertain step
on dangerous paths—Your peace and comfort
in all our sorrow, suffering and pain.
Your inspiration through the Holy Spirit
in our fellowship with You. We do not want to
venture into the unknown without You.
As always, be our Good Shepherd
who leads us to green pastures and beside
the still waters where we will find Your peace.
Help us to be obedient as we follow You
to our eternal destination.
Do all this in Your grace and through Jesus Christ
and the Holy Spirit.
Amen.

Hallelujah! God Is King!

The Lord reigns forever; He has established
His throne for judgment. (Psalm 9:7)

Through the centuries kings and rulers have come and gone: Saul, David, Solomon, Caesar, Nero, Hitler, and Stalin—to name a few. Rulers govern their kingdoms for a short while and then disappear. All worldly rulers reign for a limited time only: political leaders, heavyweights in the business world, technological giants. Then their time passes and they are quickly forgotten.

The people of Israel needed more than a temporary, human king to reign over them. Even though they had earthly kings, they knew that God was truly their King. They knew that they could always depend on God. He is always the same: yesterday, today, tomorrow and for all eternity. In a thousand years' time people will still look up to Him for His kingly reign to lead, judge and support them.

God is eternal! He is guiding the world and is in control of all things—even if it is beyond the sight of human eyes and the understanding of human minds. Because of Jesus' earthly life we know that God's rulership is not the kind of imperial might that earthly megalomaniacs longed for and wanted for the world. His reign is of love, saving grace, peace and truth. This is also from where He will return again in all His glory to come and claim His own.

King of kings and Lord of lords, we bow before You in worship
because of Your loving rulership over our lives. Amen.

Read Psalm 8:1-9

Worship God in His Majesty

O Lord, our Lord, how majestic is Your name in all the earth! (Psalm 8:9)

We often say, quite thoughtlessly, "What a small world we live in!" How wrong we are! Just think about this fact: The land mass of the African continent can fit the United States, Europe, China, India, Argentina and New Zealand on it, and you would still have 100,000 square kilometers to spare!

The people in the Bible did not have modern ways of transport and so often led isolated lives. Every nation had its own "god." "Jehovah!" or "our Lord!" was the name of the God of Israel. It was consequently somewhat challenging to declare that "His name is glorious over all the earth." Of course they knew that their God was bigger than the borders of their limited little country. He was also the God over all the nations. That is why God was not just "our God" but also "the God of all the nations."

These days we know about the existence of other planets, stars, heavenly bodies and distant galaxies. But no matter how impressive our knowledge of outer space is, we know that God is the Creator of all the world. All of creation belongs to Him and every part of it reveals something of His character to us.

So stop focusing on insignificant things. See the wonder of the world and the greatness of God. Delight yourself in His presence. Worship the God whose name is Wonderful over all the earth.

Lord God, allow me to see Your majesty every single day. Amen.

With Your Whole Heart

I will praise You, O LORD, with all my heart;
I will tell of all Your wonders. (Psalm 9:1)

I am sure that you have been to a theatre production or a sports event and got the impression that the people's hearts weren't in what they were doing: they just seemed to go through the motions. It looked as if their thoughts were somewhere else, and as if they could not wait to finish the task.

The person who wrote Psalm 9 was grateful to God for the mighty acts of redemption that He had performed. He knew that with all the injustice in the world, there must be someone who will ensure that law and order prevail. That is exactly what God does and the writer wanted to testify of his deepest thankfulness to God.

You and I should be doing the same. We are the product of what God has done for us. Christ is revealed in you continuously through the work of the Holy Spirit. Bit by bit you are becoming a new creation through the work that God is doing in you. He has also done good things in your life through other people.

Therefore, praise Him with your whole heart. Put everything you have into your praise and worship. Let your heart overflow with praise and thanks, and joy. He did not hold back from loving you completely and so you must not merely go through the motions when you respond to His blessings and grace. Put your whole heart into it.

Eternal Father, it is my delight to praise You. Let Your Spirit help me to do so with my whole heart and my whole being. Amen.

Read Psalm 9:1-21

Joy in God

Praise be to the name of God for ever and ever;
wisdom and power are His. (Daniel 2:20)

Many people see a name simply as a label that they can use to identify a person. Many people are also given nicknames like Shorty, Goliath, Buddy, etc. Many people hold positions in life with important titles: Judge, Mayor and Your Honor.

There are many names of God. The Israelites referred to God as Jehovah or the Lord. The Canaanites, who lived in Israel before the Israelites emigrated from Egypt, worshiped many idols, but the Most High was a name that was above all names. He was exalted above all other gods. The Israelites, who had been set free from slavery, liked this name and began to use it to refer to their God. It was applicable because not only is God far above all the people who worship Him, He is also exalted far above all the other gods that people might have thought of worshiping.

Do not be satisfied with a lesser god, and above all, do not allow anything else to take God's place in your life: a sports hero, a singer, or a politician. "Things" also do not have what it takes to be a god: possessions, riches or even the nation to which you belong. Only Jesus Christ, who is now sitting on the throne in heaven, is high and holy enough to deserve your love and loyalty. Give it to Him with joy in your heart. He will never leave you nor let you down (see Heb. 13:5).

Loving Lord Jesus, Almighty God,
we fall at Your feet in joyful worship. Amen.

Praise God for His Redemption

I will praise You, O Lord my God, with all my heart;
I will glorify Your name forever. (Psalm 86:12)

There are people who shamelessly boast of their achievements. They conveniently forget all their faults and failings. We have all achieved many things in our lives, but some people rely on what they have achieved much more than others do.

The psalmist had a far better perspective on life. He was so excited about what God had done in his life that he was determined to tell other people about it. God performed mighty acts of salvation for him and he felt that he had to tell the world about them. Indeed, it is because of the testimony of these people that so many people all over the world know about God's wonderful acts today. The prophets passionately told of the things God had done. The apostles, with the written and the spoken word, told of what God did through Jesus Christ. Because they spoke of God's marvelous acts of salvation, those who heard experienced His mighty works in their lives too.

Maybe you know Jesus Christ because of the testimony of another. If Christ has done anything wonderful for you, you should tell others of His wonderful acts of salvation. You might just speak to someone who is waiting for a testimony so that God's redemptive acts can come to fruition in his life too.

Lord Jesus, be with all those today who passionately
tell others of Your acts of redemption. Amen.

Read Psalm 2:1-12

God's Sense of Humor

The One enthroned in heaven laughs;
the LORD scoffs at them. (Psalm 2:4)

Many people around us have a sparkling sense of humor. A God-honoring sense of humor helps you to stay grounded in a world that often seems to be off balance. D. F. Malherbe, a South African writer and linguist, calls humor "a laugh with a cry." Humor is able to see the absurdity in life and keeps a person humble. Often cartoonists reflect the ridiculous things that politicians say or do and that helps to reveal their human weaknesses and foibles.

God also has a sense of humor: why else would He have made the giraffe, the toad or even people? He empowers the weak and brings the arrogant to their knees. He waters the seed of self-destruction that over-ambitious people often plant when they lay their evil plans.

You do not need to be afraid that the world will completely turn into chaos. The Lord mocks those who plan to usurp Him. He scoffs at the empty arguments of those who claim He does not exist.

On Easter Sunday when God raised Christ from the dead, perhaps there was a hint of a smile because of the reaction that it caused among those who had crucified Him. In the end all secrets will be revealed and hidden agendas will be exposed. The truth will shine like the rays of the sun. Love will take its rightful place and peace will triumph.

Loving God, grant me the grace
to laugh, to love and to trust. Amen.

Thus Far, and No Further!

He rebukes them in His anger and terrifies them in His wrath, saying, "I have installed My King on Zion, My holy hill." (Psalm 2:5-6)

It is quite possible that at some time in the past you have looked at a completely chaotic situation and said to yourself, "When will this ever come to an end?" It might even sometimes seem to you that God has completely forgotten about the whole situation here on earth, or that He is powerless to do anything about it. It becomes very difficult to trust God in the midst of circumstances that border on chaos.

The writer of Psalm 2 quite possibly intended it to be a coronation psalm for the king. People used to believe that the monarch was very close to God and that God had appointed him to his position. In the face of all the enemies who were determined to prevent the king from ascending to his throne and taking authority, God still placed him there and he was still God's loyal servant or son. In this way God thwarts all evil plans. No matter what they do, ultimately God says to them, "Thus far, and no further!"

Christians ought to understand and welcome the judgment of God. It is the final intervention that He makes into all the chaos, strife, confusion, anarchy and foolishness. When God takes authority over an evil situation, no matter how painful His intervention might be, it opens the way for healing, light and restoration.

Most holy God, confirm Your singular rule in our chaotic world today. Amen.

Which Side Is God On?

God is present in the company of the righteous.
You evildoers frustrate the plans of the poor,
but the Lord *is their refuge.* (Psalm 14:5-6)

It is a fact that evil people often enjoy prosperity while things go badly for good people. If it is true that God is a God who wants people to live righteous lives, why does He not reward the good people with prosperity? If God were to do that, life would undoubtedly be wonderful. Not only do evil people seem to get ahead, but they often do so at the expense of good people. Through passing centuries this apparent injustice has upset believers.

Not all evil people prosper. Many of them end up behind bars. And there are lots of good people who prosper. In spite of this very confusing picture, it is an important truth that those who choose to obey God and live good lives do so because they believe in God Almighty, and not because they want to receive earthly rewards. They believe that God really does care for them, that He does in fact sustain them and that He often rewards them with more than they deserve. The central fact is indeed that God is on their side in the conflict against evil. Their faith also teaches them that evil is strong and resourceful and that is why things do not always go well for them.

Jesus experienced the evils of this world. He did not end up in a palace with lots of servants and luxuries, but on a cross. Now God has exalted Him to the highest place. This is the God who is on your side.

Merciful God, help me not to envy
the wicked when they prosper. Amen.

God's Good Gifts

I said to the Lord, "You are my Lord; apart from You I have no good thing." (Psalm 16:2)

When you were a child you probably thought that all good gifts came from your parents or from Santa Claus. But when you grew up, you became the one who made good things happen for other people.

The believer, however, knows that God is the giver of every good and perfect gift. When you put your life in God's hands, you will appreciate and understand what He really does in your life. He gives you infinitely more than just gifts. He has given you a rich inheritance. If you have been privileged enough to receive a good education, remember that you did not educate yourself. This was simply a result of the structures of society. God has given you good things like the church where you can grow in faith. Then there is the Bible that was written by people who were inspired by God and which has been passed on and translated by committed and diligent students. It was created to help you and guide you.

The most precious gift that God has given you is your salvation through Jesus Christ. He lifted you up out of the mire of sin and placed your feet on an immovable rock of faith and He gave you spiritual gifts. All of this compels you to worship Him and in turn serve other people so that they too can partake of His good gifts. You will see that there is no end to the good things that come from God. Just sit and prayerfully meditate on them.

God of love and mercy, may Your Holy Spirit help me to appreciate the good gifts that I receive from Your hand. Amen.

Read Psalm 16:1-11

God Takes Care of Your Future

Lord, You have assigned me my portion
and my cup; you have made my lot secure.
Surely I have a delightful inheritance. (Psalm 16:5-6)

We often used to sing the old hymn when we were small: *Count your blessings, name them one by one, count your many blessings and see what God has done*. It is good to meditate on all the good things that God has caused in your life.

The greatest blessing that God has given to any person is, however, not a gift, an opportunity or even assistance. The gift is God *Himself*! He is immeasurably greater than any gift. In fact, He is greater than the sum total of all His good gifts. Even if He never gave us any other gifts, it would still be worth it to seek Him.

David, who wrote today's psalm, was king: he was powerful, successful, rich and popular. In his reign the kingdom extended farther than under any other king at any other time. Calculated in human terms, he had everything. Nonetheless, all the success did not mean as much to him as God. David knew that in God's hands his future was secure.

If Jesus Christ is your Redeemer and Savior, if He is more precious to you than anything else, like David you can be certain that your future is secure. As long as you have Jesus! So place your future in His hands and let Him work out His sovereign will in your life.

Omniscient Father, my past, present and
future are in Your loving hands. Amen.

The Finger of God

When I consider Your heavens, the work of Your fingers, the moon and the stars, which You have set in place, what is man? (Psalm 8:3-4)

Your fingers are an integral part of your body. You use them to eat, to take hold of all kinds of instruments and tools, to point, draw and type. When someone is clumsy we say, "He has butterfingers."

The writers of the Bible extended the image of the fingers on a human hand to God. In today's verse we read that the heavens, moon and stars are the work of God's fingers. When Moses demonstrated miracles in Egypt, the Egyptian magicians said to Pharaoh, "He does them by the finger of God" (Exod. 8:19). When God gave Moses the stone tablets on which He had written the Ten Commandments, it was said that they had been written by the finger of God: "The tablets of stone inscribed by the finger of God" (Exod. 31:18).

Jesus said that He cast out evil powers by the finger of God: "If I drive out demons by the finger of God, then the kingdom of God has come to you" (Luke 11:20). God's finger represents His almighty power that was at work when He created the world, when He gave the law to guide His people and when He healed the sick.

The finger of God is at work in your life too. Sometimes He points out a specific direction to guide you. Sometimes He puts His finger on the sinful places in your life to bring you to repentance. When you are sick, He lays His finger on you to make you whole again.

Father, thank You for lovingly guiding my life. Amen.

Read Psalm 8:1-9

What Is Man?

What is man that You are mindful of him, the son of man that You care for him? (Psalm 8:4)

I spent many of my childhood years growing up at the foothills of the Drakensberg Mountain Range in South Africa. Mountain climbing was one of our favorite pastimes. We could often be found competing with one another to see who would be the first to reach the highest peak and look out over the panoramic view. Each time we felt a sense of achievement and victory. But at the same time there was a sense of humbleness at the immensity of God's creation. On top of the highest rock, the town lay beneath us like a dot on the landscape. It made us feel small and insignificant.

Next to God, people are minutely tiny—despite our achievements and the way we talk as though we own the world. Yet, in the vast expanse of the universe, with all its amazing and overwhelming truths, God chose to care for us.

You are the crowning glory of God's creation and the focus of His love. His attention is on you more than on any other creature. You are His child, made in His image. He longs to form His image in you more and more as He makes you more like Christ. He wants to speak to you. He wants to guide and direct you. He wants to see you grow in His grace and love. He created you to bring Him glory and honor—to proclaim His glory. He yearns for you to have fellowship with Him. The best way to do this is by honoring your fellow humans.

Lord, may Your image be more and more established in me. Amen.

When God Seems Far Away

Why, O LORD, do You stand far off? Why do You hide Yourself in times of trouble? (Psalm 10:1)

One of the worst things about being in trouble is that you feel totally helpless and you can do nothing about it. It sometimes seems as if there are people "out there" who are conspiring against you. At the same time you feel isolated and alone. But worst of all is the feeling that God has abandoned you.

If you, as a Christian, have ever felt like this, know that it is absolutely normal. The writer of Psalm 10 felt exactly the same way. He was surrounded by evil-minded people who were out to get him. They were cunning, vicious villains who made his life very difficult. He felt that God, who should have been defending him in this situation and who should have been bringing about his enemies' downfall, had hidden Himself when he needed Him most.

He was in the process of learning one of the most difficult lessons a person can learn: that problems are part of life. Yet the psalmist did not forsake his faith in God. He asked God to come out from His hiding place and do something about the evil and the trouble that he was wrestling with.

But no matter how difficult and confusing life might be, God might conceal Himself for a little while. He wants you to seek Him in the darkness so that you will know without a doubt that He still loves you.

Merciful God, help me to continue to seek You in the darkness until I find You. Amen.

Read Psalm 12:1-8

God Keeps His Promises!

"Because of the oppression of the weak and the groaning of the needy, I will now arise," says the Lord. "I will protect them from those who malign them." (Psalm 12:5)

People's lives can be threatened by all kinds of dangers. Sickness can attack; natural disasters destroy: floods, tsunamis, earthquakes and fires. Road accidents are everyday occurrences; crime and violence increase daily; there are political uprisings, terrorists and hijackers, and wars.

But we cannot live in constant fear of these things. Of course we must take every necessary precaution, but above all we should be seeking the protection of God. King David wrote the psalm on which we are meditating today, and he knew all about danger.

It seems that he lived in constant fear for his life. But he also knew the danger born from lies and the groundless boasting of arrogant people. The tongue can be just as deadly as the sword. We need to be protected from the braggarts who think that they can rule the world through propaganda and misinformation.

The only way in which we can know peace of mind in similar circumstances is through the surety of God's protection, by living in Him through faith and trusting Him at all times. Jesus was able to sleep while a storm was raging around Him because He had entrusted His life to His Father. He could trust Himself to the Father when He was hanging on the cross because He could look beyond the fear of death to the glory of eternal life.

Lord, I call on Your promise
and Your faithfulness. Amen.

God Watches Over You

O Lord, You will keep us safe and protect us from such people forever. The wicked freely strut about when what is vile is honored among men. (Psalm 12:7-8)

There comes a time in our lives when it feels like God is far away. That is how many people feel when problems arise in their lives. Some people have financial problems; others develop health problems; and still others have marital problems. It even seems as if the pressure comes down on you from all sides.

We need to remember, always, that God's concern for us cannot ever be measured by the intensity of the problems that overwhelm us. It is also not calculated according to the number of blessings or prosperity that we experience. He does not watch over the righteous as a reward for their righteousness. You cannot earn God's love, no matter how good or exemplary your life is. The Lord watches over you simply because He has chosen to love you. He constantly watches over you and His love for you never wavers.

God watches over you in every situation. He watches over you in love, when you are sick and when you are well; when you are tired and worn out; when you are confused and weary; when you are outcast and defeated; when you are joyful and jubilant; when you are strong and successful; when you are calm and tranquil; when you are busy and diligent—He watches over you in love always!

Father God, watch over those today who feel alone and abandoned. Amen.

Read Psalm 16:1-11

God Is Never Far Away

I have set the Lord always before me. Because He is at my right hand, I will not be shaken. (Psalm 16:8)

Alfred Delp was a Jesuit priest who was executed by the Nazis because he resisted their régime during the Second World War. When he was in prison, he wrote:

> *I was inwardly very focused on God. I have many questions to ask Him and many things I want to tell Him. But there is one thing that is as clear and tangible to me as never before: the world is filled to overflowing with God. This realization wells up in you as if it flows out of the pores of things. But we are often blind to them. In good times and bad we just remain bogged down. We do not experience these through and through to the point where they flow forth from God Himself. This is what creates our true relationship with good and evil. God wants to sanctify every situation and He expects and asks of you to respond in love and worship.*

Ten weeks later he was hanged. Alfred Delp was aware of God's presence in his prison cell. King David was also fully aware of God's presence every day.

You can experience His presence too. Whether you are at work or at play; whether you are rushing around or relaxing; whether you are praying or wrestling with a difficult situation: remind yourself that God is with you. He is never far from you: how far are you from Him?

Stay with me, Lord, especially when it is hard for me to stay close to You. Amen.

God Remains Faithful!

Your faithfulness continues through all generations;
You established the earth, and it endures. (Psalm 119:90)

In 2002 an important summit was held in Johannesburg. The theme was Sustainable Development. Important people from all over the world attended the summit. It was also known as Earth Summit 2002 and it addressed the problem of the squandering of the earth's natural resources through over-developing resources such as minerals and forests.

How can Earth continue to exist with more than eight billion people that need to live here? This is a serious problem. The summit looked at the economical and political issues as well as scientific and social problems. But they probably didn't look at the spiritual aspect.

They forgot that God created the earth and that He created it with the ability to renew itself. In the long run it is a spiritual issue. The Bible looks beyond the physical planet and looks at the Creator of the universe. The Bible proclaims that, "You established the earth, and it endures." It also declares, "Your faithfulness continues through all generations." Those who have placed their trust in God look past the *How?* problems of the moment to the *Who?* question of all time. They know that God established the earth. They believe that He will sustain it. He will guide humanity to responsible stewardship of the earth's resources. Because they trust in God who remains faithful from generation to generation.

I praise and thank You, Creator God, that You in Your faithfulness
will continue to sustain and renew Your creation. Amen.

 Read Genesis 13:1-18

A Sacrifice to God

Abram moved his tents and went to live near the great trees of Mamre at Hebron, where he built an altar to the LORD. (Genesis 13:18)

Mother Teresa of Calcutta was one of the most significant people of the twentieth century. Malcolm Muggeridge wrote a book about her life and called it *Something Beautiful for God.* This phrase sums up her whole life. She gave her whole life to God—a beautiful sacrifice to God.

Abram went to live in Hebron where he built an altar to the Lord. It was his gift to God who had given him so much in life and who had performed such mighty deeds for him. Abram is still honored in Hebron today.

When we do something for God, our lives attain its highest purpose. It might be singing a beautiful song that glorifies God; writing poetry for Him, or performing deeds of compassion and care. Paul dedicated his life to proclaiming the Gospel. Jesus died on Golgotha, and one way to view the crucifixion is to see it as a sacrifice to the Father.

Communities have built great churches, constructed hospitals, and sent missionaries to far off places as their offering to God. One congregation sponsored a worker to go and live in a poor neighborhood and called him *Our man for others*! Others have taught the illiterate and shared their faith in God with them as their offering to God. Some sacrifices to God are big and others are small. But all of them are beautiful to God. What offering are you bringing?

Lord, my God, accept in Your mercy my humble sacrifice. Amen.

God Rules with Sovereignty

Melchizedek was … priest of God Most High, and he blessed Abram, saying, "Blessed be Abram by God Most High, Creator of heaven and earth. And blessed be God Most High who delivered your enemies into your hand." (Genesis 14:18-20)

There are many different faiths and religions in the world and each one has its own god or idol. The followers of each god believe that *their* god is the best. This causes much conflict and misunderstanding.

King Melchizedek was a king and priest in Jerusalem. He was a Canaanite and therefore a stranger to Abram. He met with Abram to congratulate him on a military victory and to bring him a gift. The Canaanites had many gods and "God Most High" was the name of the highest of their gods. In this way they were saying that they worshiped the greatest and most sovereign God, greater than all the others, no matter how great the followers of other gods thought their gods to be.

Today people still worship many gods, both of the spiritual and secular kind. Christians worship Jesus Christ and know Him as the name that is above all other names. They exalt Jesus even when people around them are worshiping the gods of pleasure, sex, money, food and power. We are convinced that He is sovereign and that eventually, "at the name of Jesus every knee should bow, in heaven and on earth and under the earth, and every tongue confess that Jesus Christ is Lord, to the glory of God the Father" (see Phil. 2:10-11).

Almighty God, may the day come quickly when all people will recognize the true glory of Jesus and worship Him alone. Amen.

Our God Sees All Things

[Hagar] gave this name to the LORD who spoke to her: "You are the God who sees me," for she said, "I have now seen the One who sees me." (Genesis 16:13)

Some people, when they are overwhelmed with problems, feel "lost." Their problems look huge and solutions so difficult that they can't find answers. They do not know where or to whom to turn and they don't know where to start. To add to their crisis, it seems to them as if no one is interested or willing to help them.

Hagar probably felt that way when she came to the spring in the desert and God appeared to her and commanded her to return to Abraham and Sarah. She was completely and utterly lost, but God in His grace appeared to her out of nowhere and promised her a future that would form part of His plan of salvation. Immediately she knew that she could not vanish out of God's sight—not even in the middle of the desert and deep in the midst of trouble.

God also sees you. You can never drift out of the range of His all-seeing eye, even when you are overwhelmed by problems and difficulties. John Newton proclaimed that the inconceivably amazing grace of God could save a lost son and runaway child like him. God knows exactly where you are! He sees you, whether you are standing on victorious ground or caught in the mire of sin; in joy or despair, when you laugh or cry, God watches over you constantly.

Omniscient God, thank You that You always watch over me, a worthless sinner. Amen.

The Only True and Living God

The LORD is the true God; He is the living God, the eternal King. (Jeremiah 10:10)

About forty years ago a group of theologians emerged presenting the theory or doctrine that "God is dead!" It caused quite an uproar at the time and the propagators of the theory ended up making quite a lot of money from their writings. But it did not last. Their books had only just hit the shelves when the Charismatic revival began. God was busy demonstrating that He is alive and the Holy Spirit was confirming this!

Many of the gods people worshiped in biblical times were statues. They were, as Jeremiah pointed out, only stone, wood or metal. They possessed no real life nor did they give it—they were completely lifeless.

The God of Israel was the living God. He performed mighty deeds. He breathed life into people, provided food for them in the desert and led His people to the Promised Land. When they disobeyed Him, He punished them. The other gods were imitations and counterfeits. But the God of Israel was the true God!

It is imperative that you distinguish between the true and living God, and the false gods that are worshiped today. Even money can become an idol and cause many problems. Many people never see further than the physical needs they have and become like animals. Other people exalt their nation or people to the status of God and consequently lose sight of the fact that only Jesus can offer true life. He alone is the Truth—remain in Him!

Lord God, thank You that You are the true, living God. Amen.

 Read Jeremiah 23:21-25

God Both Near And Far

"Am I only a God nearby," declares the LORD,
"and not a God far away?" (Jeremiah 23:23)

There are, unbelievable as it may sound, people who think they are favored by God. They maintain that their prayers are always answered—and in the way that they want them to be answered. God always gives them the right guidance at the right time, pours His blessing out and answers every question that they ask. It looks as if, with all due respect, they have God figured out.

Jeremiah thought that the false prophets of his day were like these people. They diminished God to their level so that He became an object that they could present when they had need of it. They lost sight of the fact that He is also far—the Most High and Holy God who inhabits eternity, whose name is Holy. The exalted God of the universe, the Creator of the heavens and the earth and the Father of Jesus Christ cannot simply be adopted and appropriated for oneself.

God is always exalted high above us and seeks our worship, obedience and submission. God does not belong to us—we belong to Him! He is not something we possess—we are His possessions! It is fitting that we develop an attitude of awe in the face of His majesty, greatness and glory, His sovereignty and power. You will understand your place in God's universe when you bow before Him in worship and acknowledge Him as your Creator, your Savior and your King.

Holy Father, I praise and thank You that I can
worship You in Your glory and majesty. Amen.

You Cannot Flee from God

"Can anyone hide in secret places so that I cannot see him?" declares the LORD. "Do not I fill heaven and earth?" declares the LORD. (Jeremiah 23:24)

Hide and seek has been a popular game with children for countless generations. It is exciting to find a good place to hide and then wait, listen or peep to see how the seeker tries to find you. But when we become adults, life is not child's play anymore. Sometimes we want to run away and hide from everyone. But no one can hide from God!

The false prophets and people of Jeremiah's day tried to do so. Their religion was just a game to them. Even though they portrayed an image of living close to God, they used their hypocritical faith as a screen to hide behind. They were too blind to see how futile their attempts were.

God is omnipresent! He sees every crime done in secret, every hypocritical action, every corrupt deed. He hears the lies and the half-truths that you sometimes make up to cover up your sins. But you only deceive yourself. God is everywhere and there is nowhere you can hide from Him. There is also no place where you can be closer to Him. Because He sees your every move and is intimately acquainted with your every motive, it is foolish to try to get away from Him.

Open your eyes and see Him in His glory, love and mercy. Open your ears and listen to His voice of peace. Allow Him to come into your life. Live in His Light.

Omnipresent Father, help me to rediscover Your presence in every moment. Amen.

 Read Jeremiah 23:30-40

God Is Commander in Chief!

You must not mention "the oracle of the Lord" again, because every man's own word becomes his oracle and so you distort the words of the living God, the Lord Almighty, our God. (Jeremiah 23:36)

When the forces of the European Union took assumed the duties of NATO's (North Atlantic Treaty Organization) armed forces in Kosovo, a new general was appointed. He was not only the general of the forces of his own country, but the commander in chief of the combined military forces too.

The Bible teaches us that the Israelites knew that God was their Commander in Chief who led them through times of war and who ensured their success. However, Jeremiah and other prophets had an even greater vision. They saw God as far more than just the national commander. He was supreme over the armies of all other nations: the Commander in Chief! Other Bible translations use the title Lord of Hosts: the hosts of the combined armies of the whole world—of heaven and earth!

God is still the Commander in Chief! He retains control over all human forces: economic, political, academic, military, industrial, commercial—and spiritual.

The Almighty God has command over forces that are stronger than evil. The universe is under His supreme authority. God and God alone is the Commander in Chief! He is, by grace, your Redeemer, your Friend and your Guide.

Supreme Father, I pray that each day You will deepen my knowledge and understanding of You! Amen.

God's Silences

[Hananiah] said before all the people, "This is what the Lord says: 'In the same way will I break the yoke of Nebuchadnezzar king of Babylon off the neck of all the nations within two years.'" At this, the prophet Jeremiah went on his way. (Jeremiah 28:11)

Many people still need to learn the life skill of keeping quiet, which is invaluable in many situations.

Jeremiah had a clash with another prophet, Hananiah, in the temple. Jeremiah expressed that God would break the might of the Babylonians and would bring the exiled Israelites back to Jerusalem after seventy years. Hananiah, a false prophet, insisted that it would happen within two years. After their public debate, Jeremiah said nothing more, and went on his way. But in Jeremiah's silence there was a message from God: we will wait and see what God will do. A few months later Hananiah was dead and it took seventy years before the exiles returned.

In Ecclesiastes, we read that there is a time to be silent and a time to talk (Eccles. 3:7). There are also times when God remains silent so that people can meditate on His words and see what will happen over the course of time.

There are many opportunities when you and I can fruitfully remain quiet. There are times when you need to be a witness for Christ. But there are also times when it would be better to say nothing. Sometimes you just need to be silent before God—that might be the moment when He speaks to you.

Lord, through Your Holy Spirit teach me when to speak and when to be silent. Amen.

Read 1 Peter 1:1-9

God Protects Our Inheritance (1)

In His great mercy He has given us new birth into a living hope through the resurrection of Jesus Christ from the dead, and into an inheritance that can never perish, spoil or fade—kept in heaven for you. (1 Peter 1:3-4)

There are people who have nothing to live for apart from their own interests here on earth. They do not truly "live." They believe that in the end, life is extinguished, just like a candle. Many intellectuals, as well as many illiterate people, believe this with their whole hearts.

People who believe in Jesus and who have received salvation believe something completely different. They look forward to a wonderful life on the other side of the grave. They aren't fearful or skeptic but longing and joyful. They believe in a God who is not limited to this earthly life. He promises His followers eternal life. Through the triumphant resurrection of Jesus, God showed His power to overcome death and transform it into something beautiful.

Our lives are filled with poverty, evil, suffering, sickness, disappointment and sin. That is not all that God has to offer His children. The fullness that Jesus Christ came to share cannot be limited to time and space. His resurrection points us to an eternal life that is more complete, and more filled with love than this earthly life can ever be. This is the inheritance of the children of God! Look to the future with all the hope of your heart, with joy that you are His child and with faith in your God.

Eternal Father, I thank You that I can keep my eyes focused on the future that You have prepared for me. Amen.

God Protects Our Inheritance (2)

Though you have not seen Him, you love Him; and even though you do not see Him now, you believe in Him and are filled with an inexpressible and glorious joy, for you are receiving the goal of your faith, the salvation of your souls. (1 Peter 1:8-9)

You may have seen a building or landmark destroyed before. It's a sad affair. It feels as if a piece of the world that you have known and have learned to trust, has been taken away. But nothing on this earth is permanent. People come and go—as do buildings, roads, railway lines and monuments. The Bible says in Psalm 102:25-27, "You laid the foundations of the earth, and the heavens are the work of Your hands. They will perish, but You remain; they will all wear out like a garment. Like clothing You will change them and they will be discarded. But You remain the same."

There is a deep desire in people for permanence. We seek security, familiarity and comfort. But you will never find these on earth—only in heaven! There the incomplete bits and pieces of our lives will be brought together. There, everything that is good but which has been lost will be found again, taken up and treasured.

The unanswered questions of your heart will be answered; the unspoken words will be spoken. Broken hearts will be mended and tears wiped away. God will be exalted in glory. His promises will be fulfilled, His healing will be completed and His love will fill everyone and everything.

Lord, help me not to keep looking back with sorrow but to focus on the things that will last forever. Amen.

 Read 1 Peter 2:11-24

Fear God!

Show proper respect to everyone: Love the brotherhood of believers, fear God. (1 Peter 2:17)

The fear that we must show towards God is not the kind of fear that fills us with terror. It is fearful respect, but which ultimately goes far beyond respect. A sports team might fear their winning streak might end. They respect the power of their opponents.

Proverbs 1:7 says that, "The fear of the Lord is the beginning of knowledge." The original Hebrew word can be translated as "wisdom." It means to honor God who is awe-inspiring. Honoring God is one of the most wonderful sources of knowledge and wisdom. To honor God in a special way is the foundation of all knowledge, the central source of all wisdom.

If you truly put God first, you will find that most other things will just fall into place. Faith in God leads to confidence that God is working in all areas of life.

To fear God brings you into fellowship with other people who also fear God—and who at the same time love Him. Through the sincere honoring of God you will gain a healthy perspective on marriage, sex and family life. It will provide you with a frame of reference for everything in life. You will know Him as the One from whom you, with gratitude, receive all the abundance and gifts in life and as the person you can turn to when things go wrong.

Loving Father, thank You that I can fear, honor and love You. Amen.

God Works in Secret

"This is what the kingdom of God is like. A man scatters seed on the ground. Night and day, whether he sleeps or gets up, the seed sprouts and grows, though he does not know how. All by itself the soil produces grain—first the stalk, then the head, then the full kernel in the head. As soon as the grain is ripe, he puts the sickle to it, because the harvest has come." (Mark 4:26-29)

We often use the expression, "There's more to this than meets the eye." It is often heard where things happen behind the scenes. The reshuffling of positions in a large organization often happens without any explanations given for the changes. Relationships between people are often maintained through respect for confidentiality.

Christians often speak as if God is only involved when something dramatic happens: a miracle that has taken place; a sudden increase in converts; or a church that grows in a spectacular way. The parable of the seed that grows tells us rather that the kingdom of God often grows slowly, silently and in secret. God does not announce His coming from the rooftops. While the farmer is sleeping, the seed grows without him knowing.

If you trust God completely you can know that He causes all things to work together for good, even if you do not understand His methods. He is in the process of bringing His perfect purpose to pass for this world, just as He is busy working in the secret places of your life. God works in His own, secret way and according to His own timetable. You must just trust Him.

God, I trust You unconditionally
even when I don't understand it all. Amen.

Read John 5:18-29

The Mirror Image of the Father

"I tell you the truth, the Son can do nothing by Himself; He can do only what He sees His Father doing, because whatever the Father does the Son also does." (John 5:19)

Children grow into maturity by imitating the behavior of other people, especially that of their parents. Some children look like their parents—they talk and act like them.

Jesus taught that no one could come to the Father, except through Him. In both His teachings and His actions, Jesus taught the people much about the Father, and made it clear that He wanted His followers to know the love of the Father as He knew the love of the Father. Through Jesus, God drew near to His people physically, but also invited people to draw near to God spiritually, putting their trust in Him and knowing the love of the Father—the love which Jesus has known from eternity past.

By identifying with Jesus, you also submit yourself to God the Father. By living with the same attitude and disposition as Jesus Christ, you learn to know God and begin to live according to His commandments. By following in the footsteps of Jesus, you create a life for yourself in God. By praying the way Jesus prayed, you come into contact with God. By dying to yourself you come into a new life in God, just as Jesus lived in Him.

Lord Jesus, through Your Holy Spirit,
help me to become more like You. Amen.

God Is Seen in Christ

He is the image of the invisible God, the firstborn over all creation. (Colossians 1:15)

A teacher once gave her primary school class a project: to paint anything they wanted. Most of the little ones painted a family member—mostly their mothers. Some painted their pet dogs. But when she came to one painting, she was completely bewildered. "Karen," she asked, "what is this?" The answer was, "Miss, it's God!" "Oh, but no one really knows what God looks like," answered the teacher. "I know, Miss, but when I'm finished with this picture, they will know!"

In our theology class we often tried to debate what God is really like—and we could never come up with an answer as satisfying or better than the one the Bible gives us. The Bible teaches us that God is like Christ and Christ is exactly like God. The person wandering through Galilee and performing miracles; walking through the streets of Jerusalem; who died on the cross and rose again from the dead: in Him we see the perfect image of God. He is in Christ: wise, compassionate, holy, busy renewing people.

He forgives, heals and brings the best out of people. He is full of love. See Him, powerful in His fight against evil; diligent in His obedience to God the Father. We cannot see God the Father—but we can see Jesus Christ, and in Him we see all that we need to see of God.

Loving Father, help me to understand more and more of Jesus so that when I see You face-to-face I will already know and love You. Amen.

August

The Power of God in Us

For it is God who works
in you to will and to act
according to His good purpose.
~ Philippians 2:13

Heavenly Guide, I so much
want to begin this month with
faith, hope and love in my heart.
I so much want to believe unconditionally:
like Abraham and Enoch and Moses and
all those in the gallery of heroes in Hebrews 11.
But so often I am more like Thomas;
I first want to feel and see;
my faith is often limited to my senses.
I so much want to believe the unseen
and quietly profess:
"My Lord and my God!"
I so much want to experience perfect hope,
hope that all the ardent and noble ideals
of my heart will be realized;
that my spiritual life will grow in knowledge,
love and truth, so that I will be able
to distinguish what is truly important.
Keep the spirit of optimism burning in my heart.
I want to say to You with the honesty of dying words:
"Lord, You know everything.
You know that I love You!"
I want to love my neighbor with a sincere, unselfish love
that breaks down all the walls that divide us
and make reconciliation a glorious reality.
In this month, guide me to a true understanding of
faith and hope and love!
In the glorious name of Jesus.
Amen.

Respect the Scriptures

All Scripture is God-breathed and is useful for teaching, rebuking, correcting and training in righteousness. (2 Timothy 3:16)

The Bible is an essential manual for the Christian. From it you draw guidance, admonition, hope and everything else that is necessary for your spiritual development. However, it is also often abused, not only by its enemies, but also by those who acknowledge it as the Word of God. This happens especially when texts are used out of context to construct religious theories. Inevitably, these theories are divested of any true meaning. For many dedicated Christians the letter of the Scriptures is much more important than the spirit behind the words. It is disturbing to hear the Word of God loudly quoted with no regard for the message that God intended for his people.

For centuries people have explained the Bible's prophesies in the light of their own times, forgetting that the Master expressly told His followers that it is not for us to know these things. Many believe that the times in which we are now living are the "last days." This knowledge belongs to God alone. Never try to answer divine questions in human terms. You are not expected to strive after the possession of knowledge about matters that God keeps secret. Rather, you are expected to trust the Master to bring all things to their God-determined end, while living in harmony with Him.

The Bible encompasses the whole world, but it also speaks deeply to the individual human soul.

Incarnate Word, I thank You for revealing Yourself in the Word that God has made available to us in our own language. Amen.

 Read Isaiah 50:1-11

Jesus Illuminates the Darkness

Let him who walks in the dark, who has no light, trust in the name of the Lord and rely on his God. (Isaiah 50:10)

There comes a time in everyone's life when the path ahead seems dark, when difficulties overwhelm you and you become despondent because of the darkness and despair that seem to surround you. Often your circumstances are so desperate that you feel completely helpless and simply cannot free yourself. In these circumstances you are at your most vulnerable and pressurized.

Despite how far from God you feel in times like these, you must remember the glorious truth that He is actually closer to you than ever before. Your heavenly Father has assured you that He will never abandon or forsake you. He is constantly at your side, waiting for you to turn to Him for help, which He is always ready and willing to provide.

Regardless of what is happening in your life, yes, even when it is difficult to pray, never neglect turning to Christ and laying your fears and concerns before Him. Because He lived among people He is all too aware of the difficulties and problems that you experience. Allow Him to lead you and you will experience the blessing and joy of His love and peace.

O Lord, please send Your light and Your truth to me; let it guide me to Your holy mountain so that I may enter and go to the altar of God. Amen.

How Great Thou Art!

Since ancient times no one has heard, no ear has perceived, no eye has seen any God besides You, who acts on behalf of those who wait for Him. (Isaiah 64:4)

Throughout history Christianity has come under attack from every direction. The validity of our faith and even the existence of God have been challenged and questioned. Many have suffered torment and persecution for the sake of their faith and thousands have chosen death rather than to deny their God. This surely indicates the greatness and strength of God's love for the Christian and the Christian's love for God.

As you live your life faithfully in Jesus Christ, you will become more and more aware of His presence. When you place your trust in God and dedicate your life to Him, you become increasingly aware of the fact that His hand rests upon you and guides you through the maze of life. The healthier your relationship with the Master, the more aware you will be of the Holy Spirit who speaks to you and leads you through each day.

A life that is lived in, with, and for the living Christ will strengthen your faith and allow you to seize each day joyfully. Nothing else can provide you with this joy and peace. And then you can do nothing but whisper in grateful prayer, "How great Thou art!"

Savior and Redeemer, I kneel in helpless wonder before Your greatness and majesty. I truly love You, O Lord! Amen.

Read John 14:15-25

The Inspiration of the Holy Spirit

"And I will ask the Father, and He will give you another Counselor to be with you forever—the Spirit of truth." (John 14:16-17)

If one considers all the demands and expectations of modern life, it is not surprising that there are so many people who collapse under the pressure and fail to comply with the standards expected of them. Sadly, this often causes people to turn away from the Christian faith in despair, and consequently they experience the torment of wandering around in the wilderness of uncertainty.

Jesus knows human fallibility and fragility all too well. That is why He prepared His disciples for a life without His physical presence. He granted them the gift of the Holy Spirit to enable them to cope with the demands of life. And they undoubtedly needed it, because they experienced intense opposition.

The gift of the Spirit is yours too, because God has said, "I will pour out My Spirit on all people" (Joel 2:28). Jesus confirms this in the words of today's Scripture verse.

For those who are trusting Jesus as their savior, we have confidence that we will never be going it alone. The Spirit provides us with the strength to follow God's instructions, and promises to be with us in all situations. If you can call Jesus your Lord today, then you ought to find comfort and confidence in the presence of His Spirit.

O Holy Spirit, come and fill my life. Inspire me to live according to the will and instructions of God the Father and my Savior, Jesus Christ. Amen.

Choose God's Way

Surely the arm of the Lord is not too short to save, nor His ear too dull to hear. (Isaiah 59:1)

Often we live as though God does not exist. We make our own plans and work hard to accomplish them. We create goals and devise plans without any thought of what God expects of us.

And usually, when we decide to follow our own way instead of God's way, things start going awry. We run into the proverbial brick wall, and we become despondent, feeling that it is useless to attempt anything because it will just be a failure anyway.

Have you tried to live for yourself, with no regard for God or His teachings? Have you found this lifestyle to be satisfying? Do you find a sense of peace and confidence, even when things are going wrong? When we listen to God's invitation to follow Him, we get to know the One who is in control, even when things seem out of control. He is not a harsh taskmaster, but offers us strength when we are weak. He is ever so slow to punish our frequent rebellion against Him, but rather offers us forgiveness through His Son.

Do you see how different God's way is from our way? If you know the frustration of living for yourself, then come to the God who offers a better way.

Holy Master, Your way for my life may seem demanding and difficult, but it is the only and the best way for my life. I want to follow You every day of my life. Amen.

Read Philippians 4:10-20

Together with God

I can do everything through Him who gives me strength. (Philippians 4:13)

When you think of God in all His divine glory and of yourself as an insignificant little speck on earth, it becomes incredibly difficult to identify yourself with Him. Despite this, the Holy Spirit of God, who inhabits God's entire creation, also dwells with God's people in a special way. The creative power of God is at work in the lives of His people, making the impossible possible in their hearts.

When you understand that God's Spirit is with you, you can find assurance that God will help to guide you and provide you with strength to meet the challenges of life. While God's standards might seem overwhelming—perhaps impossible in your own strength—our assurance is that the Spirit even gives us the strength to grow in our obedience. The Spirit helps us grow in love, joy, peace, patience, kindness, goodness, faithfulness, gentleness and self-control. Trying to do this in our own power is futile and frustrating, yet we can do all things when God gives us strength.

Before our Savior ascended to heaven He promised that His Spirit would be with those who have accepted Him as Savior and Lord and who are willing to allow His Spirit to work through them. It is the Holy Spirit who makes God reality in the life of the Christian and who enables him to live in harmony with God.

Merciful Lord Jesus, I accept the gift of the Holy Spirit and therefore enjoy intimate communion with You, my Lord and my God. Amen.

The Will of God Alone

"By Myself I can do nothing; I judge only as I hear, and My judgment is just, for I seek not to please Myself but Him who sent Me." (John 5:30)

There are few people who have not at some point experienced the frustration of plans that go wrong. In many cases it goes much further than mere disappointment because of failure; the consequences of failure can take on immeasurable proportions. When this happens, many people ascribe it to fate, economic circumstances beyond their control, chance, bad luck, or any of a host of other reasons. Few people will admit that the fault lies within themselves, because they refuse to live according to the will of God.

God's plan for your life is good. Because you are His child and He loves you, He has promised that all things will work together for your good. Everything has a purpose, even when our human perspectives are to limited to see what God is doing.

On the other hand, we often struggle from self-inflicted wounds. Some of our struggling comes from seeking to do things in our own strength, rather than relying on God. We can also give into the temptation to live for ourselves, forgetting who our true Master is. Never embark on any endeavor that falls outside the will of God, and you will experience peace of mind knowing that even when difficulty comes, that Jesus is with you in all of your endeavors.

Eternal and loving God, I surrender myself to You completely. Lead me according to Your will from day to day. Amen.

Read 1 Chronicles 29:10-19

Integrity Before God

I know, my God, that You test the heart and are pleased with integrity. (1 Chronicles 29:17)

If you sincerely try to cultivate a regular and meaningful prayer life, you will at some time or another have experienced the problem of wandering thoughts. In the time you have set aside to be alone with your heavenly Father you may read a passage from the Bible or from an inspirational spiritual book. Then you start praying, only to discover that instead of being focused on God, your thoughts run amok.

If this has happened to you, take comfort in the thought that it happens to everyone who takes prayer time seriously. However, those who have persevered have ultimately succeeded in making their prayers a delightful reality and a powerful force in their lives.

When your thoughts wander, don't become upset or frustrated, because agitation does little to help you regain your focus. Rather, gently turn your contemplations back toward God and ask the Holy Spirit to guide your thoughts. You can rest assured that the problem of wandering thoughts can be solved as easily as turning your focus back to God, and so you shouldn't let it spoil your time of prayer.

The wonder of Christian prayer is that when you turn to Jesus you will find that He is already awaiting you. Prayer is not one-way communication; Jesus is just as eager to meet you, His beloved, as you are to meet Him.

Thank You, heavenly Master, that I may experience the reality of Your living presence through prayer. For this I praise Your name. Amen.

Where Does Your Religion Lead You?

Taste and see that the LORD is good. (Psalm 34:8)

Most churches provide some form of statement of faith, laying out their beliefs and how Scripture shapes their approach to worship. In more traditional churches, you may find certain liturgical forms of worship which you can draw hope from. Other churches may be influenced more by the charismatic movement and may demonstrate warmth, enthusiasm, and spiritual intensity. Many churches will find themselves somewhere in between the charismatic and liturgical. The point is there are many approaches to worship.

The litmus test of your way of worship is whether or not Jesus is the focal point. If Christ is at the center of your faith, you will know the deep hunger of the soul that yearns to know Him more intimately. By engaging in disciplined prayer and an intentional approach to Scripture reading, you can grow in your knowledge of the Master and His way of life. But He must always be the center.

Whatever your theological position or church affiliation, the most important thing about your faith is your personal relationship with Jesus. Knowing Him through faith, prayer and time in the Word leads to an understanding that is intimate, not merely intellectual. It will create in you a love for all people and transcendent cultural or socioeconomic differences. Take time to know Christ.

Merciful Lord, grant me a spiritual temper that
will enable me to meet You in all Your glory. Amen.

Read Micah 6:1-9

Listen to God

Listen to what the Lord says. (Micah 6:1)

Most people have an opinion on virtually every matter under the sun. Should you pose some abstract question to them, their response would probably be, "I don't really know because I haven't considered the matter, but I think that ..." If a great number of people start enthusiastically expressing immature and rash thoughts, the situation can easily become chaotic.

However, if you are sensible you will remember that behind this Babel of tongues the proven truths of God stand steadfast. In the heat of the argument these truths are seldom evident, and are also usually not expressed in devout theological terms.

God reveals His truths to those who invite Him to share in their lives, who gladly give up time to be with Him, who ponder His Word so that they can understand His will more thoroughly. Make sure that you always spend more time in the study of God's Word than you do in argumentation.

In a world that spends so much time talking, one of the most revolutionary things you can do it to listen. Make time with God's Word a priority in your daily routine. Read the Word; memorize the Word; pray the Word. Hearing God speak through His Word can be an enriching and inspiring experience and is a source of tranquility and balance in the midst of a tumultuous world.

Holy God, in listening to You I receive wisdom,
peace, balance and stability in my daily life. Amen.

Trust Through Partnership

So we say with confidence, "The Lord is my helper; I will not be afraid. What can man do to me?" (Hebrews 13:6)

If you are trying to take on life's difficulties and problems in your own strength and wisdom, it is likely that you are fighting a losing battle. This does not necessarily mean that you are grumbling or complaining, or that you are constantly asking for the sympathy of others, but if you were honest with yourself and others, you would have to admit that there are moments when you long for your burden to be lifted.

In such moments it is advisable to become quiet before God, and to realize that He is closer to you than your breathing, or your hands and your feet. The only reason why He did not come to your rescue was because you did not ask Him to. When you seek His help, you place what you are and what you have at His disposal.

You become God's partner in your everyday life. This partnership means that you should constantly do the will of your heavenly partner, and do it in such a way that destructive fear will have no place in your life.

When you have conquered fear through constructive service, you can face anyone with a peaceful confidence that is the direct consequence of your union with God. Because God is your Helper, and because you serve Him joyfully, you can step fearlessly and confidently into the future.

Good Shepherd, because You are my Helper and I serve You with sincerity, my life is filled with trust that is born from my relationship with You. Amen.

Read Isaiah 43:1-9

Jesus Will Lead You

"When you pass through the waters, I will be with you; and when you pass through the rivers, they will not sweep over you." (Isaiah 43:2)

Anyone who is a poor swimmer will know the fear of finding yourself in a pool, a river or the sea, and realizing that you are out of your depth. It causes a feeling of uncertainty, danger and anxiety, because you have nothing to hold on to and no fixed foundation to stand on. The thought of sinking and drowning only contributes to the fear and can easily change into panic.

Your pilgrimage through life can be a similar experience. There are so many situations in which you feel incompetent, vulnerable and uncertain. In the business world, you are constantly expected to act quickly and decisively, but a wrong decision or move can mean the difference between success and dismal failure. In your personal life you constantly have to make decisions and these decisions often have far-reaching consequences for yourself and for others.

The question is, how are you supposed to find calm or peace in these circumstances? There is only one way, and that is to trust in the living Christ. Know that He is sovereign over every venture you take or the various trials you endure. Remind yourself of all the times the Lord has provided for you in the past, and then act in faith and the knowledge that He is your only salvation.

Lord Jesus, I worship You as the Way, the Truth and the Life. Not my will, Lord, and not my way, but Your will and Your way for me. Amen.

How Great Is Our God?

"How great is God—beyond our understanding!" (Job 36:26)

One recurring obstacle to our spiritual development is our limited concept of God. You may believe that God loves and cares for you. You freely accept that He is all-powerful, all-knowing and omnipresent. But as soon as disaster strikes, you relegate God to the back seat. You fail to use the wisdom, calmness and strength that He has placed at your disposal. In these trying moments you find that you do not live up to that which is expected of you. Your problems appear bigger than God.

You ought to grow in your understanding of God when things are going well, in order to trust Him more deeply when difficult times come. There are several ways we can grow in our knowledge of God. Most importantly, by reading and meditating on His Word and the truths that He has shown us about Himself there. We can also grow by reflecting on how He has shown us faithfulness in the past. Additionally, there is much benefit from observing the world around you, seeing God's glory and strength through His creation.

The greater God becomes to you, the more strength you will draw from Him in moments of temptation. Faith will not be merely sentimental, but a deep trusting in a God we know. He will give you the assurance of His presence at all times. Know that your God is great, and you will possess a lasting faith!

Great and wonderful God, grant me a spirit and
attitude of appreciation for Your greatness, so that
my spirit and perspective may be broadened. Amen.

Read Romans 8:1-17

The Reality of the Living Christ

The Spirit Himself testifies with our spirit that we are God's children. (Romans 8:16)

Regardless of what church you belong to or the specific doctrines you believe, knowing Jesus personally is always most important. Without knowing Jesus, you might live what externally appears to be a very moral life, but on the inside you will simply be spiritually dead.

Undoubtedly, Jesus was both a significant historical figure and a controversial religious teacher. But to understand Him properly, you must also understand that He is the inspiration and driving force behind innumerable lives. Jesus may have lived two thousands years ago, but He is also very alive today.

Wanting to know Jesus should be the highest priority in your life. It isn't enough to be merely interested in Him or curious about His teachings; you ought to be entirely discontent until you truly know Him and His power in your life.

When your greatest passion is to know Christ, you cannot help but become more aware of the reality of His promise to always be with His people. Pray to Him in your silent struggles; share with Him your unspoken burdens. If you have ever tried to ignore His presence in your life, seek forgiveness and know that by His grace and mercy He will never abandon you.

Merciful and loving Master, I praise and thank You for Your presence at all times in my life. Amen.

Be Patient with Others

When He saw the crowds, He went up on a mountainside and sat down. (Matthew 5:1)

The wonder of Jesus' ministry lies in the fact that He had time for everyone. Despite the immense pressure that heavily burdened Him, He was able to accomplish more in three short years than what we accomplish in a lifetime. And yet He was never hurried, impatient or tense. When reading the Gospels you can share in that feeling of peace and calm that He radiated to everyone.

There are many false teachings that will claim to be Christian, appealing to people through emphasizing material assets. Prosperity, luxury and happiness are promised and guaranteed to those who follow. Unfortunately many people are drawn to Jesus because of what they can get from Him, rather than for the sake of Jesus Himself. If their expectations do not materialize, their interest in Jesus fades as quickly as their hopes to find material wealth or to get rich quick.

If you are faithful to your calling as a follower of Jesus, you should never show impatience or irritation when you are dealing with the problems of other people. Despite your busy life, Christ will always give you the time to do His work. Trust Him unconditionally and you too will be able to treat people with the same patience, compassion and empathy that He did. In this way you will become a source of peace for others.

Lord Jesus, I open myself to Your Spirit of peace, patience and encouragement in my interaction with other people. Amen.

Read 2 Corinthians 3:1-11

Lasting Glory

And if what was fading away came with glory, how much greater is the glory of that which lasts! (2 Corinthians 3:11)

Some things are made to last, while others are created only to fulfill a passing need. Both kinds of things may appear attractive and enduring. Only time and use will show how one differs from the other. This is true of every aspect of life, and our spiritual lives are no exception.

There are many forms of the Christian faith that appeal to people because they emphasize material assets, which people usually desire. Prosperity, luxury and happiness are promised and guaranteed to those who follow Christ's precepts. Unfortunately many people are drawn to following Jesus because of what they can get from Him, rather than for the sake of Jesus Himself. If their expectations do not materialize, the glory of their faith fades along with their expectations.

The true glory of the Christian faith intensifies as the years pass. A young disciple may be extremely enthusiastic about his faith and his zeal for the Lord may be a joy to see. But all the beauty of youth cannot compare with the fullness of character that is part of someone who has followed Christ through decades.

The eternal Christ brings joy and sanctification to every person who truly knows Him. This glory develops slowly, like an oak tree rather than like a mushroom, but it always reflects the lasting glory of the living Christ.

I pray, Lord my God, that my life will reflect Your lasting glory, for the sake of Your exaltation and my spiritual growth. Amen.

The Big Mystery

I … present to you the word of God in its fullness—the mystery that has been kept hidden for ages and generations, but is now disclosed to the saints. To them God has chosen to make known … the glorious riches of this mystery, which is Christ in you, the hope of glory. (Colossians 1:25-27)

There is a certain degree of mysticism in many religions, and this has even been seen in some people's approach to Christianity. Since the days of the early church, there have been those who claimed exclusive access to deeper insights about God. Likewise, they emphasize that with this secret knowledge their followers are able to achieve a higher spiritual experience.

God offers knowledge to all people indiscriminately Paul tells us that the greatest mystery of God was how He would bring about the salvation of His people—salvation, not from physical enemies, but from their sin and rebellion that often kept them far from the blessing of knowing God and drawing near to Him. The mystery has been revealed, and we now know that Christ died for our sins, and through faith we can not only be find salvation, but now have a personal relationship with God.

If you have trusted in Christ, we know that God has given you His Spirit who works in you and through you. He guides you and grows you, helping you live like Christ. God is no longer a distant reality for you, but He has drawn you near to Himself and now He abides with His people. Take courage to know that you don't need some exclusive knowledge to know God; through Christ, God is already near.

Holy Jesus, open my life to Your immanent presence. Amen.

Read Isaiah 40:27-31

Source of Inexhaustible Power

Those who hope in the LORD will renew their strength. They will soar on wings like eagles; they will run and not grow weary, they will walk and not grow faint. (Isaiah 40:31)

Familiarity is a great threat to our spiritual lives. It is possible to become so familiar with religious clichés and phrases that they lose their deeper meaning. The spiritual discipline that once fortified your faith may have become an obstacle that prevents you from growing spiritually. You may have addressed God as "Father" for so long that you have come to think of Him as Lord who closes His eyes to your sins, thus forgetting that He is also a God who punishes sin. If you have lost your sense of wonder and awe for the greatness of God, you have lost something for which there is no substitute.

The way that Christians renew their strength is by hoping their on Lord. It is impossible to spend time contemplating the wonder of God revealed through Jesus Christ and not find some new strength. Strength comes from our hope, and that hope is cultivated in the soil of intimate and deepening knowledge of our Lord.

Perhaps you have been running and you find yourself becoming weary. Perhaps you have been walking, and growing faint feel like an understatement. Regardless of the specifics of your circumstances, the promise extended to you is that you can soar like an eagle. Hope in the Lord, and you too will renew your strength.

Through hope in You, heavenly Father,
my strength is renewed so that I can grow
spiritually to be more like Your Son, Jesus my Lord! Amen.

Freedom Comes with Responsibilities

Live as free men, but do not use your freedom as a cover-up for evil; live as servants of God. (1 Peter 2:16)

The word *freedom* is a much-abused word. It is used to muster rebellious people together, and heinous crimes are committed in the name of freedom. Those who follow false leaders promising freedom, usually find themselves trapped in a new form of slavery.

True freedom can only be experienced if the human spirit is liberated from hate, cruelty and envy, because true freedom possesses a spiritual quality that is known and experienced by everyone who loves and serves God.

Many people live in slavery. However, they may be unaware of the bindings that constrain them because they have grown so accustomed to them that they have simply become habits. Their preconceived ideas are reflected in their negative attitudes. Their hate and bitterness all reveal the slavery that constrains them.

The message of the Christian gospel brings freedom for everyone who is held captive by destructive influences. Christ forgives our sins and frees us from the shackles of the evil one. This is a gift, part of God's perfect love, if it is accepted in faith. As you experience the blessing of God's deliverance, you will be transformed into a new person who lives in harmony, peace and love with God and others.

Perfect Jesus, through Your Spirit I am freed.
Because I know You, I have become truly free. Amen.

Read Philippians 1:1-11

Love Is the Answer

This is my prayer: that your love may abound more and more in knowledge and depth of insight, so that you may be able to discern what is best. (Philippians 1:9-10)

Decision-making is a process that is often the source of much perplexity. It may influence your future and well-being, or that of those whose interests you take care of. It may have a bearing on your business, your personal life or your career. Whatever the circumstances, the fact remains that unless you have a stable and level-headed approach to the problem, you run the risk of being overwhelmed by the anxiety of uncertainty and indecisiveness, and your fear of the consequences of your decisions.

There is no doubt that you need the guidance and wisdom of the Holy Spirit to provide you with clarity of thought and vision. He views matters from the perspective of eternity, while you can only observe the here and now. For this reason, and also so that you can obtain peace of mind, it is essential to pray constantly for the guidance of the Holy Spirit.

To prepare yourself for this you need to have an intimate personal relationship with the living Christ, so that your thoughts can be focused on His will. The more you love Jesus, the closer you will live to Him, thus enabling Him to speak to you through the Holy Spirit.

I thank You, Redeemer and Savior,
for the assurance that he who loves You is
Your child, and can know the God of love. Amen.

It Is Your Responsibility

Come near to God and He will come near to you. (James 4:8)

The depth and quality of your spiritual life is your responsibility. Some may say they yearn to know God more, but they take no steps in life to draw close to Him. They may say they desire a more robust prayer life, but rarely set aside time to be alone with God. A true desire to know God must be accompanied by efforts to draw near. God planted a yearning for Him in your deepest being. This hunger to know Him better is one of His greatest gifts to you. He is constantly calling: "Come to Me!" and it is in your answer to this call that your Christian perseverance is truly revealed.

To accept your Christian responsibility is a solemn undertaking, and if you accept it half-heartedly you are depriving yourself of communion with God. When you think about who God is and the extent of love He has shown you, the only appropriate response is a devotion that encompasses your entire life. Unfortunately, when believers are lukewarm, God feels distant to them and they inevitably feel deeply dissatisfied.

God will never require you to give up something without giving you something better in its place. When He asks for your devout life, He gives you eternal life in return. By accepting the responsibility for your own spiritual growth, you continually move closer to your Master and Redeemer.

Holy Father, in Your strength I accept the responsibility for my own spiritual development. I want to make use of all the instruments of Your grace that You put at my disposal. Amen.

Read Psalm 34:12-23

Your Divine Companion

The righteous cry out, and the LORD hears them;
He delivers them from all their troubles (Psalm 34:17).

The dreadful feeling of loneliness is a devastating experience. Many people struggle with loneliness caused by a variety of circumstances: the loss of a loved one; the fear caused by serious illness; struggling with problems all by yourself when it seems as if no one can help you. These are but a few of the situations in which people despair in their loneliness.

It is precisely when you find yourself in these circumstances that you are most vulnerable. It is then that Satan sows seeds of doubt, discouragement and despair in your heart. Those who succumb to it feel that there is no future and no hope, and it is not long before they slump into the depths of self-pity and despair.

In the Scriptures, as well as in history, it has been proven time and again that you are never alone, because the hand of God rests upon you. You can hold on to His assurance that He is always with you.

When it seems as if life is treating you unfairly, don't give up hope, but rather lay your fears and worries before the living Christ. Open your heart to the influence of the Holy Spirit and He will fan the flame of hope yet again, so that the tiny flame that threatened to die out will become a bright light to illuminate your path.

Powerful Redeemer, grant me the strength to keep my hand
firmly in Yours even under the most difficult circumstances.
Lead me from the darkness into Your wonderful light. Amen.

When Life Gets Complicated

In all your ways acknowledge Him, and He will make your paths straight. (Proverbs 3:6)

Sometimes life becomes complicated in very covert and subtle ways. Small and apparently inconsequential things are neglected because other things demand your attention. Eventually you are confronted with an array of unfinished tasks, irritations and confusions.

To simplify your life and create a blueprint for success, you need a goal towards which you can work. A life with a multitude of goals achieves little, because you waste all your energy without accomplishing anything. Therefore, focus on a positive goal and bring order to your life.

A sure way of complicating your life is to take on a task for which you lack both the time and the energy. There are people who cannot refuse a request, with the result that they leave many tasks unfinished. Determining your priorities is crucial if you want your life to run smoothly and productively.

Creating such a list of priorities is important when planning your life. This should not be done in a vacuum, but you should seek God's guidance. Compare your priorities to what you see in Scripture. Pray deeply and frequently over this list, asking the Spirit to lead you. Ask wise brothers and sisters about it and value their input. If you take these steps, you'll be on your way to a life that is organized and also honoring to God.

Heavenly Master, I ask that You will grant me an uncomplicated and inspired life under the guidance of the Holy Spirit. Amen.

Read Psalm 55:16-24

Faith or Worry? The Choice Is Yours

Cast your cares on the Lord *and*
He will sustain you. (Psalm 55:22)

It isn't hard work that causes mental, spiritual and ultimately physical breakdown—it's worry. Work that is free of worry is stimulating and enjoyable. It gives substance to your daily life, and also confers a feeling of belonging to the human family and contributing to the well-being of the human race.

If you are worried you cannot achieve anything constructive. Worry alienates the willing worker from his rightful inheritance and true purpose and satisfaction of life. However, the greatest tragedy of worry is that it estranges you from God. Faith and worry cannot cohabit in the same life. If your faith is a living reality there will be no space for worry, but if worry is the dominant force, faith will wither and die.

Worrying can easily become a habit. Only a radical adjustment of your thought patterns can free you from worry. Having a practical faith in the omnipotence of God and His purpose for your life is essential. The conviction that all things work together for the good of those who love God should be the dominant thought in your mind. Then you will experience the renewing power of a living faith, which is the death-knell of all worry.

Merciful Lord, from today onwards I am
determined not to allow worry to spoil the beauty
of my life or to destroy my faith in You. Amen.

When Your Load Is Too Heavy

"Come to Me, all you who are weary and burdened, and I will give you rest." (Matthew 11:28)

In today's times so many people live under incredible pressure. Tension and stress take their toll on young as well as old. Children and young people are under immense pressure to excel in their studies and in sports.

Business people struggle to keep head above water in an extremely competitive environment. The elderly experience an increasingly uncertain future and constantly worry about their security. People of all ages are exposed to all kinds of temptations that promise only disaster for them and their loved ones.

Professional counseling, medical treatment and medication have become common remedies for people suffering from tension. In many cases these are only temporary measures that are merely a crutch to help people stumble through life. And still the tension keeps increasing.

There is only one infallible way of coping with tension and stress, and this is Christ's way. He, who also lived and worked under immense pressure, offers you the peace of God that surpasses all understanding. It is a peace that banishes all anxiety and fear and gives you the ability to cope with life in the strength of the Master. Accept His gift of peace and rest.

I praise and thank You, Lord my God, that the peace and quiet of Jesus fills my life even amidst life's greatest tensions and pressures. Amen.

Disciple and Discipline Are Synonymous

*Therefore, if anyone is in Christ,
he is a new creation. (2 Corinthians 5:17)*

There are people who desire to have a religion that suits their personal lifestyle. They seek a church that is broad-minded and liberal, and that places few demands on them. Unfortunately, these people might experience some Christianity, but rarely experience Jesus.

When Jesus describes His followers as disciples, He is teaching us that to be a Christian requires a dedication that changes our entire life. Trusting Christ means obeying Christ, and that means a whole new lifestyle. This includes admitting weaknesses in your character, confessing your sins and failures, and realizing that you are dependent on God. It is this realization of your own inadequacy that brings about a turning point in your pilgrimage.

When you feel you are struggling to follow the Jesus and your spiritual life isn't what you want it to be, go to the Lord and seek His help. Even though the Lord is faithful to help, that does not mean that we can become passive in our spiritual growth. Discipleship implies discipline, which means that as we ask for help we must also be actively submitting to the Lord, setting our thoughts on things that are above and heeding the conviction that the Spirit brings. Perseverance is possible when we know the Lord is with us.

*I thank You, merciful Master, for the strength that
You give me through Your Holy Spirit. Amen.*

Your Savior Is Always There for You

Because of the Lord's great love we are not consumed, for His compassions never fail. (Lamentations 3:22)

In our lives there are often times when everything seems hopeless and lost. We succumb to illness; adversity descends upon us; fear overwhelms us; or we experience the pain of death's ultimate separation. These things leave us with a feeling of loneliness that borders on despair. What does one do in such circumstances and how do you cope with life?

Some people are extremely fortunate in experiencing the support of their family and friends in such times. Others who are less fortunate are not as blessed. And even though you may have people who stand supportively around you, there are still times when even that support falls away, because at some point they have to return to their own lives and their own families.

When life plunges you into some sort of a crisis, you should never forget God's goodness and faithfulness. You are His child, whom He has chosen, and in His Word He reassures you of His constant presence. The living Christ is at your side at all times and under all circumstances. He will guide you from the darkness into His wonderful light of hope and peace. Walk with Him and be filled with His love.

Heavenly Companion, even though I sometimes feel lonely, I know that I am never alone, because You have promised never to forsake or abandon me. Amen.

Read Romans 8:1-17

Secure in Christ

There is now no condemnation for those who are in Christ Jesus, because through Christ Jesus the law of the Spirit of life set me free from the law of sin and death. (Romans 8:1-2)

When the strength of your Christian faith threatens to wane, you start looking for all kinds of excuses for the apparent deterioration. Such excuses are not difficult to find, but it seldom happens that you turn the spotlight of truth upon your own inner being. Only if you allow the Holy Spirit to reveal the truth to you, will you discover the causes of your spiritual deterioration.

You will discover that your faith is inadequate because you have allowed something or someone to take Jesus Christ's place in the center of your life. When your awareness of the presence of Christ starts to fade and your intellectual approach becomes confused, your awareness of Jesus starts disappearing.

Scripture teaches us that we have been united to Christ, even when we do not feel it. When you trust in this truth and make Christ the focal point of your faith, you find the boldness to resist the temptations of sin and the freedom to serve God. Awareness of Jesus' closeness will be a source of comfort and joy. This is much more than merely an emotional experience. Your entire life changes because Jesus work through you and you are secure in Him.

Savior and Master, I humbly plead that my life will reflect Your life in the world in which I live. Amen.

More Christlike Every Day

Instead, speaking the truth in love, we will in all things grow up into Him who is the Head, that is, Christ. (Ephesians 4:15)

It is a glorious truth that by believing in Jesus Christ as your Redeemer and Savior you can experience redemption from your sins. This is the foundation of the gospel. But you should never forget that after you have accepted Jesus Christ as the Lord of your life, the process of growth should continue. If you ignore the necessity of growth, your spiritual life will start to flounder in the ocean of disappointment and despair.

In His mercy, God has put many resources for spiritual growth at our disposal, but we should be careful not to let these resources become an end in themselves. Communion with fellow believers is essential, but communion that is not centered on Christ serves no purpose.

Studying the Scriptures is a source of inestimable inspiration and guidance, but you must remember that the purpose of the Scriptures is to point the disciple to Christ. Good works are undoubtedly agreeable to God, but these things are only the fruits that spring from knowing Christ. In themselves they do not necessarily lead to Christ.

Spiritual growth can occur only when you strive to be more like Jesus. This should be the yearning of every disciple. Spiritual growth demands your everything in the service of Christ.

Fill me so completely through Your Holy Spirit,
O Master, that my life will reflect Your glory. Amen.

Read Psalm 130:1-8

Avoid Unnecessary Worry

Out of the depths I cry to You, O Lord; O Lord, hear my voice. Let Your ears be attentive to my cry for mercy. (Psalm 130:1-2)

Have you ever taken a moment to ponder how patient God is? He continually offers His children love, forgiveness, comfort, encouragement, assistance and an array of other gifts that allow us to live a life of comfort and certainty.

He promised to be with us always. He has even offered to live *in* us. Despite all of this however, how often do we only ask for His help after we have exhausted all other sources? How often do we, like the psalmist, only call to Him from the depths?

The wonder of it is that God—unlike people—never tires of us. He is never impatient and His love remains constant. However difficult our circumstances are, He is always there to hear our cries for help and rescue us.

People could spare themselves a great deal of worry and fear if they would immediately turn to Christ for help when a problem crops up. There is no point in being secretive or hesitant, because Jesus has invited all those who are tired and overwhelmed to come to Him so that He may give them rest. Do it, and worry will no longer reign supreme in your life.

Beloved Savior, whether I find myself in a stormy crisis or in the peaceful sunshine, I bring all my worries to You. You have proved that You have the solutions for all of them. Amen.

The Living Word

Then He opened their minds so that they could understand the Scriptures. (Luke 24:45)

There are many people who regard Bible study as a bit of a nuisance. They have been taught that it is a duty, and consequently they struggle through the pages and breathe a sigh of relief when they have read the prescribed passage.

Others find that they don't understand what they are reading, or that their daily problems destroy their inclination to read the Bible. Many people read the Bible only in the evening after a day's work, when they are tired and cannot possibly take in what they are reading.

If you are having problems with your Bible study because of these or other reasons, it might be worthwhile to consider that perhaps you are spending more time reading *about* God than spending time *with* God.

It is necessary to understand that Jesus isn't merely a character in the story of the Bible, but the main character. When we study the Word, we see glimpses of the same God we pray to. We see pictures of the same Jesus who we know as savior. When you realize that the Bible is the story of your God, your faith and prayers find new vigor.

If you draw near unto God in this manner, you will find that the Word starts to assume new life and meaning, because you are no longer merely reading a book. Instead you are *living* the Word together with its Author!

Incarnate Word of God, I open myself to You,
so that You can fill me with Your Spirit
and Your Word, and truly live in me. Amen.

September

Grow in Your Relationship with God

"Remain in Me, and I will remain in you.
No branch can bear fruit by itself;
it must remain in the vine.
Neither can you bear fruit
unless you remain in Me."

~ John 15:4

Living Lord Jesus, source of
abundant life and true growth,
I plead before You that I will not cease to grow
before I have reached spiritual maturity.
And that I will continue to grow
until I meet You face to face.
Help me to give Your Holy Spirit free reign in my life
so that I will make progress day by day
in Your school of sanctification.
Grant that I will live on victorious ground each day.
May I not be ashamed to live out my faith in public,
so that the world can see Your image
in my life and glorify You for it.
Help me to remain in the Vine so that I can bear fruit
that fits with my faith in You.
Help me, so that in the world
I can be a faithful witness of Your love
because I have experienced that love firsthand.
Let Your Holy Spirit be my Teacher and
make me a doer of Your Word and
not just an idle hearer who deceives myself.
I pray this with thanksgiving in the name of Jesus.
Amen.

A New Creation

If anyone is in Christ, he is a new creation; the old has gone, the new has come! All this is from God. (2 Corinthians 5:17-18)

No one can know everything. Even though many people specialize and might know everything there is to know about a certain subject, there will be many more subjects of which they know little. When you begin to study the existence, nature and character of God, you realize what an unending field you are entering. Countless books have already been written about God by dedicated students, but God still remains beyond comprehension.

The irrefutable fact is that people can only get to know God better if they have a personal relationship with Him. Faith in God becomes a reality when you personally accept Him into your heart.

Books are very valuable in helping us to understand God, but they only tell of the journey of a fellow traveler on the Christian road. To understand the nature, character and personality of God requires much more than an academic treatment. It needs a personal encounter and experience with God. It was for this reason that Jesus Christ, the Messiah, came to earth.

The New Testament is full of wonderful promises to those who have been united with the Lord. Jesus says, "Remain in Me, and I will remain in you!" (John 15:4). Because we are united with Christ, we have been drawn into a deep and rich knowledge of Christ.

Holy Guide, I thank You that through the knowledge that Your Holy Spirit shares with me, I can grow in my knowledge of You, the Spirit of the Father. Amen.

Read Luke 24:13-29

Grow in Christ's Presence

As they talked and discussed these things with each other, Jesus Himself came up and walked along with them. (Luke 24:15-16)

If Jesus is not a present reality in your life, you must question if you truly know what it means to believe in the God of the Bible.

To know Christ and to live with an active awareness of Him is a central part of the Christian life. For many, there may have been emotional moments in the past where Jesus felt especially close, such as when attending an evangelistic gathering or powerful moments alone in prayer. However, these moments are not the norm, and Christ can easily feel far off during the trials and demands that accompany our daily routines. How can have mountaintop experiences on a daily basis?

The place where this reality is seen most is in your thought life. If you have accepted Jesus as your Lord and Redeemer, then He should be a feature of your thoughts on a regular basis. We should strive to have the mind of Christ, looking at the world around us through His perspective. He becomes both the lens through which we see the world, as well as the object of our sight.

Even in the everyday, mundane tasks, you will encounter the living Christ and He will become more and more of a living reality in your life.

I praise and thank You, living Christ, that I can constantly be aware of Your living presence. Amen.

Keep on Growing

Grow in the grace and knowledge of our Lord and Savior Jesus Christ. (2 Peter 3:18)

One of the greatest experiences in life is new birth in Christ. It is an experience that is well known to all sincere Christians, but which can take place in different ways.

Many people, when they experience spiritual rebirth for the first time, express themselves with great enthusiasm and look sideways at anyone who does not share their joy.

But spiritual rebirths can happen in different forms. There is the sudden repentance where the forgiven sinner immediately changes to a devout child of God. Then there is the spiritual renewal that happens gradually.

There are great numbers of Christians who cannot remember the date on which their lives were given to the Lord, but the quality of their love and service leaves no doubt about their spiritual experience.

True Christianity is a process of growing toward Christ. The important thing is that Jesus Christ needs to be acknowledged as Redeemer and Savior and we should love Him with all our heart and soul, and strength.

Once this surrender to Christ has been made, spiritual development must follow as a consequence. There needs to be growth in every area as well as the gaining of new experiences with the Lord. Failing to grow spiritually may lead to backsliding, or eventually serve as proof that we never knew Christ in the first place.

Lord and Guide, make me so aware of Your abiding presence that my spiritual life will never cease to grow and develop. Amen.

Read 1 Corinthians 13:1-13

Are You Done with Childish Ways?

When I was a child, I talked like a child, I thought like a child, I reasoned like a child. When I became a man, I put childish ways behind me. (1 Corinthians 13:11)

Unfortunately maturity does not always come with age, and that applies to our spiritual lives as well. Many people who have grown old have maintained a childish approach to life. Attitudes that are understandable for a child are not acceptable for an adult.

The child who always demands to have his way can grow up to be a stubborn and selfish person. A child who always gets everything he asks for can start to believe that the world owes him a living. This type of person claims everything he can lay his hands on as his own. Too many people carry the unpleasant characteristics of their childhood into their adult years.

While physical growth is a normal process for the average person, spiritual and moral growth requires great discipline and surrender to the will of God. There can be no growth toward spiritual maturity without the acknowledgment of the presence of God.

Yesterday we read that we should, "Grow in the grace and knowledge of our Lord and Savior Jesus Christ" (2 Pet. 3:18). It is impossible to walk in fellowship with Jesus and still possess a self-centered spirit. Jesus Christ is the road to abundance of life and spiritual maturity.

Holy Lord Jesus, through the leading and inspiration of the Holy Spirit, help me to mature in my spiritual life. Amen.

Fellowship with God

Lord, who may dwell in Your sanctuary?
Who may live on Your holy hill? (Psalm 15:1)

What can a person do to draw near to God? Through centuries people have longed to see His face. We know instinctively that we are called to have an intimate walk with God.

Some people have followed the path of knowledge. They assume that if you read books and study theology you will understand more about God, and therefore will be able to live in communion with Him. Others become involved in church activities and make sure that they are indispensable to their local communities.

Fortunately, many people realize that a life of prayer, devotion to God's Word, and commitment is the road to God and they spend much time alone with God.

The psalmist answers his own question on who may dwell in God's sanctuary, "He whose walk is blameless and who does what is righteous, who speaks the truth from his heart and has no slander on his tongue, who does his neighbor no wrong and casts no slur on his fellow man" (Ps. 15:2-3).

You cannot boast in an appearance of religious fervor, or parade your church activities if there is evil in your heart. True fellowship with God is born from integrity, faith, truth and sincerity. You find these qualities when you receive Christ as your redeemer and commit your life to Him completely. Make sure that your actions do not slander your faith.

Lord, deepen my righteousness and purify my heart. Amen.

Read 2 Timothy 1:3-12

Discover Your Gifts

For this reason I remind you to fan into flame the gift of God, which is in you through the laying on of my hands. (2 Timothy 1:6)

It is a sad fact that many people allow joy and peace to disappear from their lives because they neglect the gifts that God has given to them. They are intimidated by the achievements of others and convince themselves that they can never do anything worthwhile. Therefore, they refuse to attempt anything new.

God has given each one of us at least one gift. And if this gift is developed, other gifts will come to light too. Unfortunately, very few people find the hidden talent inside them. Because of sheer ignorance, laziness or a lack of understanding on how to uncover those talents.

There is little that can be done for those who are fully convinced that they did not receive any gifts. Their treasure will lie hidden and undiscovered forever as a result of their unbelief. Those who are lazy will always complain about their lost chances and pretend that their failure means nothing to them. It is only the Holy Spirit who can stir up their spirits to new life and action.

To discover the gifts of God in your innermost being requires sensitivity to the guidance of the Father and willingness to take risks and be creatively active for Him. It takes courage, but God never disappoints those who place their trust in Him. Follow the guidance of God and He will enrich your life.

Father God, grant me the desire and the courage to obey You so that I can discover the gifts that You have bestowed on me. Amen.

Bear Fruit

"He will be like a tree planted by the water that sends out its roots by the stream. It does not fear when heat comes; its leaves are always green. It has no worries in a year of drought and never fails to bear fruit." (Jeremiah 17:8)

Trees that grow next to strong flowing streams and rivers not only look beautiful, they also bear an abundance of fruit. The Nile is a massive river that meanders through the Egyptian desert. For seventy to eighty meters on either side of the river, there are lush plants that grow richly. Beyond that, the barren desert stretches out as far as the eye can see.

Huddled together along the river are small communities, where there is vegetation, agriculture, commerce and tourism. That narrow strip of land bears rich fruit and supports millions of people.

It is the same with the people who trust God. Jeremiah was such a person. He was fed and watered by God Himself, he carried God's message and pointed the whole nation toward God. While few paid any attention to his message, it brought God to those who did. By trusting in God, he believed in spite of spiritual drought around him. By anchoring his faith firmly in God, he was in a position to serve the whole nation who read his message.

You grow the most when you give to others. Your faith becomes more certain when you see how God works in someone else's life as a result of using you as His instrument.

Lord Jesus, may we be fruitful disciples for You to Your glory and honor. Amen.

Read Jeremiah 17:5-13

How Deep Are Your Roots?

"He will be like a tree planted by the water that sends out its roots by the stream. It has no worries in a year of drought and never fails to bear fruit." (Jeremiah 17:8)

The vast, endless area that is known as the Karoo in South Africa normally has a scant rainfall. The rain that does actually fall there drains away very quickly or dries up in the intense heat. Only short, stubby shrubs grow and are food for the widely farmed sheep.

In the northern parts of the Karoo, the mighty Orange River flows and its path creates a region of rich green foliage in the surrounding semi-desert. This gives life to a variety of plants, trees and flowers. The trees grow tall because they are watered by the constant flow.

This is how Jeremiah saw and understood faith in God. He is not comparing good people with evil people, but someone who trusts in the strength and love of God, compared with the person who trusts in human strength. Human strength is as unreliable as rain in the Karoo. Faith in God is fed by a river that never ceases to flow; a source that awakens life wherever it flows; and it fills the surrounding area with hope and peace.

The question that we need to answer is: How deep are my roots? Are they anchored deeply enough in the grace, strength and love of God to give stability when the winds of life blow hard? Do other people find peace and hope in the shadow of my life?

Lord my God, keep me anchored in Your power and love through faith in my heart. Amen.

Be Faithful to Your Calling

Do not conform any longer to the pattern of this world, but be transformed by the renewing of your mind. Then you will be able to test and approve what God's will is— His good, pleasing and perfect will. (Romans 12:2)

Discipline is never pleasant. Some people think that discipline limits them and cramps their style. They seem to find it easier to live a carefree life. They go with the flow and are comfortable among the masses who have no opinion. They do this rather that changing and accepting good standards that will lead to responsible behavior.

Our Savior, in His personal invitation to you to accept abundant life (see John 10:10), laid down with great clarity the standards that He expects of you. There can be no compromising of Christian principles, because that would mean deviating from the path that Jesus has laid out for us. The consequences of this behavior are clearly spelled out by Jesus when He says, "He who is not with Me is against Me" (Matt. 12:30).

In our present world, there is more than enough evidence of the lowering of standards and it is the duty of each person who calls himself a Christian to do their part to set things right by carrying out the will of God.

Through your surrender to the lordship of Jesus Christ, you open your life to the Holy Spirit. The Spirit will use you as an example of conformity to Christ to those who are seeking salvation in a dark world.

Use me, Lord Jesus, as a catalyst for love and peace in Your world. Amen.

Read 1 Thessalonians 3:1-13

Grow in Love

May the Lord make your love increase and overflow for each other and for everyone else, just as ours does for you. (1 Thessalonians 3:12)

As children develop, their interests also grow, and in their late teen years they go through a rapid growth spurt. Later, intellectual growth becomes of the utmost importance. In adulthood the progress of our careers is zealously pursued. During the middle years, most growth seems to take place where we want it the least: around our waists! And then the growth of our savings becomes important so that we can retire comfortably.

It is also important to grow in love. The prayer of Paul for his congregation in Thessalonica was that their love for one another would grow abundantly. It would seem that this is the one area in which we can never grow enough and where we need to cut back the least.

Christian love has been described as the greatest thing in the world. Christians who are mature in their faith are also those who give the most love to others. Those whose faith is meager and unstable love the least.

It is one thing for Christians to love one another, because they agree about most things. It is much more difficult to love "everyone else." It is something that only Christ can awaken in you, because in the long run it is only His love that can be revealed in you.

He loves *in* and *through* you and as His love increases and grows in you. He enlarges your capacity to love.

Jesus, source of all true love, increase my capacity to grow in Your love. Amen.

Christ—Our Goal in Growth

Instead, speaking the truth in love, we will in all things grow up into Him who is the Head, that is, Christ. (Ephesians 4:15)

The comment that some people will never grow up can also be a compliment. It implies that they have discovered the secret of eternal youth. They have kept the sparkle in their eye, the bounce in their step and they have the ability to communicate effectively with younger people. The passing years rest lightly on them and they draw joy from every moment of their lives.

To say that some people never grow up also has a negative side. Although these people have become physically older, they are still immature in their minds and spirits. The characteristics of immaturity are clearly identifiable: there is a reluctance to forgive; grievances from the past that are not easily forgotten; unceasing pettiness replacing the truth. Unreasonable sensitivity makes healthy human relations difficult, and with the passing of time the pettiness changes to bitterness and destroys the love that is essential to spiritual growth.

The comforting fact is that you have a choice about how you will grow and mature. If you live only to please yourself, you will remain immature. But if you allow Christ to develop your mind, your character and your spirit, time will not be an issue for you because you will live and exist in the sphere of His timeless reality.

Support me, O Holy Spirit, as I conform to Jesus every day so that I can become mature in His service. Amen.

Read Proverbs 9:1-12

Understanding Life

Instruct a wise man and he will be wiser still; teach a righteous man and he will add to his learning. (Proverbs 9:9)

Spiritual growth should result in the broadening of your intellectual perception and in a deepening of your understanding of life, because it involves every aspect of your everyday life. To have the kind of spirituality that does not care for the world around you is not in line with Christianity.

When Jesus was on earth, He taught people to love one another and to believe in God. But He also commanded them to give clothes to the naked, to feed the hungry, to comfort those who mourn and in addition do all kinds of good works.

It has sometimes been said that some Christians are so heavenly-minded that they are of no earthly good. This might sound like a harsh criticism, but it is unfortunately the voice of experience. Many of Christ's disciples fail to apply their faith practically because their spiritual concept of life has not deepened and broadened their love.

As you grow in grace and your love for God increases, your good works should also increase to reach out to places of ministry. The Christian faith is expressed in service. As your knowledge of Christ increases and your love for Him deepens, you will become more and more aware of the greatness and wonder of the life to which the Lord has called you.

Lord Jesus, as my love for You increases, I grow in my appreciation and understanding of life. Amen.

Christian Sanctification

"They are not of the world, even as I am not of it. Sanctify them by the truth; Your word is truth." (John 17:16-17)

Jesus Christ was unique and divine and yet He was a perfect, sinless man. While Jesus walked this earth, He paid tax; He was tired and hungry sometimes; He won debates; He loved children very much; He could be frank and direct with those who used theological arguments to further their ideologies, and He mixed with people of every rank of human society. Yet He possessed certain qualities that separated Him from other people.

It could never be said of Jesus, nor later of His disciples, that they meant nothing to the world. Their sincerity and holiness were very practical and were never wasted on meaningless religious arguments.

The practical sincerity and holiness of Jesus influenced the hearts and minds of the people who became His followers and were not dependent on outward show. Because His teachings were timeless, they come to the people of our day with the same freshness that they had when He first spoke them by the shores of the Sea of Galilee.

Christian sanctification is not a monotonous, oppressive practice that destroys a person's personality. It is a way of living that is filled with glory because we know that Christ dwells with us.

Paul said that Christ lives in and through us by faith. Therefore, live in Christ and enjoy the fullness of faith.

Savior and Redeemer, help me to be all that You want me to be through Your indwelling presence. Amen.

Read 2 Corinthians 5:1-10

A Praiseworthy Goal

We make it our goal to please Him, whether we are at home in the body or away from it. (2 Corinthians 5:9)

Many people find the thought of living to please God and being acceptable to Him, unrealistic. They are so caught up in dreams and schemes about their own personal issues that they never stop to ask themselves if God should be acknowledged in their plans.

To live in a way that is acceptable to God may seem limiting and frustrating to you. Some things that you want to do will be forbidden because they are no longer suitable. Thus your lifestyle will be restricted.

You are concerned that much of the enjoyment and pleasures of life will pass you by because you will have to stop doing and thinking things that are unacceptable to God. You will have to start thinking and doing those things that are acceptable to a holy and righteous God.

What is often not realized or acknowledged is that God never expects any person to abandon any action or thought without replacing it with something better. A spiritual vacuum should not exist in your life. Either you serve God or you please yourself. To serve God requires a continuous and conscious commitment; to please yourself requires no effort and delivers little of lasting value.

To live on the higher spiritual plateau creates a quality of life where Christ becomes even more real to you. Then you will find your greatest joy in living as He wants you to.

Loving God, I strive to live in Your presence so that I can learn Your will and obey it. Amen.

Without Training

"How did this man get such learning without having studied?" (John 7:15)

We usually expect of a person who teaches a certain subject to be well trained in it. It is in part their superior knowledge that gives them the authority to be able to teach a certain subject. A teacher who shows a lack of knowledge and ability quickly loses the respect of his or her pupils.

The educated leaders in Jerusalem were amazed at the way in which Jesus could teach people. He had had no formal training as a rabbi. He had no formal qualifications. He was educated at home within His family circle. He lived close to God through prayer. And He avidly studied the Scriptures. His knowledge of the Father was personal and intimate, and that was more valuable than any academic knowledge. He spoke with conviction and authority because He knew God.

You do not need lots of academic knowledge and training to become a disciple of Jesus Christ. It is much more important that you know Jesus personally. It is also true that many disciples are much more effective than they would otherwise have been because they study and learn about Jesus and the Christian lifestyle.

The Holy Spirit can use dedicated theological studies to build up the followers of Jesus in their most holy faith—and He often does so out of grace.

Holy Teacher, bless all those who are studying to be pastors and teachers. Amen.

Read 1 Peter 2:1-10

Spiritual Milk

Like newborn babies, crave pure spiritual milk, so that by it you may grow up in your salvation. (1 Peter 2:2)

It is not always easy to start living a Christian life. Old habits die hard. Sinful thoughts do not simply disappear like mist before the sun. To grow in this new life is a slow and demanding process. It is easier to fall back into the old lifestyle than to grow in the new spiritual life. Disciplines of worship are difficult to establish and maintain.

The Bible often refers to new converts as little children who feed on milk. Those who tried to help new Christians on their spiritual journey saw themselves as nursemaids who fed the newborn babies pure milk. Peter draws attention to the fact that they need to be fed with the pure spiritual milk of the Word so that they can grow spiritually.

It is essential that you receive food from the Word of God when you are a new believer, as well as when you move on to a diet of solid food. Some parts of the Bible are more easily digested than other parts. Some people might consider the Gospel of Mark as milk, while Romans is seen as solid food by others. It is important that you continue to grow spiritually, and that mainly occurs through faithful study of the Bible.

It helps you to learn to know God as He is, to learn to know yourself and to know the world in which you live. It enables you to move forward and to continue growing until you have reached maturity in Jesus Christ.

Spirit of God, feed me with the Word, today and always. Amen.

Reach for Your Goals

Not that I have already obtained all this, or have already been made perfect, but I press on to take hold of that for which Christ Jesus took hold of me. (Philippians 3:12)

Many of us become discouraged because our spiritual lives are stagnant. A biography of a hero of the faith might inspire you, but when you compare your own experiences with his, you become discouraged.

This despondency might make you feel like an average, lukewarm Christian who lacks the power, inspiration and joy of true faith. Be assured that you are not alone in this feeling of spiritual insufficiency because there are many others who feel the same way. You need to regain your vision of Christ and believe in the glory of a life that is lived to honor Him. If your faith is weak, you must realize that the fault lies with you and not with God.

Maybe you thought that high spiritual standards are unattainable and as a result you have lowered your own. You might have begun by pleasing yourself instead of living to please the Lord. It might be that you have tried to manipulate the teachings of Christ to fit in with your own way of thinking rather than accepting the truth of His teachings.

Discover once again the full impact of a dynamic Christian faith and accept the challenge of living in the Spirit of Christ. Then you will reach the spiritual goals you are aiming for.

Holy Lord, I believe that I can achieve my spiritual goals through the power of Your Holy Spirit. Amen.

Read Galatians 2:15-21

Christ in Me!

I have been crucified with Christ and I no longer live, but Christ lives in me. (Galatians 2:20)

Many people find the requirements of the Christian commitment too demanding. When they weigh up everything that Christ expects of them, they become discouraged and lose all hope. In such circumstances, they run the danger of abandoning what they see as an impossible struggle against overwhelming forces—and as a result they miss out on the opportunity to live a life of meaning, purpose and fulfillment. Because that is what a life in Christ is all about!

When you surrender your life to Christ, it is important to know that Jesus does not want you to fight the battle on your own. Jesus will never expect you to accept His way of life without equipping you to do it. He will never call you to do something in His name without granting you the ability to fulfill it.

While surrender to Christ and His standard for your life requires you to unconditionally abandon those aspects of your life that are at odds with Christian standards and principles, the Spirit of the Living Christ is in you and He will make it possible for you to live according to Christ's teachings. With God on your side, all things are possible.

Never lose sight of the fact that Christ lives! By maintaining a personal, intimate relationship with Him you will experience the blessings of a life of abundance.

Thank You, Lord Jesus, that I can remain in You so that You will remain in me. Amen.

The Sower and the Seed

"Listen! A farmer went out to sow his seed." (Mark 4:3)

The sowing of seed is as old as creation itself. Long before farmers sowed seed, nature did so itself. It is also universal. Everyone has sowed or planted something somewhere. Sowing is an activity of hope. You sow and hope for a good harvest.

Galilee, where Jesus told the parable of the sower, is a rocky area with adequate soil and sufficient rain. People could expect a harvest even though the earth was not very fruitful. The farmer in the story is God. He sends out His Word like a farmer who sows seed. While He does it in hope, there is still an element of risk involved. If you have ever sowed seeds you will know all about the uncertainty involved as you wait to see if anything comes up. The Word of God goes out and it has the ability to germinate and bring about life, joy, love and hope.

God is continually sowing His seed. It goes out to young and old, men and women, rich and poor, educated and illiterate. It goes out through the words that are spoken in various situations. It goes out as the written Word, the Bible, and through sermons about Scripture.

God's Word also goes out in a personal form. If you have heard or received the Word and if it has brought about growth in you, then you too become a sower of the Word. Your presence, your lifestyle, your words, your character, and above all your faith speak of Christ.

The people around you are the soil. That is why we must sow the pure seed of a mature Christian.

God of the Word, spread Your
Word over the whole world. Amen.

Read Mark 4:1-9

Where Does Your Seed Fall?

"Some fell along the path, and the birds came and ate it up. Some fell on rocky places. ... Other seed fell among thorns. ... Still other seed fell on good soil." (Mark 4:4-5, 7-8)

It is often said that it takes all sorts to make a world. It has always been so and it will always be so. Different kinds of people listened to Jesus. Some were fat and others were thin; some were very clever and others were less intelligent. There were those who drank in every word that Jesus spoke, but others got confused and did not understand His message.

Jesus knew what it meant for seed to fall on hard and unfruitful ground. There were hearers who were hard, cynical and unwilling. They had built up an inner resistance to God and refused to respond to the words of Jesus.

Others were shallow: they listened to what Jesus had to say, thought it was wonderful and started to believe. But their response did not last long. Others again were too involved in a life of pleasure and worldly possessions to respond to Jesus. All these things prevented God from being able to work in them.

Are you also restraining the work of God in your life? Do not allow a hard, cynical attitude to obstruct God's work. Do not be satisfied with a shallow faith that quickly withers. Do not allow money or worldly pleasures to keep you from enjoying the true, deep, rich life of friendship with Jesus.

Lord Jesus, plough the soil of my soul so that Your seed can grow bountifully in me. Amen.

Spiritual Fruitfulness

"Still other seed fell on good soil. It came up, grew and produced a crop, multiplying thirty, sixty, or even a hundred times." (Mark 4:8)

Farmers know that each different field of the same farm varies in fruitfulness. Although weather does play a role, it is largely the fruitfulness of the soil that determines how good the harvest will be. The better the ground is prepared, the better the harvest will be.

How well do you hear, receive and use the Word of God? His grace is offered to you freely, as it is to every other person. But what do you do with it?

You can receive a message from God and simply say, "That is great," and then continue your normal way of life, until another message comes along. On the other hand, you could hear God speak in such a way that you feel you need to adapt your attitude to certain things, or even that you should change your whole lifestyle.

You might also find that you are touched to the very core of your being by the Word of God to such an extent that your whole inner being is transformed from being focused on yourself to being Christ-oriented.

There are also those who experience the grace of God in such power and compulsion that they go out and dedicate their whole lives to sowing the seed. The question that you and I will have to answer before God is: how fruitfully have I sowed God's seed through my life?

Word who became flesh, help me not only to hear Your Word, but help me to obey and cherish it with all my heart. Amen.

Read Mark 4:26-34

Small Can Be Beautiful

"It is like a mustard seed, which is the smallest seed you plant in the ground. Yet when planted, it grows and becomes the largest of all garden plants." (Mark 4:31-32)

It seems like we are all impressed by size. The biggest building; the biggest car; the biggest plane in the sky—these things awaken admiration in us. We accept that the biggest is the best. But the kingdom of God is full of surprises. It often turns human thinking upside-down.

In our Scripture verse for today, Christ is glorifying the little things. He says that even though the growth of seeds is controlled by invisible forces, even the smallest seed can grow into a mighty tree. With God all things are possible.

The disciples came from a tiny country on the edge of the mighty Roman Empire. They would soon venture out to spread the gospel message to the whole known world. It would bring them many trials because they would be opposing the powerful religious authorities in Jerusalem and the secular might of Rome.

From a small and insignificant beginning that started with a group of fishermen from Galilee, God gave them the potential to achieve a greater future than they ever thought possible. Jesus said to them, "Look at the extent of the end and not at the humble beginning."

Christ says the same to us. No matter how insignificant your work for God might seem, He views things in terms of the results they can bring about.

Lord, make the work of Your kingdom a powerful accomplishment in our day. Amen.

Find Stability in God

Set your minds on things above, not on earthly things. For you died, and your life is now hidden with Christ in God. (Colossians 3:2-3)

The things that happen in the world and in your life can have a major influence on you and on those who are dependent on you. They can influence your vision and determine the pattern of your life. The decisions that you make might be controlled by the way things stand at that particular moment. The problem, however, is that you cannot always trust these things. History has shown that humanity is fickle and changeable. Furthermore, the circumstances in the world are continuously changing.

To live a life of stability, it is necessary to look beyond human thinking. It is necessary to look to Jesus Christ as your mentor and guide in everything that you undertake.

Many people will scoff at this point of view. But there is no doubt that if you make Christ your focus in life, you can have a confidence that God is working all things for good, if when things look otherwise.

When you finally accept that God's will is perfect for your life, and when you disregard your own plans and you give your life unconditionally to Him, you will become aware of the shortcomings of the world as well as the fallibility of people. Then God's holy plan for your life will unfold. No matter how the world changes, Christ is the same yesterday, today, and through all eternity.

Eternal God, we worship You as the Father who never changes. Amen.

Read Colossians 3:5-17

The Old and the New

You must rid yourselves of all such things as these: anger, rage, malice, slander, and filthy language from your lips. Do not lie to each other, since you have taken off your old self with its practices and have put on the new self, which is being renewed in knowledge in the image of its Creator. (Colossians 3:8-10)

Many wrong attitudes and emotional outbursts are sinful.

Paul knows what damage anger, hate, envy and cursing can cause among people. It leads to the destruction of relationships and wipes out mutual trust. It causes unhappiness if it happens between groups of people who are working together for Christ. It is the remnant of the "old self," of the person's life that has not yet been fully sanctified by the grace of Christ or the sensitivity of love.

When people put on the "new person," they yield themselves to the influence of Christ and learn how to control their hatred, malice, and their tongues.

We need to examine ourselves and ask the Holy Spirit to show us if we still have an unhealthy amount of the "old person" that overrules our words and actions.

If you have given yourself unconditionally to Christ, then you know how important it is to allow the Spirit to work in you and your life to build up a new perspective of purity and holiness. The "new person" is known through his self-control, caring, tenderness, awareness of the needs of others and has a desire to build up relationships rather than to break them down.

Loving Lord, help me to clothe myself with the new person and to bury the old person forever. Amen.

Sitting on a Gold Mine

This is what the LORD Almighty says:
"See, I will refine and test them." (Jeremiah 9:7)

Have you ever been to a gold mine? You go down into the earth in an elevator and see the small opening that is left behind when the gold-bearing ore is removed like a page that has been torn out of a book. You also see how tons of rocks are taken up to the surface. There they are crushed and processed until they are eventually ready to be placed in the furnace.

Later, the yellow smelted liquid is poured into molds the size of bricks. Tons of rocks are needed to make one small bar of gold.

Jeremiah tells us that this is how God treats people. Disasters befall them, adversity threatens them and tragedies erupt. They will know what it is to be crushed and to feel the heat of the furnace. But through the process, God is busy purifying them.

Life is a mixture of success and failure, of joy and sorrow, of victory and defeat.

Christians are also subject to the same problems and disasters that all other people face. View these things as a gold mine out of which Christ is calling you to bring the pure gold of faith, hope and love into existence.

They came to the place where they could see God doing His sanctifying work in the midst of their pain. May God allow us not to miss the gold-mining process in our own lives.

Merciful God, purify and sanctify me
more and more from day to day. Amen.

Read John 8:31-47

Grow Through Obedience

"If you hold to My teaching, you are really My disciples. Then you will know the truth, and the truth will set you free." (John 8:31-32)

At the turn of the previous century there was a talented Christian student named Robert Newton Flew. When he was a young man, he was offered a very attractive academic position in Canada. It would give him the opportunity to pursue and develop his intellectual gifts and be financially very lucrative.

But he committed his life to Christ and the ministry, and declined the offer with these words, "The path of study and the white light of generations who have walked that road is extremely attractive. But I cannot help but feel the drawing power of that 'extraordinary Man on the cross' and to know that He has other plans in mind for me." Christ called him and he knew that he had to obey.

Jesus Christ said that the true test of discipleship is obedience. You might insist that you love Him. You might be wonderfully touched by worship services. You might fulfill many duties in the church. You might know a lot about the Bible. You might be by nature a helpful person. But finally the conclusive question is, "Were you obedient to the voice of Jesus?" Perhaps the question carries more weight if it is put like this: "Are you willing to obey Jesus even if it costs something?"

To obey Christ might mean that you need to do something within or outside the Christian community to challenge the evil of the world while still obeying Him.

Lord Jesus, strengthen those who find it difficult to obey. Amen.

Never Give Up

"Sir," they said, "from now on give us this bread." (John 6:34)

In the autumn of 2006, the Western Cape in general and Cape Town in particular experienced a series of serious power cuts. This threw the city and the province into chaos. We trust in a never-ending supply of power for industrial, household and business interests. The same goes for water, food, gas and transport.

The provision of food in the early Middle East was definitely not guaranteed. Drought and famine were common experiences. When Jesus said to the people who had been fed with the five loaves and fish, "I am the bread of life. He who comes to Me will never go hungry, and he who believes in Me will never be thirsty" (John 6:35) they begged, "Sir, give us this bread!" One miracle was amazing but they knew that they needed far more than that: they needed a continuous supply for daily bread and spiritual food.

Some people suffer from spiritual malnutrition because they do not regularly draw from the supply that Jesus gives to them. But our Savior never withholds it from us. Perhaps you are trying to survive on a spiritual diet? If that is the case, you might not be as near to God as you would like to be?

It is necessary for you to go and sit down at the feet of the Lord and be satisfied. To persevere in living in Christ, you need to take in the food that He offers you on a regular basis.

Word who became flesh, ensure that my desire
for the Bread of Life will never wane. Amen.

Read John 4:1-26

Do You Know the Gift of God?

"If you knew the gift of God and who it is that asks you for a drink, you would have asked Him and He would have given you living water." (John 4:10)

The problem many people have with their faith is that they are looking for the wrong things. They long for success and they think that God is the right button to push for that. They want to do good, and presume that God will reward them if they do so.

Jesus asked the woman at the well for a drink of water. She neither saw the spiritual insight of the request, nor did she know who Jesus really was. That was why she did not realize that Jesus was offering her much, much more than what He had asked from her. As a result, they talked past each other on two different levels.

When people first come to know Jesus Christ, there are few who are aware of the greatness of the God whom they seek. They are also not prepared for the requirements that He will place on them. It is completely normal to come to Him when you are looking for help. Remember then that when you do so, He comes into your life and offers you far more than what you ask of Him.

At the same time He invites you to become a partner in a friendship that will lay duties on you that are far beyond your expectations. As you grow and increase in spiritual stature, your capacity to receive will expand and your capacity to love will grow at the same time.

Savior and Redeemer, thank You that I can experience the greatness of Your love. Increase my ability to receive and to care. Amen.

Purified Through Obedience

Now that you have purified yourselves by obeying the truth so that you have sincere love for your brothers, love one another deeply, from the heart. (1 Peter 1:22)

Not only is life sometimes difficult and unfair, it is also cruel and greedy. We are tainted by the society around us. We become involved in its evil ways and are drawn into its disparaging schemes. Our greed, judgment, lust and pettiness pollute any good that we try to do. Our own internal desires and drives, our arrogance and pride and our love of ease holds us back. Even when we try to do good, we yearn after the enticements of Egypt.

The people to whom Peter wrote this letter were obedient to the truth. This does not mean that they obeyed the Ten Commandments and that as a result they remained pure. The truth that they obeyed was the truth that came to them through the gospel of Jesus Christ. They believed in Jesus Christ as the truth of God and of life.

To believe in Jesus meant that He had forgiven their sins and had cleansed them. They had turned over a new leaf and because they had been born again they had become new creations in Jesus Christ.

You too can be cleansed. No matter how stained you are; no matter how badly you trespassed in the past, by surrendering yourself to Jesus you can be purified. Your conscience can be cleansed, your soul can be purified and your thoughts can be healed. All that is required of you is to trust in Christ for the forgiveness of sins and start over with Jesus as your Savior.

Holy Savior, cleanse me and keep me pure. Amen.

 Read John 4:19-26

Now Is the Time!

"A time is coming and has now come when the true worshipers will worship the Father in spirit and truth." (John 4:23)

One of the great dangers of faith is that we will become so relaxed in the unending grace of God that we think any time that suits us will be good enough for allowing God into our lives. In this way, people postpone their repentance to God. People who put off their conversion until the eleventh hour, often die at half past ten!

The Bible has a completely different picture of God. It shows that He is always ready to intervene in any situation. He did so with creation, the Exodus, the coming of Christ and He will do so again.

Jesus told many parables about the landowner who returned suddenly and his servants found themselves in a difficult position because they thought that he would return later. Our God is the God who unexpectedly intervenes in situations. God might come at any time! He might speak to a servant and through that change the course of the history of the world. Not next week—today!

The Bible creates the image for us of the future that is hastened to the present moment. He is the God of the past, the God of the future, but also the Lord and God of the present: every moment belongs to Him!

For the woman at the well, her daily drudgery was to fetch water. But it gave Christ the opportunity to confront her, to claim her life and to make a new person of her. Today, He comes to you. Are you ready for Him?

"Behold, I am coming quickly. Amen. Even so, come Lord Jesus." (Revelation 22:20)

October

Follow Him

Not only was the Teacher wise,
but also He imparted
knowledge to the people.
~ Ecclesiastes 12:9

Redeemer and Savior, Jesus Christ,
Thank You for coming to this earth
to live among us and to teach us
to find the path to life.
You said, "I have come that they may
have life, and have it to the full" (John 10:10).
Thank You for every lesson You
taught us during Your earthly stay:
Lessons through Your perfect example
and Your enriching parables
that can even be understood by the most simple.
Life is sometimes dark, but You bring the light;
Life is sometimes lonely, but You are always with us;
Life is sometimes puzzling,
but You bring sense and meaning to it.
In this month, lead us through Your life and teachings.
Be our Good Shepherd who leads us to
green pastures and quiet waters.
Thank You that we can belong to the flock
that cost You dearly and therefore
experience life every time You act or teach us.
Make us willing learners in Your
preparatory school for eternal life.
We pray this in the name above all names—
Jesus our Savior,
Amen.

Focusing on Trivialities

One Sabbath Jesus was going through the grainfields, and as His disciples walked along, they began to pick some heads of grain. The Pharisees said to Him, "Look, why are they doing what is unlawful on the Sabbath?" (Mark 2:23-24)

Many people are under the erroneous impression that Christianity is primarily about rules and regulations. There are certain things Christians "simply don't do" and there are other things Christians "must do." Most other religions have similar codes of behavior.

The Ten Commandments that God gave Israel served to direct the children of Israel. Through the ages, teachers have tried to guide the people by theorizing which actions do and do not break the Law. This culminated in thousands of rules and regulations. Picking heads of grain was regarded as harvesting—which was work—and to work on the Sabbath was forbidden. Jesus knew that the Law was meant to bring life, not to make people miserable with guilt.

Christianity is not a set of regulations, rules and laws. It means to follow Jesus and to know that He loves you, to love Him in return, and to transform that love into love for your fellow man. It does, however, include a few disciplines, but love always rises above the law. Laws are too small, narrow-minded and soul-destroying. They lead you away from the true issue—God! God fills your heart with love and gives you the strength to live according to His standards. He wants to free you to live, grow and love.

Lord Jesus, fill my heart with love so that I will truly love. Amen.

Read Mark 2:23-28

What Is the Sabbath Day For?

He said to them, "The Sabbath was made for man, not man for the Sabbath." (Mark 2:27)

During the Second World War there came a time when the English army urgently needed ammunition. It was decided that the factories producing the ammunition would work seven days a week to increase their production. Initially there was a rise in production, but after just a few weeks the production dropped to less than when they worked six days a week. The experiment was stopped and the factories returned to working six days a week. Production again rose to its previous level.

God knew a few things when He commanded, "Remember the Sabbath day by keeping it holy. Six days you shall labor and do all your work, but the seventh day is a Sabbath to the Lord your God" (Exod. 20:8-10). Jesus was saying that God gave us the Sabbath (which is Hebrew for *rest*) as a gift and for our own benefit. It was meant to enrich human life.

Christians don't honor the Sabbath—which is on Saturday—but the Day of the Lord—which is Sunday—the day of Christ's resurrection. This is a day to celebrate Christ's sovereignty, to rest and refresh ourselves, to renew relationships, to spend some time alone and meditate on all the wonderful gifts God has given us. Don't make it a burden. Rejoice and be glad in it. Worship God and find new direction for your life from Him. Open yourself to the Spirit and begin to truly live.

Let Your disciples throughout the whole world rejoice in Your resurrection and Your glorified Presence among us. Amen.

What Is Your Answer?

Always be prepared to give an answer to everyone who asks you to give the reason for the hope that you have. (1 Peter 3:15)

You probably feel that you don't know enough about the Bible to get involved in religious arguments. It is a broad subject with many pitfalls that are to be avoided. Furthermore, few unbelievers are convicted through clever arguments.

In spite of this, Peter told the early believers to be ready with a meaningful response if they were asked why they believed in Jesus Christ. He didn't command them to run off and obtain degrees in theology. He knew that there would be sincere people who wanted to know more about their faith and confidence in the future.

The future was a real factor for Peter's believers because they could be killed for their faith at any moment. Some people were amazed that Christians could face death so courageously, but they knew that they would be with Christ after they died.

We must also know the reason for the hope that lives within us. You don't have to be clever to give a simple, direct answer when asked. "I believe in Him because He has carried me in love over the years," would be a good starting point. Knowing the Bible better will take you a step further. Always be ready to share your faith with someone else because it could be the turning point in that person's life.

Teach me, faithful Savior, to always be ready to answer questions about my faith. Amen.

Read 1 Peter 3:13-22

Gentleness and Respect

Do this with gentleness and respect. (1 Peter 3:15)

Christianity today tends to think of Jesus in terms of how He has helped us. We primarily think of Him as our Friend, Redeemer, Helper in need, Shepherd, Healer, Advisor and Guide. We call Him "Lord" but hopelessly underestimate His glory.

The New Testament Christians could never have done this. They were forced to declare, "Caesar is Lord!" By doing so they would be pledging their highest allegiance to a politician, who was just an ordinary human. They knew that they couldn't declare, "Jesus is Lord" and say the same of the Caesar. They refused to acknowledge that Caesar was Lord and were persecuted and killed.

To exalt Jesus as Lord and to declare this was to sacrifice your life for your faith. For this they were burnt at the stake. To make Christ Lord of your life at that time meant more than simply using the name "Lord" as a comfortable crutch to lean on.

Christ offers to be your Friend and Helper. But at the same time He expects to be "Lord" of your life. This means that you allow Him to take full control of your life and to direct your life every moment. It means to submit to Him in loving obedience and to accept that He now gives the commands. He becomes the object of your greatest loyalty—above political rulers, before your spouse, before your boss and before your community. Make sure who is "Lord" of your life.

Jesus Christ, my Redeemer, You are Lord of
my life, both now and forevermore! Amen.

When You Have to Walk Alone

*God has said, "Never will I leave you;
never will I forsake you." (Hebrews 13:5)*

Christian fellowship is essential for spiritual growth. To belong to a warm, caring fellowship inspires us and strengthens our daily walk with the living Christ. To try and walk the Christian way alone, without the support of living Christian fellowship, is to become prey to spiritual failure. You need the support of fellow Christians to help you as you carry your cross.

If, however, your spiritual dynamic depends on emotional gatherings, the day will come when you realize that you don't possess a living faith, but rather a masquerade of a religion that will let you down in a time of crisis. Then you will realize that you have to depend on God and not on people.

You have to accept full responsibility in every area of life. No one else can do it for you. When you have to make decisions, you alone are responsible for the consequences. Choose very carefully because you can't digress from the path you have chosen.

When you set out on the final journey of life, you have to travel alone. No one can accompany you. You have to walk that path alone, and yet, you are not alone because the Master has promised to be with you as you enter the great unknown. As a disciple, you have the privilege of knowing Him as the companion who will stand by you until the end of your life—and beyond!

*Faithful Savior, even though I sometimes have to walk alone,
You are my constant companion. I thank You for this! Amen.*

Read James 4:1-10

True Christianity Balances Life

Humble yourselves before the Lord,
and He will lift you up. (James 4:10)

All Christians desire to live balanced lives. They want to remain calm in the midst of chaos; to think clearly when conflicting viewpoints fight to win their trust; to see both sides of every problem.

Unfortunately this experience proved that it is easy to nurture an ideal, but very difficult to live it out in practice. What you do and what you are often causes inner pressure and throws you spiritually off balance.

It is very important to accept that life must have a spiritual foundation and that it can only be lived successfully if this fact is accepted. This foundation is more than intellectual approval of a creed or dogma—no matter how much it might express the truth. It is accepting the living Christ in your life and allowing Him to speaking into your actions and thoughts. The glorious fact that Jesus Christ lives makes Christianity the most powerful force in the lives of today's disciples.

It is only when you start a relationship with the living Christ through love, grace, daily prayer and meditation that your thoughts can turn toward Him and you can become aware of His guidance and accept His practical way of living. In this relationship the battle of your life becomes subjected to your living Lord and your life becomes balanced and Christ-inspired.

I rejoice, Lord Jesus, that through Your grace
and love I can live a well-balanced life. Amen.

Love That Conquers

Your attitude should be the same as that of Christ Jesus. (Philippians 2:5)

The sad fact is that we live in a world where the attitude and behavior of many leave much to be desired. Corruption, scandals and violence are the order of the day and most decent, right-minded people are astounded by the decline of societal standards and the degeneration of behavioral patterns.

The normal human reaction to this is the temptation to handle the situation with similar attitudes and to fight fire with fire. However angry you may be about present circumstances—especially if you have been a victim—as a Christian, you can't allow yourself to stoop to their level. It might give you temporary satisfaction, but it isn't a lasting solution to the world's problems.

Jesus Christ clearly demonstrated that His way was the best and always will be. The only way to handle evil is through the path of divine love.

Love is not a sign of weakness, as some would have you believe. If we consider Christ's courage and endurance on the cross, nobody can dare to call Him weak. As it was then, so it is now: only the forgiving love of Christ can and will conquer the powers of evil.

Father God, You are love. This is clearly spelled out at the cross. Amen.

Read Ephesians 4:1-10

To Find God!

There is ... one Lord, one faith, one baptism; one God and Father of all, who is over all and through all and in all. (Ephesians 4:4-6)

Through the ages people have searched for God. They saw His majesty in the heavens, studied His handiwork in nature, and experienced His timing through the galaxy. God was "out there" the whole time. He was someone separated from the human race, introduced as a kind-hearted God who was quick to forgive and slow to judge. In moments of testing He was asked for help and comfort—but He was always the One placed apart from the human race.

The coming of Jesus totally changed this concept of God. The living Christ teaches us that the eternal God is not a distant Godhead, but rather the Holy One who makes His home with His people.

Jesus, who is in perfect harmony with the Father, invites people to the same relationship. Jesus said, "I am in the Father and the Father is in Me." Then He invited His followers to abide *in* Him.

The amazing truth of Christianity is that our knowledge of God doesn't not begin with us working our way to God, but rather by God coming to us. Christ lived among us, and died to put away our sins. He sent His Spirit to indwell His people, and the Spirit draws us to the Father. While God may be transcendent, He is anything but distant. Rather, He draws near to us, and bids us draw near to Him.

Master and Savior, come through the Holy Spirit and make me aware of the indwelling Presence of the eternal God every day. Amen.

Tell Me a Story!

He taught them many things by parables. (Mark 4:2)

When you were a small child you probably enjoyed bedtime stories and this was the best part of the day. When the one story was finished, you pleaded for another. And when you were tucked in, your parents would switch on the TV and watch—a story!

The whole Bible is the story of God's dealings with His people and with the world. The Gospels tell the story of Jesus' life, crucifixion and resurrection. Acts and the Letters of the Apostles tell the story of God's ongoing activity through His church. Jesus didn't come to proclaim a philosophy, or to lay down a set of rules. He didn't bring a political system to life. He told stories. And the things He did resulted in stories that have been told over and over again. We still tell these stories and they still spark the imagination of young and old.

The stories Jesus told were stories about life. They are about people—working people, foolish people, clever people, strong people, and sinful people. They are also about God—a loving God; a wise God; a sovereign God.

You also have a story. Indeed, you *are* a story! If you believe in Jesus Christ and follow Him, He helps you write a new story—the tale of human struggle, failure and growth, with the glory of God, the grace of Jesus and the tender touch of the Holy Spirit. When you eventually stand before God, He will say, "Tell Me your story!" What will your story be like?

Help me, Good Shepherd, to write a story
with my life that will gladden Your heart. Amen.

Read Mark 4:1-9

On the Shore at the Water's Edge

Jesus began to teach by the lake. The crowd that gathered around Him was so large that He got into a boat and sat in it out on the lake, while all the people were on the shore at the water's edge. (Mark 4:1)

In court great emphasis is placed on what the witnesses say. Some are regarded as "good" witnesses, others as "trustworthy" and others as "unreliable." The manner in which they tell their story, whether they appear honest or devious, and how their story survives under cross-examination are all factors the judge takes into account when he decides to accept or reject a witness.

The Gospels consist of stories that were told by witnesses about the actions and words of Jesus Christ. Mark wrote about what Peter told him—and Peter was there. Therefore, Mark's story is authentic. In our reading for today we see details that could only have been observed by an eyewitness. Peter remarked that Jesus "sat in" the boat to teach the people. He remarked that the people were on the shore. Such facts are not simply made up. You can believe and trust the four Gospels. You can have faith in Jesus on the basis of the trustworthiness of those who recorded Jesus' first actions. God entrusted the truth of His eternal message to ordinary people.

Jesus never wrote a book, because the people who saw and heard Him and conveyed the message were living embodiments of the truth. And you are too. Jesus conveys the same message through your life, and for this reason you must be a trustworthy witness.

Holy Jesus, make me a trustworthy witness. Amen.

Be Prepared to Suffer

Since Christ suffered in His body, arm yourselves also with the same attitude, because he who has suffered in his body is done with sin. (1 Peter 4:1)

Above the west door of Westminster Abbey in London are ten small statues, each one in its own slot. They all represent people who died for their faith in Jesus Christ during the twentieth century. One is a South African, Manche Masemola. She was born into the Pedi tribe and grew up in an environment where Christianity was regarded with aversion. She became a Christian during a missionary outreach in her area. Every form of physical persecution, including violence, was used to make her abandon her faith. She said to a priest, "I will never deny my faith, even if they behead me. I will be baptized in my own blood." Her parents took her to an isolated place and she was beaten to death.

You will hardly be called to such martyrdom. But you can ask yourself some serious questions about how far you will be willing to go to obey Christ. If a romantic relationship required you to sacrifice your faith, would you be willing to do it? If your superiors at work required you to abandon your faith, would you do it? If the only job you could find would require you to violate your beliefs, would you let your faith fit in with it? Followers of Jesus all over the world make these decisions daily. How prepared are you to suffer for Christ?

Holy Spirit of God, thank You for helping me to calculate the cost of my discipleship. Amen.

Read Matthew 28:11-20

The Great Commission

"Go and make disciples of all the nations." (Matthew 28:19)

Many businesses believe in the saying, "If you aren't growing, you're dying." They are continually on the look out to buy similar companies and expand their own activities so that their profits increase.

Jesus commanded His disciples to become apostles. Earlier He had invited them to "Follow Me!" and now He sends them to "Go and make disciples of all the nations." Their task was commissioned to them by One who received His authority from God. From that moment on the church of Christ knew that its mission was to make new disciples, more disciples and better disciples. The church either takes steps to grow, or it faces deterioration and eventual death.

This is still the church's God-given task. It is also the challenge that Jesus sets for each one of His disciples—to make more disciples. It is not solely the responsibility of the church body as a whole; it is the responsibility of each one of us. You do this by talking about Jesus every time the opportunity arises. You do this through the spiritual edification of those who are already His disciples. You help followers to be better followers. You do it when you pray for those who are battling a faith struggle. You do it when you pray for missionaries. You help to make disciples when you support missionaries financially and when you help to spread the gospel through reading material, radio and television. You can't evade this command because it is Christ's "Great Commission" to you!

Lord, help me to make more disciples for Your kingdom. Amen.

The Threefold Name

"Go and make disciples of all nations, baptizing them in the name of the Father and of the Son and of the Holy Spirit." (Matthew 28:19)

Christianity is much more than the awareness of God or acknowledging Him. It is more than saying, "Yes, there is a supreme being!"

It means having a personal relationship with God who came to us in the form of three persons. Don't worry if you find it difficult to understand the concept of the Trinity. Christianity is about becoming a disciple of the One who came from God the Father.

We can only know God the Father through God the Son. He shows us the Father who sent Him. But you can only know God the Father and Jesus the Son if the Holy Spirit has worked faith in your heart—faith that Jesus is the Son and that God is His Father and yours. This Spirit works in you and enables you to know Jesus and to come close to God the Father.

Therefore, the disciples you must go and make are those who do not yet know God. They have to know Jesus Christ as their God and they have to be receptive to the work of the Holy Spirit in their lives so that Jesus can live in their hearts. They have to be taught about Jesus and become learners of the Holy Spirit and people of God. Faith must grow in them daily. Christ must mold them as they grow in knowing God as their loving Father.

Father, Son and Holy Spirit, teach me to know You better and more intimately each day. Amen.

Read Ephesians 5:15-20

Look Back and Be Thankful

Give thanks for everything to God the Father in the name of our Lord Jesus Christ. (Ephesians 5:20 NLT)

The middle of the year has come and gone. It is fitting to stop for a moment and consider how the year has been for you so far. Maybe it has been a year of problems and troubles; or maybe it has brought you prosperity, success and achievement. Maybe you had to say goodbye to someone who was very close to you. Maybe there was the birth of a child or the marriage of someone special. Most years our lives are a mix of good and bad.

Take a few moments today to thank God for all the good things that have come to you from His loving hand. Even if you have had an awful year, there will still be things you can thank Him for. Write them down on a piece of paper. If things have generally gone well, it is just as important to list them so that you don't forget. Include family-related blessings too. Also thank Him if you have profited financially or been promoted at work.

Possibly some of your prayers have been answered; maybe there has been healing in the family; or a small miracle has taken place. If you have grown spiritually in a time of suffering, thank God. If you have advanced in your particular career, it's also something to thank God for. To think earnestly about these things will help you to see your setbacks from a different perspective and you will notice the hand of God in your life.

Loving and gracious Lord Jesus, every year I have endless things to thank You for. Amen.

Chosen to Suffer

To this you were called, because Christ suffered for you, leaving you an example, that you should follow in His steps. (1 Peter 2:21)

In the movie *Fiddler on the Roof,* Tevye, the main character, sings, "If I were a rich man." He asks God, "Would it spoil some vast eternal plan if I were a wealthy man?"

God's "vast eternal plan" has nothing to do with who is rich and who is poor. His plan is the salvation of humankind. To fulfill this plan He sacrificed His Son out of love for the world. Jesus, in turn, appealed to His disciples when He said, "If anyone would come after Me, he must deny himself and take up his cross and follow Me" (Matt. 16:24). By the time Peter wrote our reading for today, many had already died for Jesus and many more would follow—including Peter himself.

God has also called you and me—not to a life of peace, power and prosperity—but to a life of self-denial, service and love for others. For some believers this may lead to suffering and even death. To follow Jesus is not a walk in the park. It sometimes includes mockery and rejection. It is sometimes a lonely path on which you must lay down certain things that others take for granted.

Some have taken up the cross by going to a far-off mission field. Others have cared for the sick and helped the poor. Each one of us has a cross to bear. The question is: Do you carry your cross in a worthy manner as you follow the great Cross-bearer?

Give me grace, Lord Jesus, to carry the cross that You have laid upon me, without grumbling. Amen.

Read Galatians 3:21-29

Different Spiritual Experiences

You are all children of God through faith in Christ Jesus. And all who have been united with Christ in baptism have put on Christ, like putting on new clothes. (Galatians 3:26-27 NLT)

Self-created spiritual segregation is a great danger for Christians. When some people become part of the "new life in Jesus Christ" and become aware of His power and love, they tend to think that the way they received this experience is the only way. With the enthusiasm of their new-found faith they find it difficult to accept that other people have similar experiences, in a different manner.

The truth is that dedicated churchgoers and zealous evangelists all have witnessed God's power and love rise above man-made divisions. God works in the lives of all believers, regardless of the doctrinal differences that may feel so significant to us. We must not act like our brothers and sisters are outside of God's grace, just because we do not see eye to eye on all issues. Rather, in so far as we share in the reality of Christ as our savior, we should love our fellow believers, regardless of points of disagreement.

The core of any Christian experience is that the living Christ is accepted in the heart and mind of the believer and that finds expression through love and service to Him and other people. If this is your experience, be grateful for what you have, but allow others to rejoice in His Redemption even if they see some matters differently from you.

Lord, keep me in harmony with all who love You. Amen.

The Path of the Lord

Anyone who runs ahead and does not continue in the teaching of Christ does not have God; whoever continues in the teaching has both the Father and the Son. (2 John 9)

Many people are confused by the various interpretations of the Word of the Lord. The sad fact is that this state has caused many divisions within the church of Jesus Christ. Our Master's prayer for perfect unity among all believers is ignored by those who regard themselves as authorities and believe that their way of interpreting Scripture is the only way.

The hidden danger is that this attitude provides the breeding ground for the destructive influence of Satan, whose most effective method of attack is from within the church, and not from outside.

If you experience uncertainty in this area, it is necessary for you to investigate both the teachings and the teachers. If they are not Christ-centered and grounded on His all-encompassing love, you can be sure that they are not from God and must be rejected.

It's not always easy to understand this issue. It is necessary to pray for God's gifts of wisdom and discernment to enable you, through His Holy Spirit, to get a clear understanding of every situation. In this way you will discover the true teaching of Christ in a new way.

Lead me on Your path, Lord Jesus, and grant me a clear understanding of Your teachings. Amen.

Read Luke 19:45-48

The Power of Your Faith

Every day He was teaching at the temple. But the chief priests, the teachers of the law and the leaders among the people were trying to kill Him. Yet they could not find any way to do it, because all the people hung on His words. (Luke 19:47-48)

The Christian faith has been continuously attacked throughout the ages. Cynics have mocked it, and individuals have been persecuted and martyred because of it. Even some people who call themselves Christians have sowed doubt in the minds of others regarding the teachings of Christ and the interpretation of Scripture.

In spite of all these attacks, the Word of God has remained entirely indestructible. The truth that Christ brought to light is untouchable, and any attempt by mere people to undermine it cannot succeed.

To play your part in upholding the name of Jesus Christ, it is essential that you maintain a personal and intimate relationship with Him and make sure that your understanding of Scripture is pure and correct.

In this way you will receive strength from the living Christ and you will be able to resist the pressure that is placed on you by those who seek to undermine your faith. Your knowledge of God's Word will give you the ability and assurance to oppose any argument that is aimed against His teachings. For this you need a lot of mercy and firm faith.

Thank You, Redeemer and Savior, that Your Word carries me through in the face of great opposition. Amen.

Praying in the Dark Valley

The Lord will rebuild Zion and appear in His glory.
He will respond to the prayer of the destitute;
He will not despise their plea. (Psalm 102:16-17)

Every child of God experiences a time when it is difficult to pray. As believers, we sometimes feel like we are losing grip on the anchor of our lives—our confidence in God's faithfulness. God, who has always been a reality in our lives, suddenly seems distant and unreal.

Many Christians don't recognize the immeasurable importance that this time can have for them and their spiritual growth. They incorrectly think that God no longer cares about them, that He doesn't hear when they cry out to Him and that He won't answer them.

These times are an opportunity for growth, and that can only happen by drawing our hearts and minds back to the truths we know about God. Pray that He will make these truths feel real to you, that you would trust Him more deeply. Know that God is there in the dark times, even when we cannot see Him. Even when prayer feels difficult, remember that one day the darkness will pass and we will clearly see our God who has been there all along. When God feels distant, we know that He is near.

God always listens to your prayers—those you pray in times of sunshine, but also those prayed in the dark valley. He won't scorn your prayer—He will answer you.

Hearer of prayer, help me not to focus on myself and my problems; but to search harder for You and to do Your will until You transform the darkness in my life into light. Amen.

Read John 20:26-31

To Not See and Yet to Believe

Jesus told him, "Because you have seen Me, you have believed; blessed are those who have not seen and yet have believed." (John 20:29)

We usually trust what we can see. If someone tells us something unusual, we suspect that they are misleading us—and no one wants to be misled. Even more so, we don't want others to think that we are fools who can be tricked easily. Therefore, we want to see things for ourselves—because seeing is believing.

This is exactly how Thomas felt after the resurrection. He was no-one's fool. He didn't fall for the other disciples' story that Jesus was alive. But while he was present, Jesus came. This made Thomas look like a fool. The presence of the risen Lord, the nail marks in His hands and the spear wound in His side transformed Thomas. Darkness changed into light. Skepticism changed into trust. Doubt disappeared and amazement flowed from Thomas.

Thomas probably didn't touch Jesus, or place his fingers in the nail marks or in the wound in Jesus' side. He simply believed and fell at Jesus' feet in worship. But many who saw everything that Jesus did still did not believe. Many in the crowd did not believe. The church authorities and the state did not believe. You might say, "If I was there and saw everything, I would believe!"

Two thousand years later you *can* believe because the story of Thomas sounds sincere and true. Stop for a while and join Thomas in His amazement and submission and declare along with him, "My Lord and my God!"

Gracious Jesus, help me to believe, even when I can't see. Amen.

The Need for a Deeper Love

"The most important one," answered Jesus, "is this: 'Hear, O Israel, the Lord our God, the Lord is one. Love the Lord your God with all your heart and with all your soul and with all your mind and with all your strength.'" (Mark 12:29-30)

No matter how much you might love Jesus Christ, you will always have a feeling of inadequacy when you compare your love for Him with His love for you. No one can love you as much as He loves you, but this shouldn't prevent you from striving to increase your love for Him.

To grow in love, it is very important to meet with God regularly, spending time listening to Him through His Word, and bearing your heart to Him in prayer. Both Scripture and the experience of countless disciples tell us that the Master honors these means, and those who seek Him out never find themselves disappointed. Let your love for Him grow in this fellowship, and let your life being an offering that is pleasing to Him. The sadness of giving yourself up will always pale in comparison to your love for God.

While your love may be imperfect, it will continue to grow as you become closer to your Lord. The Holy Spirit will continue to work in your heart, and love is one of the main fruits that He cultivates in God's children. As you continue to trust in the Lord and reflect on His love for you, your love for Him cannot help but flourish in time.

Faithful Savior, grant that my love for You will increase and grow through the inspiration of the Holy Spirit. Amen.

Read Luke 18:1-8

When Your Faith Is Tested

"When the Son of Man comes,
will He find faith on the earth?" (Luke 18:8)

An endless amount has been said and written about the state of the world today. Violence is on the increase and lawlessness and anarchy are the order of the day. The urgent call is being heard more and more that we are living in the last days and that the coming of Christ is at hand. There is nothing more we can do to prevent the decline of society and the destruction of the world.

Whether these predictions are true or not, despite the chaos that reigns, we can't reject the standards that Christ has set. The fact that the world is in a desperate condition doesn't give Christians the excuse to stop fighting against the influence of the evil one. We dare not just sit back and wait for the Prince of Peace to come and set the world straight again.

Christian dedication and submission for life and discipleship must be practiced in sunny weather as well as during storms. Despite the evil one's efforts to undermine the church of Christ, and the tremendous pressure that is mounting against the Christian faith, it will always be your duty to honor the name of Jesus Christ. You must cling to His power and everything He stands for, so that when He does indeed come, you will hear Him say, "Well done, good and faithful servant."

Holy Jesus, if I am tested, strengthen my
faith so that I will be able to endure it. Amen.

Appreciating Others

As we have the opportunity, let us do good to all people, especially to those who belong to the family of believers. (Galatians 6:10)

Never hesitate to express sincere appreciation. It is so easy to take for granted the work someone did with great effort and sacrifice, or to undervalue the sacrifices made for us.

Appreciation does not only delight the hearts of those who receive it, but it also brings you joy.

Guard against being self-centered and taking more from life than you are prepared to put into it. If you make a conscious effort to be aware of things to be grateful for, you will realize that there are a number of blessings that you have taken for granted.

Love, loyalty, and generosity of spirit are beautiful gifts people give to you every day. Recapture the God-given insight to see the glory of these daily acts of love that people continuously perform for you. Respond to these with your own acts of grateful love.

Never forget the mercy God has shown you. It is impossible to stand in the glory of our gracious God and still feel depressed. Allow your gratitude for God to spread out into acts of selfless love for your fellow man. This will become a source of blessing to you and others.

If you have the urge to express your appreciation or do a kind deed, don't delay or postpone it. Act as soon as possible to show your appreciation.

Help me, heavenly Father, to appreciate the love and help I receive from others, and especially from You. Thank You for all Your blessings in Jesus Christ which I undeservingly receive. Amen.

Read 1 Corinthians 15:50-58

Fight Discouragement

Therefore, stand firm. Let nothing move you. Always give yourselves fully to the work of the Lord, because you know that your labor in the Lord is not in vain. (1 Corinthians 15:58)

Discouragement is something most people, if not all, experience at one time or the other. Good intentions are misunderstood; careful plans are thwarted; earnest suggestions are pushed aside; resulting in the temptation to give up. It can happen in your spiritual and secular life, but the frustrations are the same, and it is a well-known fact that discouragement is one of Satan's most popular weapons. He persists, especially with enthusiastic people, and his only goal is to undermine Christianity.

If you want to fight against discouragement, it is of the utmost importance to make Christ the center of your life. Before starting any project, first seek God's will in your specific circumstance. Earnestly pray that He will lead you in your decisions and make His will for your life very clear. Move forward then; renewed by the Spirit and strengthened by knowing that God is with you.

You will always face obstacles, as well as people who will try to thwart your efforts. There will be moments when you sense a hint of discouragement. Search for the Master's help to support you and know that what you are attempting to do is being done for and with Jesus. Then you will triumph over all adversities with God's help.

Living Savior, I will face life with confidence, knowing that You are beside me. Amen.

It is Never Too Late

Jesus loved Martha and her sister and Lazarus.
Yet when He heard that Lazarus was sick,
He stayed where He was two more days. (John 11:5-6)

You, too, have probably also prayed for more time. Perhaps something had to be completed by a certain date and because it was important, you spent a lot of time praying about it. You might have asked God to help you to do something before the due date otherwise it would be too late. And then … nothing happened.

If you have ever had such an experience, you have probably learned the hard way that you cannot rush God.

When Jesus learned that His friend Lazarus was dying, He did a strange thing. He did not go to support and comfort His friends straight away; He stayed where He was for another two days. When He did eventually arrive in Bethany, He transformed the tragedy of Lazarus' death into an opportunity to glorify God.

There may have been many times in your life when God did not follow your schedule. You prayed fervently but it seemed as if God was too late. But God is never late. His timing is always perfect.

If you love and trust Him, He will let all things work out for your good, in His own perfect time. Instead of demanding from God to act within a certain time frame, you should allow Him to form and polish you according to His perfect will. Then you will live in harmony with Him and have peace of mind.

Forgive me, O Lord, for my selfishness.
I place my life and my wishes in Your hands. Amen.

Read Matthew 18:21-35

Cast Away Your Grievances

Peter came to Jesus and asked, "Lord, how many times shall I forgive my brother when he sins against me? Up to seven times?" Jesus answered, "I tell you, not seven times, but seventy-seven times." (Matthew 18:21-22)

It is difficult to forgive when you have been wronged or treated unfairly.

When someone scolds or ridicules you, especially in the presence of others, it is almost impossible to forgive them. When you have been treated unjustly, you automatically feel indignant. Your anger reaches boiling point and if it boils over, you're in trouble.

If you suppress ill feelings, they become an evil, festering sore in your heart, which gradually poisons your thoughts and eventually your entire being.

However difficult it may appear, there is only one way to handle these situations. In both your prayers and in your heart, you should continuously confirm that you have forgiven the person who has hurt you. Ask God for grace and strength so that through the Holy Spirit you can forgive as Jesus forgave.

Your forgiveness must not be restricted to your prayers. Jesus' command is, "First go and be reconciled to your brother; then come and offer your gift" (Matt. 5:24). You must go and tell the person who hurt you that you forgive them; only then can you obtain deliverance.

Discipline yourself to forgive those who cause you suffering. Then you can live in peace with God.

God of Love, give me the ability to forgive,
as You forgave me in Jesus Christ. Amen.

Grow, Grow, Grow!

Grow in the grace and knowledge of our Lord and Savior Jesus Christ. (2 Peter 3:18)

A newly-wed young man wanted to start planting a garden around his new house. He went to an experienced gardener to find out what to do and what not to do. The older man showed him his beautiful garden and explained what the names of the various plants were and how to get them to grow. They came to a certain plant and the older man said, "Years ago I was given a tip about these plants: they grow better if you plant them in the moonlight." "Really?" the young man asked, "Do you always do it this way?" "Oh yes, always. And I talk to them." The young man thought that the old man was kidding him, so he asked, "And what do you say to them?" "I say, 'Grow you wretched creatures. Grow!'" grumbled the older man.

The apostles give the same advice to believers—just maybe not so explicitly! We aren't told to grow as people in our own estimation or skill. We must grow in grace—God's grace! We must allow God's grace to grow Christ in us.

Allow the Holy Spirit to grow Christ's image in you. Never think that you can stop growing spiritually, however old you might be. Continue to learn more and more about Christ. You can never know Him too well or know too much about Him.

Lord my God, help me, through the Holy Spirit, to never stop growing in Christ. Amen.

Let Christ Be the Referee

Let the peace of Christ rule
in your hearts. (Colossians 3:15)

The referee is one the most important people in a sports game. He must know the rules and how to apply them. His decision must be immediate. Sometimes tensions mount and tempers get out of hand between the players. Then the referee has to intervene, and maintain law and order. Sometimes the referee has to call on another referee to help him make a decision.

The peace that Jesus gives is not only a peace that calms the storm in your heart. He must rule as the other referee does. He is given to you as a guide in difficult circumstances, where your own preferences, fears and desires can force you to make the wrong decisions. Friends and loved ones can also give you the wrong advice. Rather refer the matter to Jesus. His knowledge is perfect, His wisdom is incredible and His peace can diffuse all disputes.

If you are pressured to make decisions that are outside your ability, turn it over to Jesus. You can never calculate the consequences ahead of time because you don't know the future. Let the peace of Christ reign over all your thoughts and trust Him. Know that you are in the best hands!

Lord Jesus, help those who are battling with difficult decisions
and let them look to You for the right guidance. Amen.

Called to Peace

As members of one body you were called to peace. (Colossians 3:15)

Organizations choose teams to achieve certain goals. A commercial firm may send a team to a certain area if it wants to improve matters there. But it will send a completely different team to clean up a mess.

In the early days of Christianity local groups of believers—or churches—had diverse members. Some were Jews who had converted to Christianity. Others were "heathens." Some were slave owners, while others were the slaves themselves. There were men and women; rich and poor. As a result there were many points of disagreement and sometimes conflict arose. The life of the community was marred by quarrels. When Paul encouraged the Christians at Colossae to live in harmony, he reminded them that they were called, or chosen, by God to live in unity and peace with each other.

The love that Christ shares is to encourage Christians to live in peace with each other; however much their economic backgrounds differ. It isn't simply a case of "liking" each other. It is a challenge to accept others as children of God and brothers and sisters in Christ.

We are also chosen by God to live in peace. The peace of Christ must not only reign in your heart, but also in family, church, and social relationships as well as in your work situation. You must contribute to unity and hope, just like the Master did.

Lord my God, make me an instrument of Your peace. Amen.

Read 2 Peter 1:1-10

Keep Learning

Grace and peace be yours in abundance through the knowledge of God and of Jesus our Lord. (2 Peter 1:2)

A middle-aged professional man said on one occasion, "When I was young I thought that going to university would teach me everything there was to know about my field of study and that it would be enough for my professional career. Now, fifteen years later, I realize that I am still learning and that my degree was only the beginning of a lifetime of study and growth."

It's the same for the disciple of Jesus Christ. The day you give your life to Christ is only the beginning of a long process of learning about Jesus and growing in Him. You read about Christ in the Bible, or you listen to a sermon about Him. You apply it to your life and work and realize how the Holy Spirit empowers you to a deeper faith and a consecrated way of living. Then you suddenly discover something new about Christ and the process continues. Sometimes life is cruel and you wonder how God can allow certain things to happen to you. But then you discover what it means to walk with God and you continue again, but with greater strength.

Never think that you know everything. No matter how far you have already traveled, there is still another piece of road that you must walk. The riches of Christ are "unsearchable" (Eph. 3:8). However much you might have learned and know about them, you will discover that there are always hidden treasures to be discovered. Keep learning and allow the Holy Spirit to teach you.

Holy God, lead me daily to new truths about Yourself. Amen.

Who Reigns in Your Heart?

Let the peace of Christ rule in your hearts. (Colossians 3:15)

Some people have wayward hearts. They are tossed to and fro by stormy passions, jealousy and spite. Others are consumed by anger and bitterness. Many people have a burning desire to take revenge. Others are driven by greed and malice.

Paul knew what it meant to be driven by hatred. On occasion he had been granted permission to kill Christ's disciples, "Meanwhile, Saul was still breathing out murderous threats against the Lord's disciples" (Acts 9:1). Then he met Christ, who replaced his internal conflict with peace, harmony and purpose. In place of the bloodshed he previously sought, he now strived to spread the peace of Christ wherever he went. Christ calmed the tempest in Paul's heart by calling, "Peace, be still."

Allow the peace of Christ to reign in your heart. Allow Him to speak His words of peace in your storm of rage, revenge and hatred that threatens to take over your heart and life and cause chaos in your thoughts. If you don't find peace here, you might find yourself at war with God, other people and yourself. This might already be the case. Let Christ calm the storm in your life. Let His peace take over your heart and life and calm your passions. Don't be tossed to and fro by hatred and bitterness. Allow Christ to put His strong, calming hand on the steering wheel of your life.

Take over my life anew, faithful Savior,
and replace passion with Your heavenly peace. Amen.

November

God's Unending Love

"Love the Lord your God with all your
heart and with all your soul and with
all your mind. This is the first
and greatest commandment."

~ Matthew 22:37-38

Holy God, our loving Father, through Jesus Christ
I come before You to plead for my urgent need:
Help me to love You.
Kindle my love and let it grow every day.
Thank You that Your love casts out all fear and
that You are able to draw love from my wicked heart.
Rule over my emotions, Lord,
despite my disloyalty to Your love.
Purge in the fire of Your love every wrong desire in me.
You are the perfect source of love.
Grant me the grace to love You fearlessly;
with a love that will stand the test of eternity.
I often rebel against Your love,
but without it I am nothing.
God of love, have mercy on me, a poor sinner.
Grant me a new vision of Your love so that I will know
and be able to obey Your will for my life.
Open my heart and protect Your love in me.
Grant that I will live up to
the full measure of Your love.
Grant that I will love through my will, my words,
my thoughts and my deeds.
Thank You that Your love has not left me alone,
but reached out to me and
brought me home to Your love.
God of love, come into my life and
ignite me with Your love,
so that I can love You and
my fellow man the same way You do.
God of love, I pray in Your name!
Amen.

Love Is the Best of All

Now I will show you the most excellent way. (1 Corinthians 12:31)

There is only one thing that can bind the church together in perfect unity, and that is love. After Paul said this, he continued with a song of praise. Our reading for today is one of the most wonderful chapters in the New Testament when we grasp its full meaning.

Paul maintains that a person can possess all the spiritual gifts mentioned in the previous chapter, but if a gift is not used in love, it is worthless. One may speak "in the tongues of men and of angels" and be as articulate as one can, but without love this is nothing more than the sound of a clanging cymbal. One may "have the gift of prophecy" and understand its deepest mysteries, but without love this means nothing. Paul's words can be compared to a modern sermon with two kinds of speakers: the prophet of doom and the pastor who is concerned about the immortal souls of the congregation and aims to draw them back to God in love.

Paul goes on to say, "If I have all knowledge ..." Only the kind of knowledge that can be brought to life by an ardent love can lead people to a true knowledge of God. You may have "a faith that can move mountains," but without love, you are nothing.

There is barely any other portion of Scripture that demands as deep an examination of the Christian faith as this passage does. Let us go forward in prayerful admiration to the God of love.

Father of love, give me the grace to examine honestly
the quality of my love for You and my fellow man. Amen.

Read 1 Corinthians 13:1-4

Love Is Patient

Love is patient. (1 Corinthians 13:4)

The Greek word *makrothumein* is used in the New Testament to mean *patience*—being used most often to speak of patience with people. It applies to a person who has suffered an injury and has the power to avenge, but chooses not to do so. It describes someone who is slow to anger. It is used for God, and His relationships with us.

When dealing with people, however vindictive or unkind they may be, we are called to practice the same patience that God exercises with us. Patience is not a sign of weakness, but of strength, the only road to victory.

No one spoke of President Abraham Lincoln with more disdain than Edwin Stanton. He called Lincoln "a vulgar, common clown." He gave him the nickname "Original Gorilla." But Lincoln did not react to this. He made Stanton his Minister of Defense because he considered him to be the best man for the job. Through all the years he treated Stanton with respect. The night that Lincoln died and his body lay in its coffin, Stanton looked at him with teary eyes, and said, "Here lies the greatest ruler of men that this world has ever known." Lincoln's patience and love had triumphed in the end.

When Jesus Christ was jeered and mocked, when a crown of thorns was placed on His head, when He hung on the cross and died in the company of criminals, the world was seeing the greatest Man who ever lived. His patience with and love for us is still unchanging today.

Thank You, Savior and Lord, that Your
patience with me is never-ending. Amen.

Kindness and Love

Love is kind. (1 Corinthians 13:4)

Origen described this kind of love as "kind-hearted to everyone." Jerome called it "the gentleness of love." There are many Christians who seem good, but are not kind. A little girl once prayed, "Lord Jesus, make all the bad people good and all the good people kind."

There were few men more devout than Philip II of Spain and yet he instigated the Spanish Inquisition and thought that he was serving God by torturing and murdering those with differing views.

According to Paul, there are spiritual cannibals among Christians who devour each other, "If you keep on biting and devouring each other, watch out or you will be destroyed by each other" (Gal. 5:15). Love that is not tempered by kindness is not truly love. Christ attracted people to Him not only through His love, but also through kindness—even towards tax collectors and prostitutes.

Most modern-day Christians would probably have chosen the side of the scribes and the church authorities, rather than support Jesus in the case of the woman caught in adultery.

Love is convincing only when it is accompanied by genuine kindness.

Kind Lord Jesus, teach me the virtue of
kindness as I emulate Your way of life. Amen.

Read 1 Corinthians 13:1-13

Love Knows No Envy

Love does not envy. (1 Corinthians 13:4)

Noël Coward claims, "There are really only two types of people in the world: those who are millionaires, and those who want to be." There are also two kinds of envy. First there is the kind that covets the possessions of others, simply because of human weakness. The other kind is much more serious: people become jealous because someone else has something that they do not have. It is not so much that they want to have it, but rather that they resent the other person for having it.

Such lovelessness can hardly sink lower than this. Envy eats at the soul. It ruins your health and robs you of your peace of mind. Finally, it completely destroys you.

Chaucer, in his *Canterbury Tales*, identifies two types of envy: People who are distressed over the goodness of others and people who rejoice over the sorrow of others. Envy means begrudging another person anything good. These people will do everything to undermine others, without having the faintest idea that they are actually undermining themselves at the same time.

The Pharisees and the scribes in Jesus' time were jealous because the people were following Jesus and listened to Him. They would have done anything to destroy Him. They thought they had achieved their goal when they nailed Him to the cross. But love triumphed.

Let this be a lesson of confirmation for us—to never allow envy to prosper at the expense of love.

Humble Savior, grant that I will learn by Your example never to be envious of the good things others have. Amen.

Boastful Pride

Love does not boast, it is not proud. (1 Corinthians 13:4)

The Chinese have a proverb that goes: "If you want to know how important you really are, draw a bucket of water, clench your fist, push your arm into the water and take it out again. The hole you leave behind in the water is a symbol of your greatness." There is definitely an aspect of humility in love.

Real love is not proud. Loving people are filled with discretion even when they have achieved great things. St. Augustine who observed, "Do you wish to rise? Begin by descending. You plan a tower that will pierce the clouds? Lay first the foundation of humility." Christian humility is based on an accurate image of oneself, a vision of Christ and an understanding of God's greatness.

Some people love others and think they're doing them a favor. Real love knows how to say, "I was wrong and I'm sorry." Arrogance refuses to accept the blame. Many relationships have been wrecked because people are too proud to admit their faults.

In the spiritual realm pride is an enemy of grace. This was amply demonstrated by Satan's rebellion against God and Judas's refusal to acknowledge his mistake in time. Judas preferred to commit suicide rather than accept the grace of his Lord. Peter, on the other hand, was able to confess, "You know that I love You!"

Pride demands the love of others. Genuine love is always in awe of unconditional love.

God, grant that I may follow the example
of the Master and wash the feet of others. Amen.

Read 1 Corinthians 13:1-13

Love Is Never Rude

Love is not rude, it is not self-seeking. (1 Corinthians 13:5)

There is a certain type of Christian who takes delight in being abrupt, almost brutal. There is power in this behavior, but no kindness. These people usually act grim, proper and come across as loveless. It seems as if they are scared to be friendly or kind for fear of undermining their Christianity.

John B. Lightfoot once described one of his students, "No matter where he goes, his face will always be a sermon." Christian love shows kindness that never forgets that politeness, tact and friendliness are excellent virtues. The underlying strength they reveal is gracious love and kindness.

Loving behavior is always well-mannered. Paul explained in his letter to the Corinthians, "Everything should be done in a fitting and orderly way" (1 Cor. 14:40).

It is possible for a Christian to be strong-principled and firm, and yet be compelled by love to be kind. You will be a much better witness for Jesus Christ if you always behave in a kind way towards people.

Holy and gentle Lord Jesus, may I always
be a true witness of Your love. Amen.

Love Is Not Angered

Love is not easily angered. (1 Corinthians 13:5)

The Christian with real love in his heart will never be impatient with others, because not being able to control your temper is a sign of failure and defeat. When you become bitter and lose your temper, you lose everything: your authority, your self-respect, your respect for others, your argument, and above all, your friend.

Rudyard Kipling calls this the measure of a man: If you can keep your head when all about you are losing theirs and blaming it on you, you'll be a man. When you are treated unfairly, do not allow any room for revenge and bitterness. Christ set the example for us: on the cross He prayed for the very ones who had crucified Him.

With a calm and restrained attitude we can overcome the world. Anger and a quick temper bring about sad endings to the good relationships in our lives.

A young boy made his mother very angry. They were both enraged because they were both quick-tempered. The mother sent him to his room, saying he should pray that Jesus would take his bad temper away. She listened at the door while he prayed, "Lord Jesus, please take away my bad temper. And while You are at it, please take my mother's away too."

We are extremely offended when someone hurts our self-esteem and tend to brood over it. The result is hatred and bitter thoughts. Staying angry with someone is a waste of time and emotional energy.

Father of mercy, please grant me the grace
not to become unnecessarily angry. Amen.

Read 1 Corinthians 13:1-3

Love Is Not Selfish

Love is not self-seeking. (1 Corinthians 13:5)

There are two types of people in this world: those who only think about their rights, and those who think only of their duties; those who are always laying claim to these rights, and those who think only of their responsibilities; those who always think about what life owes them, and those who are never able to forget what they owe life. If people thought less about their rights and more about their duties, most of the world's problems would be solved.

In life there are the "takers" who grab everything they can out of life and relationships to their own selfish advantage, and never give anything back. Then, there are also the "givers" who always offer generously of their best for the enrichment and benefit of humanity. The paramount example of such a giver is our Lord, who gave Himself to the utmost degree, yet never laid claim to a privilege or made self-serving demands of others.

We should be asking what we can contribute to life through love and ministry, rather than asking what we can get from life. The Jordan River flows through Israel. Three subsidiary streams join together and a concrete canal was constructed to channel this water. Because the water was no longer purified by filtering through the soil, deadly salts were left behind and caused the fish to die. There is no shortcut to success. When the elevator is out of order, you must take the stairs.

Good Master, protect me always against
selfishness, through Your Holy Spirit. Amen.

Learn to Forgive

Love keeps no record of wrongs. (1 Corinthians 13:5)

Some people keep a balance sheet of wrong and right things done to them. But one of the greatest Christian virtues is learning the art of forgiveness.

Many people nurse their anger and keep it aflame, despite the fact that they are hurting themselves. Christian love teaches the important lesson of forgiving and forgetting. C. S. Lewis speaks of this as "surprised by joy!"

Jesus did not just command us to forgive and forget: He Himself demonstrated this when He forgave His murderers on the cross. My love for God is demonstrated and confirmed through my love for my neighbor, "If anyone says, 'I love God,' yet hates his brother, he is a liar. For anyone who does not love his brother, whom he has seen, cannot love God, whom he has not seen" (1 John 4:20).

One day some children were playing in the park. A young boy came down a slope on his skateboard, the picture of sheer joy. At the bottom of the hill he lost control, crashed into the sidewalk and landed head-over-heels on the grassy verge. He was not hurt but when he stood up, he was furious. He walked back to the sidewalk and kicked it with all his might. Naturally he hurt himself more and started to cry. We don't like accidents, especially when they are offensive to our self-respect. But it is a waste of time to refuse to forgive and forget.

Lord Jesus, help me to follow Your example
of how to truly forgive and forget. Amen.

Read 1 Corinthians 13:1-13

Love Takes No Pleasure in Evil

Love does not delight in evil but rejoices with the truth. (1 Corinthians 13:6)

We will probably understand this verse better if we take it to mean that love finds no pleasure in anything wrong. It is not so much taking delight in doing things that are wrong, but rather the malicious pleasure that causes us to enjoy hearing about someone else's misfortunes rather than their successes. This is one of the peculiar and sinful characteristics of human nature.

We find it much easier to weep with those who are weeping than to delight in someone else's joy. It is generally so much more pleasurable for us to hear a juicy story of someone else's fall than to listen to the wonderful story of their success or victory.

Love delights itself in the truth. But this is easier said than done. There are times when we definitely do not want the truth to triumph and other times when the truth is the last thing we want to hear. Christian love has no desire to conceal the truth, because it has nothing to hide. It is grateful and happy when truth triumphs.

"So if the Son sets you free, you will be free indeed" (John 8:36). Christian love has none of that jealous rivalry that worldly people seem to thrive on so much.

God of love, please let my love be honest and without any ulterior motives. Amen.

Love Endures

Love always protects. (1 Corinthians 13:7)

This aspect of love shows that Christian love can cover anything. This love will never bring another's mistake out in the open. It will make an effort to quietly make things right. Today's Scripture means that Christian love can endure insults, trauma and disappointments. It describes the kind of love that was in Jesus' heart: His enemies hated and despised Him. But He never stopped forgiving and loving them.

Johan Cilliers describes it well, "Here is something to think about: Every morning you faithfully put out the garbage bag for the municipal workers to remove it. But just before the trucks arrive, you run outside, bring the bag back into the house and add it to the growing pile in your kitchen. It stinks, the neighbors are moaning, your circle of friends has noticeably grown smaller, your family are all looking for reasons to move out ... but, undisturbed, you carry on bringing the garbage in, going back on your promise ... Absurd? Yet many people do just that in their unwillingness to forgive.

We allow the trash of other people's sins to permeate our houses, our churches and our spirits. We don't want Christ's forgiveness to take away the misdeeds of others, and our own, once and for all. We would rather transform ourselves into a black bag of unforgiveness. We choose garbage over forgiveness."

God of grace and forgiveness, let Your Spirit
cultivate in me the gift of forgiveness. Amen.

Read 1 Corinthians 13:1-13

Love Trusts Completely

Love always trusts. (1 Corinthians 13:7)

This characteristic of love has two aspects: In our relationship with God it means that love trusts in God's Word; it believes in His promises without reservation; and every promise that begins with "They who ..." becomes personal and is actually saying, "This is for me!"

In our relationships with our fellow men, Christian love always believes the best of others.

When Thomas Arnold became the principal of Rugby School in England, he adopted a completely new way of doing things. Before him, terror and tyranny reigned at the school. Arnold called the boys together and explained that in future, they were going to have much more freedom. "You are free," he said, "but you are also responsible. My intention is to leave you mainly to yourselves and your honor. I believe that as long as your every move is monitored you will grow up to know only submissive fear. When you are eventually given freedom, you won't know what to do with it."

The boys found it difficult to believe. When they were summoned to own up to their misdeeds, they still offered all the old excuses and told all the old lies. "Boys, if you say so then it must be true—I'll take your word for it," was Arnold's only response. The day dawned in Rugby School when the boys said to each other, "It's scandalous to lie to Arnold—he always believes us." Love improves individuals by believing the best of them.

Lord Jesus, make my faith in the triune God unshakable. Amen.

Love Never Lets Hope Die

Love always hopes. (1 Corinthians 13:7)

Jesus Christ teaches us that no one is beyond hope: He proved this in His behavior towards one of the criminals who had been crucified with Him. This is great encouragement for all sinners. Love that hopes is a virtue that surpasses all others. No situation is so hopeless that you have to give yourself over to despair. When you do this you belittle the grace of God.

Christian hope is not the same thing as "positive thinking." A Christian's hope lies in this knowledge that even in my utmost need God is still there; even in my deepest loneliness I am not alone, because the Good Shepherd is with me. Those who believe in God expect eternal hope, but those who do not believe will meet a hopeless end.

Adam Clarke was one of the greatest theologians of his time, but at school he was a slow learner. A respected guest once visited the school. The teacher pointed to Clarke and said, "He is the dumbest pupil in this school." Before he left, the visitor went up to Clarke and said softly to him, "You may be an important student one day, son. Don't be discouraged, just try hard and keep on trying." The teacher had no hope but the visitor was hopeful. Eternity may one day reveal what those few words of hope meant for Clarke and the kingdom of God.

Loving Master, thank You for the hope that is aflame in my heart. Grant that it will never die. Amen.

Read 1 Corinthians 13:8-13

Love Reigns Supreme

Love never fails. (1 Corinthians 13:8)

In the reading for today, Paul says three things about Christian love: Firstly he emphasizes the importance of the permanence of love. When all the earthly things have passed away, love will still endure.

In Song of Songs there is one of the most wonderful truths about love, "For love is as strong as death, its jealousy unyielding as the grave. It burns like blazing fire, like a mighty flame. Many waters cannot quench love; rivers cannot wash it away" (Song of Songs 8:6-7). The one unconquerable thing in life is love. When love comes into someone's life a relationship is established that time cannot destroy and that outlasts death.

Secondly, Paul emphasizes the absolute perfection of love. We are looking into a dim mirror. The Corinthians understood this comparison even better than we can. Corinthian mirrors were made of highly polished metal and at best gave only a dim reflection. Much of what we know about God is still a riddle and a mystery to us. Our knowledge is like that of a child. But our love will lead us to the day when the veil will be removed and we will see God face to face. We cannot reach that day without love, because only those who love will see God.

Thirdly, Paul emphasizes the absolute supremacy of love. Faith and hope are important, but love is so much greater. Faith without love is cold and heartless, and hope without love is rigid and grim. Love transforms hope into certainty.

God of love, help me never to lose my focus on love. Amen.

Love and Obedience

If anyone obeys His word, God's love is truly made complete in him. (1 John 2:5)

We often find it difficult to submit our will to the will of God. We want to tell God what His will should be and attempt to bring His will into line with ours. The problem is that we are too full of ourselves and our own dreams and schemes. Even though we know that we need to open ourselves up and allow God's love to fill our hearts, we still find it difficult to let go and let God do His will in our lives.

The love of God comes into our lives completely. It is not a reward for carefully obeying every command of God. It is an undeserved gift that we are not entitled to. We can try as hard as we like but we will never be worthy of it in any way. All we can do is open ourselves to His love and allow Him to take complete control of our lives. When we do this, God fills us to the brim with His love. When God's love attains its perfect purpose in us, we find ourselves able to obey His every command. Obeying Him is pure joy for His willing subjects.

With His love perfected in us, we are able to love Him in return, and also our fellow man whom He sends across our paths.

We love in obedience to God's Word, not through any strength of our own, but rather in and through His love. The question is: Has His love reached its fulfillment in you?

God of love, fill me with Your love that it will be a joy to me to obey Your commands. Amen.

Read 1 John 2:1-11

Live in the Light of Love

Whoever loves his brother lives in the light, and there is nothing in him to make him stumble. (1 John 2:10)

In the business world there are certain products with added value. If you are willing to pay extra, you get them as a luxury. You buy an economy-class ticket on an airplane, and if you pay more, you can travel business class. For a first-class ticket you will have to dig even deeper in your pocket.

There are many people who think that the Christian faith works in a similar way. You live a respectable life, you don't do anything seriously wrong, and you go to church regularly on a Sunday. Doing a good deed for the church or for someone else is an "optional extra." It actually doesn't work like that. Loving other people is not an extra option—it is the essence of being a Christian. Walking in the light of Christ means spreading His light across the whole world. It means loving the important people as well as the less important ones.

Living in the light means showing kindness not only to church members, but also to people of other religions. We should treat others with dignity, and let them feel that they are valuable to God.

It means treating troublemakers as children of God too; and dealing with them patiently and carefully, in the same way that you would relate to the "pleasant" people. When you love all people in this way, your love can reach out to "the unreachable" through them.

Lord Jesus, grant that the measure of my love for You will be evident in my love for my fellow man. Amen.

Where Does Your Love Lie?

Do not love the world or anything in the world. If anyone loves the world, the love of the Father is not in him. (1 John 2:15)

For many people something that they enjoy doing becomes their hobby. Some may have a particular love for dogs. Others enjoy rugby. Certain people admire antique furniture; others have a passion for films, books or gardening. All of these pastimes are relatively harmless as long as we do not allow them to take up all our time.

When you love God "with all your heart and with all your soul and with all your mind" (Matt. 22:37), it is hard to imagine developing an obsession about the world or anything in it. But you must be on your guard. The "world" in this sense is neither the physical universe nor the world of people. It is the sum total of all the forces that conspire against the kingly authority of God. Greed, lust, power, pride and hate are the signs. Money in particular has the power to enslave you. Your desire for money can become so strong that it takes control of your life. Then greed will rule your life. Paul wrote to Timothy about the consequences, "For the love of money is a root of all kinds of evil. Some people, eager for money, have wandered from the faith and pierced themselves with many griefs" (1 Tim. 6:10).

To resist the temptations of the world, you must fill your mind and your heart with the knowledge that God loves you. Let His love rule your heart and nothing else will ever have the power to enslave you.

Lord Jesus, through the help and leading of the Holy Spirit, I subject all my interests to Your authority. Amen.

Read 1 John 3:1-10

His Overflowing Love

How great is the love the Father has lavished on us, that we should be called children of God! And that is what we are! (1 John 3:1)

Most parents love their children very much. Some smother their children with love. They go to extremes, giving their children things that they don't actually need or want. They often deny themselves the privilege of owning something so that they can provide for their children. They give these children everything that money can buy. They lavish them with love, encouragement, support and comfort. Other people complain that these parents are spoiling their children.

God, our Father, does not just love us. He showers us with His love. He does not spare Himself or do a careless job. His love is not sporadic or on-and-off, as ours so often is. It is constant, steady, wise and heartfelt. He gives us everything we need—and more! He never grows tired of loving us; He never takes the day off; He is never irritated by our childishness. He always keeps our welfare and best interests in mind.

In Jesus Christ, God provided us with an example, a model and a mentor. Through Christ, God proved to us how much He loves us. God's love is personified in Jesus and goes into action through our human experience. Even when we are no longer a part of this world, He will continue to shower us with His love as if there were only one of us.

Thank You, O God of love, that I am also the subject of Your love. I pray today for those who feel that no one loves them. Amen.

We Must Love One Another

This is the message you heard from the beginning: We should love one another. (1 John 3:11)

A young disciple of Jesus Christ was called up for military service. Somewhat nervous, he knelt by the bed in prayer. Some of his conscripts were embarrassed and others openly mocked him. But he stayed on his knees, unmoved.

Close by was a man who scorned religion and made sure that everyone knew how anti-Christian he was. He took off his muddy shoes and threw them across the room. One of the shoes hit the praying man on the head. Nothing further was said, but when the mocker woke up the next morning, he found his shoes at the foot of the bed, clean and brightly polished. No one asked because everyone knew who had cleaned the shoes.

Love lies at the heart of the Christian message and its way of life. In a world divided by enmity, fear and suspicion, Christians are called to be witnesses of God's love and present it to others. Today it is needed more than ever in homes devastated by addictions and unfaithfulness. It is essential in the business industry where mistrust and competitiveness are the order of the day.

Hospitals and nursing institutions need love, because love is the foundation of all therapy. Men, women, the elderly and the youth need it. The middle-aged yearn for it. The whole world needs it. It is Christ's medicine for an ill world. You and I can be His agents of healing. We need to love one another!

Lord, bring Your love into a world that is steeped in hate. Amen.

Read 1 John 3:11-24

Life and Love

We know that we have passed from death
to life, because we love our brothers. Anyone
who does not love remains in death. (1 John 3:14)

Love is not always easy. It does not come naturally. It is, however, natural to love your family members. Some people are easy to love, and others more difficult.

Something remarkable happened with the disciples of Jesus Christ. In order for them to follow Jesus, they were filled with the Holy Spirit at Pentecost and this brought about a remarkable change in them. Their natural feelings of fear and suspicion for certain people were replaced by a love that they knew could only have come from God.

This was especially clear in their relationships with people from other nations and cultures. Because they had been raised in the Jewish tradition, they had little love for the Gentiles. Now they longed to share the love they had received from God with the same Gentiles they had previously kept at arm's length. God's love was most compassionate and nurturing. It compelled them to care and share with the Gentiles.

This brand-new adventure of love opened up an entirely new dimension in their lives. They discovered that the world was a much bigger place than they had ever known and that there were some amazing people out there. Their lives started when God's love was revealed to them and swept them off their feet. They crossed over from death to life.

Lord, help me to find Your life by
loving as You have loved. Amen.

Love Is Far-Reaching

This is how we know what love is: Jesus Christ laid down His life for us. And we ought to lay down our lives for our brothers. (1 John 3:16)

Much of our human love is a matter of "I'll love you as long as you love me." Even the love between parents and children can reach its breaking point.

In the living Christ, God's love reached new heights. Before the time of Jesus, people knew that God loved them and that He required them to obey His commandments. But before Jesus came, they did not know how much God really loved them. Jesus taught the people all about God's love. In the parables of the prodigal son and the unmerciful servant, He mentioned this love. His ministry put God's love to work—the healing of diseases, the feeding of the hungry and His charity to outcasts demonstrated His Father's love.

But it was Jesus' death on the cross that proved that God's love is unlimited. In that one act of sacrifice, God declared before humanity, "This is how much I love you. However unworthy you may be, however rebelliously you have behaved, however weak and faithless you may be, I seek to save you and win your trust with this act of unrequited love. You deserve death, because your sins have alienated you from Me. But I will die in your place. Won't you repent and return to Me in love?"

There is nothing superficial about God's love. It sets the standard, and we must try to live up to it.

Lord Jesus, Savior also of those who are full of hate, grant me a love like Yours. Amen.

 Read 1 John 3:18-24

Love in Action

Dear children, let us not love with words or tongue but with actions and in truth. (1 John 3:18)

François Fénelon became the Archbishop of Cambrai in 1695. People quickly realized that he cared about others and was the type of person they could approach with their problems. On one occasion, a number of farmers took refuge in his palace during a border war.

Fénelon noticed that one man in particular was very upset and when he asked him what the trouble was, the man said that the enemy had stolen his cow. The archbishop replied, "Don't worry, I will buy you another one." But the man could not be comforted: he wanted his own cow back. That night the archbishop and one of his servants went to the village on foot, where the man had indicated that his cow had been taken. Shortly before midnight the archbishop returned—with the man's cow! Fénelon not only preached love—he acted it out!

One sincere act of love is worth a thousand sermons. Sometimes, we can also love people by the things we say. Often a word of thanks or appreciation can reveal God's love.

There are times in life when words of love are all that are possible for us to give. But a good deed, such as the action of the archbishop, can provide a simple solution in difficult circumstances. Such action can put a struggling person back on his feet. When last did you act in love outside of your immediate family circle?

Merciful Lord Jesus, let my actions always be a witness of Your love. Amen.

Love: Active and Sincere

Dear children, let us not love with words or tongue but with actions and in truth. (1 John 3:18)

An in-depth study of the life of Jesus Christ reveals an interesting fact—that He was always practical. Read again about the miracles that He performed—how He demonstrated God's love; how he healed people physically, in addition to the deeply spiritual aspects of His ministry. One event that particularly stands out was the time when he raised a young girl from the dead—and then advised her family to give her something to eat!

True love and concern demand much more than mere words: they call for action. They require you to perform an act as proof of your love and care—even if it is inconvenient. A visit to a patient in hospital or to an elderly person in an old-age home; a card or letter of encouragement to someone who is experiencing difficult times; a phone call to someone who is feeling lonely—these are all examples of the practical expression of God's love. It brings joy and happiness to someone's life—as well as to yours.

When you show your love to others, faithfully follow the example of Jesus the living Christ, because the secret of all of your sincere and loving actions lie in His practical love.

Holy Spirit of God, help me to model myself on Jesus and love others with an active and sincere love. Amen.

Read 1 John 3:18-24

The Love Commandment

This is His command: to believe in the name of His Son, Jesus Christ, and to love one another as He commanded us. (1 John 3:23)

In the well-known comic strip series *Peanuts,* Lucy says to Linus, "The trouble with you, Linus, is that you don't love mankind." He replies, "I love mankind; it's people I can't stand!"

Many Christians find this the most difficult part of Christianity. It would be so much easier just to love God and serve Jesus Christ. If it was only a matter of loving humanity, that would also be manageable. But it is people who present the real problem for us. If only we could protect ourselves from the unpleasant people, the moody people, the proud and self-centered people, the small-minded people, the childish people, the jealous people, the merrymakers, the strangers, the quick-tempered, the beggars, the idle, the physically challenged and the manipulators—if only we could devote all our attention to loving God.

But God says, "Your neighbor and I are one. You can't have Me if you don't love your brother and your sister." And the problem is that your brother or sister may be among the lazy or manipulating ones. God has joined us together with all of humanity, for better or for worse.

Understand this: God is in your brother or sister sitting next to you. If you want to love Him, you will also have to love that person. See God in others every day.

God of indescribable love, help me to love the difficult people—for Your sake. Amen.

The Origin of Love

Dear friends, let us love one another, for love comes from God. Everyone who loves has been born of God and knows God. (1 John 4:7)

It is not surprising that God's desire is for us to love one another. He Himself is love and He wants us to be just like Him. It was out of love that He gave us His only Son to be our Savior. Jesus overflowed with love and He lived a life of love until the very end. He loved people: He instructed them, cared for them, healed and befriended them. His Kingdom is a kingdom of godly love.

His call to us is not only to reach out in love to others. He wants love to be present within the fellowship of believers. He desires for all His disciples to love one another in Christ. The people of ancient times would look towards the small communities of Christians and say, "Look at their love for one another." We do not have to strive to achieve this. We have accepted that Jesus loves us unconditionally. We have invited Him into our lives and our hearts. He has entered and is replacing our hate and fear with His love. In this way He is able to love through us.

C. H. Dodd, director of the team who translated the *New English Bible*, said, "The energy of love discharges itself along lines which form a triangle, whose points are God, self, and neighbor." God has commanded us to love as He loves us.

I ask You, Father God, for the gift of Your love through the Holy Spirit. Amen.

Read 1 John 4:7-21

Proof of God's Love

This is how God showed His love among us:
He sent His one and only Son into the world
that we might live through Him. (1 John 4:9)

When you were young, you were probably encouraged to acquire skills and gather knowledge to be able to make the most of life. Maybe you thought to yourself, "Will I be successful? Will I be happy? Will I be rich?" You accepted that these were the things that mattered in life.

The Christian faith suggests something completely different. Success, happiness and wealth are viewed as secondary to life's true purpose. Pursuing them for their own sake will cause you to miss out on what is really important in life: knowing God and serving Him. God's way of life is so crucial to our survival that He sent Jesus to live, suffer and die in order to open up the road to eternal life for us.

God's way of life is true living, as opposed to merely existing. His way revolves around love. Love comes from God and God loves us. This love is personified in Jesus Christ. God's way of life is also a source of joy, worship and wonder to us. He also gives us a way of coping with the dark side of life.

To the guilty He offers forgiveness and salvation. For the sick He gives healing. In the face of suffering He gives the prospect of life after death. In the place of human weakness He gives strength and in the darkest moments of life He sheds light. God's love is sheer grace!

God, thank You for enriching my life with Your love. Amen.

The Godly Initiative

This is love: not that we loved God, but that He loved us and sent His Son as an atoning sacrifice for our sins. (1 John 4:10)

We all think we know what love is. Human love is complicated—a mix of admiration, empathy, selfishness, lust, caring and sacrifice. We can experience in our relationships only a glimmer of what God's love is really like.

God's love is always far ahead of ours. He loved us before we loved Him. He loved us even before we were born. He loved our parents before us and He loved the human race long before He called us into being. The human race came into existence *because* God is love. We did not ask Him to love us—God Himself took the initiative. Every other form of love as we know it derives from His love.

Our love for Him and for one another is patterned according to His love. In spite of His great love for us, we hurt Him through disobedience, thereby alienating ourselves from Him. But His only response was to love us even more. He fulfilled His obligation to sacrifice His Son and through that sacrifice we were forgiven.

When we accept that He has adopted us—as unworthy as we are—then His love permeates our whole lives. It saves us, heals us, restores us, motivates us and enables us to become like Him. Praise the Lord, for He is good! His love has no beginning and no end!

I thank You, O God, for taking the initiative and loving me first. Amen.

Read 1 John 4:7-21

Make God's Love Complete

No one has ever seen God; but if we love one another,
God lives in us and His love is made complete in us. (1 John 4:12)

We so often long to be able to see God! Most religions have a physical entity that serves as a focus for the worship of its devotees. We also long to be able to see and hear Jesus and be with Him.

Perhaps this longing is just a weakness on our part. Perhaps He maintains His mystique through being invisible to us. This is how He stays God. Rather than using our imaginations or speculating, God invites us to see Him through the work of love He does in us and in others.

Our text for today suggests that when we love others, it is a clear indication that God is living in us. He is well-known and can be seen in our love for other people, which makes His love clearly visible to everyone. It has often been said that the best argument for the existence of God is the life of a godly person. It is an astounding truth: God's love can be manifest in us, and it can reach perfection if we will practice it.

Has God already begun to love through you? Have you performed a good deed, or made an effort to do someone a service? He wants *you* to manifest His love in its fullness. What an enormous challenge for all His faithful children.

Continue, Lord Jesus, and finish
what You have begun in me. Amen.

God Is Love!

God is love. Whoever lives in love
lives in God, and God in him. (1 John 4:16)

What is love? Someone walks around wearing a T-shirt with a slogan on the front: "I ♥ country music." The word *love* is represented by a heart. Many people claim to love their local sports team; others love running; others love their country and are willing to die for it; people love their families and take up an entire lifetime doing this; people love their life partners, and they love the Lord.

When the Bible says, "God is love," this means so much more than just, "God loves us." Love is the core quality of His being. All His acts are acts of love. When He judges, He judges in love. When He creates, He creates in love. When He speaks, He speaks in love. When He rules, He rules in love. Everything He does, He does in love. Love is the essential expression of His nature.

God loves you! He loves you twenty-four-seven. He loves you when you are well and when you are sick. He loves you through all the good times and the bad times. He loves you in joy and in sorrow. He loves you when everyone else has let you down and betrayed you. He loves you when you deserve it and also when you don't.

Are you living in His love—and does His love live in you?

Lord my God, how can I express my gratitude
to You for giving me Your love? Amen.

Read 1 John 4:7-21

God First Loved Us

We love because He first loved us. (1 John 4:19)

Sometimes couples in love jokingly say that the one loved the other one first. There is absolutely no doubt that God Himself took the initiative in the quest for love. He loved us first, in more ways than one.

His love is also the most enduring, because it is steadfast, while ours is fickle. He never slips up in His love. His love does not vary in its quality. He bears all our unfaithfulness and deceit. While our love hesitates and fades away, His remains constant. His love is deeper than ours. He spares no effort when it comes to loving us.

The painting of the good shepherd, who went out at night to look for the one lost sheep, is a reliable description of God's desire to save each one of us. His love is more widespread than ours. It reaches people in the depths of their sin and in the stubbornness of their refusal to respond to His love. In addition, His love surpasses ours in that no one is beyond the reach of His saving grace, no one is too evil to be restored to godliness by Him.

Never underestimate the love of God. You can see it in its fullness in Jesus Christ, and its saving power in the lives of the people around you. Feel its impact in your own life and identity. His salvation is freely available to the entire human race. There can be no doubt that your salvation was the greatest event in your life.

Even the angels cannot describe the true depth of Your love,
O God. May my life be living evidence of this. Amen.

December

The Atonement Child

Thanks be to God
for His indescribable gift!
~ 2 Corinthians 9:15

Loving Father God, thank You for showing us
Your eternal love by sending
Your Son to earth to show us the way.
We thank You for the difference that He makes
in our lives, our thoughts, our hearts,
our families and in our community.
We give You jubilant thanks for the gift of eternal life
that we have received through the birth, life, suffering,
death and resurrection of Your beloved Son.
During this festive season, bless every heart and every
home with Your boundless love and grace.
Grant Your grace in double measure to children
so that in the early morning of their lives they will learn
of the love of Jesus and they will call You Savior!
Bless our land with Your grace
so that we will all submit ourselves to Your love
and to Your Son, the Prince of Peace!
We thank You yet again for the child of Bethlehem:
He who is our light, our life, our love,
our Lord and King, now and always.
Help us, Lord Jesus, to commemorate Your birth
in a worthwhile way, so that we might join in the song
of the angels, experience the awe of the shepherds,
and relive the pure worship of the wise men.
Teach us to be joyful with sincere hearts.
Let us come home to You this month like children
who return to their parents' home for the holidays.
For the sake of Jesus! Immanuel!
The living One!
Amen.

Waiting for the Messiah

At that time there was a man in Jerusalem named Simeon. He was righteous and devout and was eagerly waiting for the Messiah to come and rescue Israel. (Luke 2:25 NLT)

Children wait impatiently for Christmas to arrive. We have all experienced that kind of excitement at one time or another. Not everything we are so impatient for comes as surely as Christmas. People buy lottery tickets and wait for their "lucky day." That day never arrives for most people. Others wait for poverty to be alleviated and find that that day is being delayed.

God's people wait longingly for Him. Sometimes He comes quickly and unexpectedly. In other situations He prolongs His coming and keeps His disciples full of anticipation, sometimes for very long periods. Simeon was an elderly man and was typical of many dedicated people in Israel who waited for the coming Messiah.

When God finally sent His Son, many didn't recognize and accept Him. But Simeon was not one of them. With patience and humility, he obeyed the promptings of the Holy Spirit and welcomed Jesus. He knew that the long wait was finally over.

There is something moving in this picture of this elderly man welcoming the small child, in whom He recognized God's greatest gift. Don't become impatient if you are waiting for God to fulfill His promises. No speculation will hasten His coming. He will come in His own time. Wait patiently for Him and trust Him completely.

Lord Christ, help me to wait patiently for Your coming. Amen.

Read Luke 1:26-38

A Village in Galilee

In the sixth month, God sent the angel Gabriel to Nazareth, a town in Galilee to a virgin pledged to be married to a man named Joseph. (Luke 1:26)

At the heart of Christianity is the restoration of our right relationship with God, but with that comes the establishing of good relationships with others. It is not based on myths like other religions. It did not evolve out of a dream or a vision. It is born out of historical facts.

These things that happened occurred in a specific place and at a definite time. It all began in a village in Galilee. It took place on solid ground and not in someone's imagination. Nazareth is still there today. There are people who earn their living there, marry and start families, bring up children and educate them there. There is nothing special or exceptional about the town, except for its historical connection with Jesus Christ.

He can, as He has always done, come to any town, city or settlement on earth. He can come to your hometown too—and when He comes, His coming is good news. He comes in humility, in everyday situations, in the day-to-day world where carpenters work and women prepare meals. He might come to your everyday world today, to your workplace, to your place of worship. He comes to save, to set free, to raise up and bring meaning to our lives.

We must acknowledge Him when He comes.

Lord, help me to be a humble, down-to-earth follower of You. Amen.

To Die in Peace

"Sovereign Lord, now let Your servant die in peace, as You have promised." (Luke 2:29 NLT)

Death is not a topic we like to think or talk about. We don't like to use the word *dead*, but rather use euphemisms like *passed away* or *departed from this life*.

After welcoming the Christ child and praising God, the elderly Simeon prayed a beautiful prayer to God that is known as the *Nunc Dimittis*. Simeon walked with God and lived a life of dedication, faith and hope.

The insight of the Holy Spirit enabled him to see that this child was God's Promised One, and for this reason he was ready to die. He accepted life from God's hand and was now ready to die "in peace."

See how Simeon addresses God, "Sovereign Lord … Your servant." Mary reacted in the same manner when the angel announced that she would bring God's Son into the world, "'I am the Lord's servant,' Mary answered, 'May it be to me as you have said'" (Luke 1:38).

God's servants accept both their calling to serve and their calling to stand aside of their service in the same faithful and obedient manner. They know that they are God's servants in life and in death. All that they desire is the privilege of being obedient to Him. They are not afraid to die because they know that they are in God's loving hands—both in life and death.

Holy Lord and Master, thank You for teaching us to die in a worthy manner. Amen.

Read John 3:10-21

Sent to Save

"God did not send His Son into the world to condemn the world, but to save the world through Him." (John 3:17)

Jesus, the living Christ, came to earth on a rescue mission. He was sent by God with a purpose. His coming into our world, His ministry and teachings, His healings and friendships, as well as His death and resurrection were all for one purpose: He came to save us!

Many people do not know in what way they need to be saved. Firstly, you need to be saved from sin. This means the sins from your past must first be forgiven. Confess to Jesus that you have sinned and trespassed against God. Then accept the forgiveness that He offers. Being saved also means maintaining an intimate, personal and living relationship with Jesus. It further means that you receive His help to turn away from evil; and, as far as it is in your ability to live a life free from sin.

Secondly, you need to be saved into a new life in which you honor Jesus, acknowledge His lordship over your life, and then become actively involved in ministry. You will discover fellowship with other believers and develop a deep sense of community in your faith. If Jesus was sent to save, then you were saved to serve.

In your ministry you become an agent who promotes salvation through Jesus Christ. You are saved to a new life in which you follow the example of Jesus, where you grow to spiritual maturity and are made complete in love through the work of the Holy Spirit.

Thank You, Lord Jesus, that You came
to save the world—including me! Amen.

Do Not Be Afraid!

The angel said to her, "Do not be afraid, Mary, you have found favor with God." (Luke 1:30)

Many people's lives are ruled by fear. There are people who are afraid of other people, of the future, of loneliness, of financial need, or sickness. Nearly everyone is afraid of death.

Mary was afraid because she didn't know why the angel was visiting her. She was completely flustered. But then the angel said, "Do not be afraid, Mary."

God had a task for Mary that would require much courage, commitment and emotional strength from her. It was a huge role, an important position and a difficult task to which God called her.

We need to hear that message again and again: Do not be afraid! It is often repeated in the New Testament. Christ says to you today: Do not be afraid! Don't be afraid of your declining health, or the state of the world's economy, or the increase in terrorism, or the rise in crime, or the spread of diseases, or worldwide hunger.

Some of the things you fear might never happen to you. Some might happen, but not on the catastrophic scale you fear. Some will happen, but humanity has the incredible ability to solve problems.

Above all the things we fear is an almighty God who is in ultimate control. He finds favor with you and He sincerely loves you. You can trust in Him and peacefully continue with the task you have been called to perform.

Father God, grant that Jesus' example will give me renewed courage for each day. Amen.

 Read 2 Corinthians 9:1-15

God's Precious Gift

Thanks be to God for His indescribable gift! (2 Corinthians 9:15)

It's easy to get caught up in the hustle and bustle of the festive season with all its glitter and glamour. It's a good idea to take a breather at times and meditate on the gift that stands at the center of it all.

Jesus Christ is God's gift to mankind. He is also the Word that became flesh; a personification of God Himself in the only form in which we could receive Him—a living person. And yet this gift is, in Paul's words, indescribable: too amazing for words! How exciting it is to receive a gift that so amazes and surprises us that we do not have the words to show our thanks. We cannot even find the words to say what we feel. The gift of Jesus Christ leaves us speechless with gratitude, awe and love.

How can we respond to such an indescribable gift? You accept it by opening your heart and life in the same way that you open your hands to receive a gift from someone else. Then you thank God for it by living a life surrendered and committed to Him. You give your life to God as a sign of your thankfulness that He gave His life for you.

Jesus came to fill this indescribable gift with words: the message of the gospel, the interpretation of its meaning and the testimony of it in the heathen world. You too can thank God for this indescribable gift He has given to you. You can do so every day with words and deeds, with your testimony and your love.

Lord Jesus, let Your Spirit teach me to be
more and more thankful each day. Amen.

To God Be the Glory!

The shepherds returned, glorifying and praising God for all the things they had heard and seen, which were just as they had been told. (Luke 2:20)

It's hard to imagine what the shepherds must have thought and felt when the angel of God brought them the wonderful news. In the merciless world in which they lived and worked, a Savior was born. These simple people were chosen by God to be the first to hear "the good news of great joy." They quickly hurried to Bethlehem to witness this miracle for themselves, and our reading today says, "The shepherds returned, glorifying and praising God for all the things they had heard and seen, which were just as they had been told."

Even in our day and age we have Jesus' assurance of salvation and hope. Scripture assures us that He came so that we could have life and have it to the full (John 10:10). He sacrificed His own life so that we could be reconciled with God. So marvelously great was and is Almighty God's love for humankind.

We have not only heard of this great act of love, but we can testify to it in our own lives: God's love is greater than human thoughts and the heart of the Eternal God is amazingly compassionate.

After a blessed Christmas it is only fitting to return to everyday life with praise and worship to the God of love.

Holy God, we honor You. We worship and praise You. We thank You for Your unending love. Amen.

Read Luke 2:8-14

Peace on Earth!

Glory to God in the highest, and on earth peace to men on whom His favor rests. (Luke 2:14)

As century follows century and human lives are engulfed by war and crime, the yearning for true peace becomes greater and greater. There is no other time of year when we see peace as more of a reality than during the Advent season.

In some instances it appears as a safe harbor to which we can flee from the cruelties of our day. The opposite might also be true. The aura of peace that is generated during the festive season is a dose of good medicine which our war-plagued and sin-torn world so sorely needs.

The message of the angels came at a time when the Roman leaders had forced the *Pax Romana* (the peace of Rome) on the whole of the Mediterranean world. There was peace, but it was the peace that was brought about through military rule of one kingdom over all the other nations. It was not the peace of which the angels sang. That specific peace depended on one man: a tiny baby in a manger filled with straw in a forgotten corner of the Roman Empire. The peace that the Romans brought was the peace of military rulership and the reign of the mighty Roman Empire.

The peace that God offered to the world was created through the honor and glory of the Son of God. It is only when He becomes Emperor in the hearts of people that true peace is born. True peace comes from within.

God, let peace come into the world and into our hearts. Amen.

Quiet Meditation

Mary treasured up all these things and pondered them in her heart. (Luke 2:19)

The birth of a baby is an emotional time in any home. Photos and other mementoes are gathered to serve as reminders of those early days. It is a time of indescribable joy.

Mary undoubtedly also cherished her memories about the birth of Christ. She, however, also had other things to worry about. There was the message of the angel who had shared with her the importance of the event. She would remember the call of God to this wonderful honor that would make her the most well-known woman of all ages. There was the visit of the shepherds and then of course also the wise men.

Many would have meditated on how Jesus was the chosen one of God. But she would also have known that God would go before her into a future that would be vastly different from her past. But above all she would have wondered about the fact that Jesus would need all her motherly love, guidance and encouragement.

At this time of the year you and I ought to come to a standstill and spend some time in quiet meditation and think about how God has worked in our lives during the past year. We should hold fast to His promises so that we can go forward trusting in His ongoing mercy, love and strength.

Lord my God, fill my heart with quiet hope and absolute trust in Jesus, my Redeemer. Amen.

Read Luke 1:26-38

Son of God

*He will be great and will be called
the Son of the Most High. (Luke 1:32)*

Most parents have wonderful dreams about the future for their unborn babies. A father might dream that his son will become an international sportstar. A mother might hope that her daughter will become a famous singer.

The thought that Mary's unborn baby would become great was not just a dream of a mother for her beloved child, it was the promise of God that had been brought by the angel Gabriel. Furthermore, the thought that her child was the son of God led Mary to the realization that she had been called by God into a special ministry.

Her Son would not be great in the conventional sense of greatness. He would be great in His knowledge of God. He would be great in the acceptance of His status as a servant. He would be great in His love and compassion. He would be great in His bringing salvation to those who believe in Him.

He would be great in His struggle to defeat evil and to free humanity from the control of sin. He would be great because He would give people life in all its fullness.

He would be great in the future of His kingdom when it would come to power and glory. He would also be great in bringing the greatness of other people to light. He turned all the accepted ideas of greatness upside-down!

*Lord Jesus, appear yet again in these
days in Your greatness and glory. Amen.*

Servant of God

"I am the Lord's servant," Mary answered.
"May it be to me as you have said." (Luke 1:38)

Are you willing to stand aside and give someone else complete control of your life? There are not many people who are prepared to do this. The power struggles that occur take place because people want to be in charge.

The angel told Mary what God's plan was for her and without arguing she accepted her role. This is one of the classic expressions of absolute submission and obedience. Before her there were others who had also bowed to the will of God: Abraham, Moses, Isaiah and Jeremiah. And after her there would be others who would imitate her.

Every disciple of Jesus is a servant of the Lord. If you are not His servant, then you are not His disciple. A certain person was once struggling to understand the meaning of the word *disciple* and cried out, "To be a disciple means to suppress your ego!" The preacher then answered, "Yes, that is exactly what it means." The ego that surrenders itself to God will find a new value and worth in serving the One who takes ordinary people and molds them into exceptional individuals. People who have surrendered their lives to God's will have graciously said to God, "May it be to me as You have said."

During this Christmas season, think about the absolute surrender and commitment that Mary made and about her joyful identification of herself as a servant of the Lord. Ask yourself, "Am I truly a servant of the Lord?"

Lord Jesus, make me Your humble
and obedient servant. Amen.

Read Colossians 2:5-15

God and Christ

In Christ all the fullness of the Deity lives in bodily form, and you have been given fullness in Christ. (Colossians 2:9-10)

The world has tried its best to put a label on Jesus Christ. One poet referred to Him as "the wan Galilean." Sometimes He is described as a great prophet, a wise man, a spiritual leader, a rabbi or teacher. Some theologians referred to Him in the Dead Sea Scrolls as "the teacher of righteousness." But all these titles fall far short of identifying Him as the human expression of God. In Paul's time, false teachers were saying that Christ was one of a series of revelations of God. "That is not right," said Paul. He is God Himself who came to the earth. He is not a messenger of God, an ambassador, or representative of God. In Christ, God Himself came to the earth: not just a part or a suggestion of God, but God Himself.

No one, apart from God Himself, is big enough, powerful enough, holy enough or loving enough to be your Savior. God did not come to this world in Christ to make it difficult for theologians to explain Him. He came to share His love with you, to raise your life to a new level, and to make you a complete person.

Because He lived, struggled, worked, suffered and died, He knows every problem and every longing in your life. He is with you, no matter what your age is; no matter whether you are sick or healthy, whether happy or sad. A prophet, a wise man or teacher cannot do this—only the Savior and Redeemer can do it.

*Lord Jesus, help me, the branch,
to remain living in You, the Vine. Amen.*

I Believe!

Sovereign Lord, as You have promised, You now dismiss Your servant in peace. For my eyes have seen Your salvation. (Luke 2:29-30)

Seeing is believing, or so the idiom goes.

One of the most important aspects of the coming of Jesus Christ into our world, was exactly this: that the invisible God could actually be seen. Other nations worshiped idols that everyone could see and take notice of. No one had ever seen the God of the Hebrews. He spoke, He acted, He created, He judged. But He remained carefully hidden to the human eye.

In Jesus Christ, God was here for everyone to see. Yet, it was just as hard to believe because to see a perfectly ordinary person as God was just as difficult as not seeing anyone. It required faith from the worshiper to see that an ordinary person could be anything more than that.

Simeon, however, opened the way for all believers who would come after him and who saw Jesus. They did not see Him only with their own eyes, but also with the eyes of faith. For some, the birth of Jesus was just another statistic. For Simeon, He was God in human form.

Some people "see nothing" in spiritual things. They consider them to be mere imagination, fairy tales, or superstitions. Others' eyes have been opened to see God from a new perspective. What do you see in Jesus?

Savior and Redeemer, thank You that I can see You and taste Your salvation. Amen.

Read Isaiah 9:1-6

A Son Is Given

To us a child is born, to us a son is given. (Isaiah 9:6)

The birth of a child is an occasion of great joy. The parents are congratulated and the baby is showered with gifts and wonderful wishes for the future.

When Jesus was born in Bethlehem, He fulfilled the age-old prophecy of the birth of a child who would do what no earthly person could do. But this son was different. He wasn't just anyone's son—He was God's Son! No human child was capable of fulfilling the hope of humankind, but God's Son was! He was God's gift to humankind. He was God's gift of obedience. No other person was ever completely obedient to God before.

If people want to be obedient, they must overcome their human inclination to be disobedient. They can't accomplish this unless they trust in the Son of God. God's Son also gives them God's love. God's kind of love doesn't come from the human heart, which is corrupted by much self-love. But these weak and errant hearts can be filled with Christ's love.

Christ lives in those who believe in Him and His love can transform them. God's Son is also God's gift of true and perfect humanity. It is only through Jesus Christ that mankind finds meaning in life.

These are God's gifts in Jesus Christ: obedience, love and humanity. Pray that these gifts will grow to maturity in your life.

Father of mercy, let Your Son be revealed
in my life more and more. Amen.

Prince of Peace

He will be called Wonderful Counselor, Mighty God, Everlasting Father, Prince of Peace. (Isaiah 9:6)

We usually refer to Christmas as a season of peace and goodwill. The song of the angels was indeed a message of peace. Our conflict-ridden world desperately needs this message more than any other message. It is ironic that with all our developments in technology, international organizations, and instant communication, we are just as plagued with war as previous generations.

The Old Testament prophet dreamed of a Messiah who would be a "Prince of Peace." The Hebrew understanding of peace was far more comprehensive than ours. While we have a slightly negative association with peace the people in biblical times thought about peace in a positive way. It was much more than the absence of conflict. Peace was to continue toiling the soil, gathering the harvest, building families, developing communities, and worshiping God. Peace was well-being, progression, and the promotion of good health and happiness.

During Advent time we celebrate the coming of Christ to this world. *Christ* is the Greek word with the same meaning as the Hebrew word *Messiah,* which means "Anointed One." God's Anointed One is coming again as the Prince of the greater peace, the peace that heals broken people, builds families, strengthens societies, encourages love and promotes well-being. Won't you consider how you can promote this peace every day?

Loving Savior, let peace reign supreme and let the entire human race strive toward it. Amen.

Read Isaiah 9:1-6

A Son Is Born!

To us a child is born, to us a son is given,
and the government will be on His shoulders.
And He will be called Wonderful Counselor, Mighty God,
Everlasting Father, Prince of Peace. (Isaiah 9:6)

Our world is inundated with problems. There is a large disparity between the poor and the rich. There are ever-growing threats of nuclear war, terrorism, drug smuggling, human trafficking, sickness, disease and overpopulation.

The prophet Isaiah had exceptional insight. In the midst of social injustice, political unrest and economic uncertainty, he told the people of his time, "The answer to all these problems lies in the birth of a child." He listened to God, studied the world around him and then made the shocking announcement that the human race was in such a mess that only someone outside the situation had any hope of saving it. The prophet said, "We need a Messiah to help us with this mess. Only God can provide a Messiah!" Seven hundred years after this prophecy, a son was born—God's answer to humanity's problems.

Today we rejoice in His Second Coming. It brings hope to a world that is sick with despair. They yearn for salvation of souls entrenched in sin, the healing of the bodies and minds of sick people, joy for those who experience sorrow. Jesus' coming is a challenge. He doesn't remove our problems but He equips us to face them and shows us the direction we need to move in.

Savior and Redeemer, provide us with wisdom
to solve the problems in our world. Amen.

The Coming Kingdom

Of the increase of His government and peace there will be no end. He will reign over His kingdom, establishing and upholding it with justice and righteousness. (Isaiah 9:7)

If you think that the world is in a terrible condition, you are probably right. It has always been this way. It is not a sign of the end times—it is completely normal. But the important question is, "Will it ever get better?"

Despite the fact that the Old Testament prophecy about a coming Messiah has been fulfilled in Jesus Christ, the world is still afflicted by poverty, oppression, starvation, greed, war, crime and terrorism. As a Christian, do you ever consider all the bad things in the world and want to give up in despair? Rather, you should do what the Hebrew prophets did. They trusted in God and looked forward to a new world where God would set all things right. In a sense their hope might seem unrealistic, because it would not be fully realized in their lifetime. Yet, in another sense, they were very realistic. Their hope was grounded, not in the abilities and merits of earthly leaders, but in the power of God's saving and renewing love. This is the only way of looking at the future in hope.

However deep the world might have sunk in the mire of sin, you must still expect the great kingdom of God. Hope and pray for that time when God's power will be revealed, when peace will reign and when righteousness and justice will triumph.

Lord Jesus, rule over this world and my heart with Your loving and just hand. Amen.

Read Luke 2:8-20

Great Joy!

The angel said to them, "Do not be afraid. I bring you good news of great joy that will be for all the people." (Luke 2:10)

The thought of inviting Christ into their lives fills many people with unworthiness and reverence and it causes them to tremble. The concept of the responsibility that they connect with Christianity causes feelings of fear and anxiety. Many people turn away from Jesus because they simply can't determine the benefit of following Him.

The situation today is no different than it was on the night of Jesus' birth. In the same way that the angel spoke to the shepherds and brought them "good news of great joy," the living presence of Christ in you is confirmation of the greatest joy that you will ever know. The coming of Jesus Christ into your life is the good news of the Christian faith. Remember that when the angels appeared to the shepherds, the angel announced the birth of the Savior and the good tidings of great joy that would be for all the people.

The living Lord Jesus Christ offers Himself to you so graciously; don't allow fear or unworthiness to rob you of the great privilege of knowing Him as your Redeemer, Savior, Master and Friend. Accept Christ into your life and experience the great joy that the angel heralded for all people.

Lord Christ, I humbly and gratefully open my heart to You. Amen.

No Room—
But God Was There

She gave birth to her firstborn, a son. She wrapped Him in cloths and placed Him in a manger, because there was no room for them in the inn. (Luke 2:7)

The accommodation could have been better, but it was all the innkeeper could offer them. The welcoming party for God's Son was small and socially unimportant, but the shepherds had sincerity that was inspired by a heavenly vision. The Caesar's decree caused an uprise, but it undoubtedly brought about the reunion of family members that would not have otherwise come together. In the midst of this joyous activity the Prince of Peace was born. God accepted the best the innkeeper could offer and the shepherds' worship gave Mary and Joseph the deep contentment of knowing that their child was born among their own people.

One of the Holy Father's wonderful character traits is that He is always constructive in the midst of destruction. In every hopeless situation, He brings a glimmer of hope. In the darkest moments of life, He brings light. God is never overwhelmed by circumstances or conditions. Those who trust in Him inherit this holy optimism.

When everything looks hopeless and you want to give up, don't give in to fear or despair. Acknowledge that God is present in the situation and that He is your loving Father and guide. Never fear because God is always with you and He brings His wisdom and light to brighten your situation—if you will only allow Him to.

Heavenly Father, I thank You through Jesus Christ that You are always there when I need You the most. Amen.

Joseph and Mary

Joseph also went up from the town of Nazareth in Galilee to Judea, to Bethlehem the town of David. (Luke 2:4)

Christmas church services usually have more people in attendance and that is something to be glad about. What exactly the reason is for their increased popularity is not so clear. Perhaps there is true thankfulness for another successful year and spared lives. The choir of the congregation sings the Christmas carols beautifully and people feel that they are being spoken to by the Word in an extraordinary way.

There is, however, one thing that we must never forget: the bright lights, festive gatherings and the beautiful songs are all gifts of the child who was born that night. And He was the child of destitute people. We would not have been able to distinguish between Joseph and Mary and other displaced people ordered by the command of the emperor to return to the place of their birth for a census and who kept troops in preparation on the borders in case there were people who did not obey his command. Mary and Joseph had no place to stay. Just like all the lonely people these days who must live and sleep on the streets, under awnings and in dark doorways and under bridges. That is how Christ was born and that is how His earthly ministry began.

With this we simply want to say: our Christmas services and our intimate celebrations at home can be empty if we forget the child.

O Lord, help me not to forget the poor and homeless—particularly the children—during this festive season. Amen.

Goodwill to All People

Glory to God in the highest, and on earth peace to men on whom His favor rests. (Luke 2:14)

This is the beginning, the middle and the end of the heavenly message to a dark, sin-torn world. Who could have thought of it—of such a song! Many sounds are heard on earth, many songs arise from the dust. But that God, the holy and exalted One who lives in the heavens, has goodwill toward people who have alienated themselves from Him—that He has such an interest in our goodwill!

If you look at your own restless, dissatisfied heart, if you look back along your path through life, if you remember the words you have spoken in the past year, then you, and I too, crumble and stammer, "How is this possible?" Is God still interested in me? Does He love me in such a way too, I who have not asked after Him? Did He send His Son to earth to rescue me too and make me holy? If this is possible then it is also possible that my life can respond to His purpose for me!

Let the angel song resound in our hearts and in our practical lives, while the wonder of this love touches our hearts and lives at this special time of the year.

Peace on earth we hear from heaven. Peace descends into our sinful hearts that bow before God in worship as we surrender ourselves to the highest and most pure love, "For God so loved the world …"

God of love and grace, thank You that You take an interest in my well-being, and thank You too for loving me. Amen.

Read Matthew 2:1-12

The Wise Men and the Star

When they saw the star,
they were overjoyed. (Matthew 2:10)

If there is one event in history that is interwoven with legend, then it is this one. People commonly talk of three kings, and a feast is celebrated in their honor each January. But there are three misconceptions: they were wise men; the number of them is unknown; and the date of their arrival is definitely not known. It is indeed possible that the Christ child was already a half-year-old or even older. We know only one thing for sure: eastern astrologers or astronomers saw a particular apparition in the starry skies that confirmed that the King of the Jews had been born.

Can something like this really happen? Is astrology not just foolishness? Are not all the people who allow their horoscopes in newspapers and magazines to prescribe whether or not they are going to have a favorable or unfavorable day a little off balance? Is there a connection between our date of birth and our lot in life?

In Deuteronomy 4:19, Moses puts it like this, "When you look up to the sky and see the sun, moon and stars—all the heavenly array—do not be enticed into bowing down to them and worshiping things the Lord your God has appointed to all the nations under heaven."

Children of God know that it was God who freed them from slavery, and that is a better message than any other. The Son of God who created the stars shows us the way.

Creator God, prevent me from putting any part of Your
creation above You in my thanksgiving and worship. Amen.

Look and See

When the angels had left them and gone into heaven, the shepherds said to one another, "Let's go to Bethlehem and see this thing that has happened, which the Lord has told us about. (Luke 2:15)

Sometimes God breaks unexpectedly into someone's daily routine. This is how He appeared to Moses, Amos, Mary and Paul. But this is not always the way in which God chooses to work. There is more than one method that God uses to intervene in a person's life.

When the angels appeared to the shepherds keeping watch over the sheep on the hills outside Bethlehem, they left the shepherds with an invitation. They needed to go on a journey to find the baby Jesus. They could have spent the night in long debates and arguments and in this way have reasoned away the appearance of the angels. They could have said, "We really wanted to go, but what is going to happen to the sheep?" But they took the message of God at face value and quickly made their way to the village. Their faith was rewarded with a vision of God.

Some people undergo a long search to meet Christ. They need to clear their way through difficult arguments or doubt and uncertainty. Others spend many years in worship and study, seeking after Jesus. Prepare yourself to meet Him this Christmas and there might just be a wonderful surprise in store for you.

Jesus of Bethlehem, cause all those who are seeking You during this Christmas time to be rewarded with a life-changing encounter with You. Amen.

Read Luke 2:8-20

Prayer on Christmas Eve

Glory to God in the highest, and on earth peace
to men on whom His favor rests. (Luke 2:14)

Heavenly Father of our Lord Jesus,
we thank You for the privilege
of being able to celebrate Christmas.
And for all that it means to us:
that You sent Your beloved Son to our world and
that He became a member of a humble family home;
That He was educated and grew up
like all other children;
That He grew to adulthood and
worked in a carpenter's shop.
That He, like each one of us,
also became thirsty and hungry,
knew temptation and sorrow and that
He was like us in all things, except that He did not sin.
That He, just like us, needed to battle to survive.
We thank You for His life and work,
His love that died for us
and the power of His resurrection from the dead.
We thank You for His glorification
and His intercession for us with You, our Father.
May He, at this time of Christmas,
move in our hearts so that this will be
a real celebration of Christ.
Help us to rejoice throughout the year
because we have found life in all its fullness in Him.
We pray this in the name of the Jesus
Amen.

The Savior Is Born!

Jesus was born in Bethlehem in Judea. (Matthew 2:1)

Our Scripture verse for today is a historical fact. Jesus was born in Bethlehem. It was in this act of physical birth that God revealed Himself in human affairs. Jesus came to demonstrate the character of God to the world in a way it had never before been revealed. That humanity found it hard to accept this revelation does not alter the value of it because, although nations have turned away from His challenge to live in righteousness, there are numerous people who have acknowledged Him as Lord and Master of their lives.

He who was born more than two millennia ago in Bethlehem is bringing about new life in the hearts and lives of men and women who have been born in this modern century. This simple yet glorious truth is often ignored or forgotten in the rush and excitement of the festive season, but it is irrefutable that if He was not at work in your heart and life that you will not fully enjoy the true joy and peace of Christmas.

Without Him, Christmas festivities become just a meaningless tradition and a time of abnormal excess and overspending.

If you want to enjoy a true and meaningful Christmas celebration, put Christ at the center of your life. For those who do so it will be a truly blessed Christmas because when the Child of Bethlehem comes to dwell in you He is the source of true Christmas joy.

Lord Jesus, when You made etrenal life possible,
Christmas became a glorious reality. Amen.

Read Luke 1:26-38

J-E-S-U-S!

You will be with child and give birth to a son, and you are to give Him the name Jesus. (Luke 1:31)

People today are inclined to name their children after movie stars, sports heroes or any other popular celebrities. A girl's name is often chosen because it sounds pretty, and a boy's because it sounds strong.

In biblical times a name often indicated the hope that the parents had for their child and what he or she would become. Family names were also carried down. The name *Jesus* means "Savior." It focuses on Jesus' role of redeeming humankind. He came to save completely. His redemption centered on the forgiveness of sin, but it also included healing, holiness, renewal, joy, the fruit of the Spirit, love and hope.

Jesus is the most beloved name in the entire universe. It means different things to different people. When you are lonely, it means friendship and love. When you are depressed, it means joy. When you are afraid, it means courage. When you are sick, it means healing. When you are guilty, it means forgiveness. When you have fallen, it means restoration. When you are in the midst of trouble, it means light in the darkness. When you die, it means life on the other side of the grave.

It is the name most of us use for God—and this is correct. Without Jesus, we would never have known God.

"Jesus, Jesus, Jesus sweetest name I know. Fills my every longing, keeps me singing as I go." My Savior and Redeemer. Amen.

Life in Christ

For to me, to live is Christ. (Philippians 1:21)

With passing time people have developed a great misunderstanding about the church. For many people, faithfulness to the church means a monotonous, dull life without any joy or delight. The critics of the church have developed a perception that Christians are somber people without any cheerfulness.

Nothing could be further from the truth! Jesus offers His followers abundant life and that can be found in no other source than the Lord Himself. He lived a full and rich life that spoke of perfect fulfillment. There is absolutely nothing in the life of Christ that could be regarded as monotonous, boring or purposeless. He is in every sense the Source of life!

To follow Jesus entails giving over our own priorities and ambitions and learning to live as Jesus lived. Rather than this feeling like a loss, we will learn the abundant life and deep-rooted joy that comes from knowing and following our Savior and our lives finding purpose through serving Him.

If you want to experience the deepest satisfaction in life, put Christ at the center of your life. Work together with Him and seek only to carry out His will. This is a gracious proposal from the Lord to let you live the life that comprises all the elements of a life of fulfillment and satisfaction (see John 10:10).

Thank You, blessed Savior, for the full, abundant and complete life that I have found in You. Amen.

Read Colossians 2:6-15

The Day When Selfishness Died

In Christ all the fullness of the Deity lives in bodily form, and you have been given fullness in Christ. (Colossians 2:9-10)

Many people are dominated and motivated by selfish interests. They appear to be irredeemably selfish. Years ago a young man responded positively to an altar call to surrender to Jesus and to go and serve in the ministry. Simply, humbly and quietly, he said to the preacher, "Two years ago I murdered my mother." "I am sure you did not murder her with your two bare hands?" the preacher asked. "No," was the answer, "but my selfishness killed her."

Selfishness breaks up marriages, drives families apart, ruins business initiatives, and prevents people from growing into responsible adults. It hinders churches from becoming effective communities for Christ.

Before Paul learned to know Christ, he was dominated by selfish desires. Christ changed it all. He made Paul His servant and from then on love ruled over him and motivated his every plan and project. Where he had been driven by selfishness, he was now motivated by love for Christ and compelled by concern for people.

Ask Christ to change you. Only He can do so. Look at yourself and confess the selfishness that rules in you and your worldly ambitions. Give it all to Christ and ask Him to fill you with His love. Apply it practically: care for others, show love for others and stop wondering what you will get out of it.

Lord Jesus who is love, cause me through the work of the Holy Spirit in me to be compelled by love. Amen.

Put Christ at the Center

May I never boast except in the cross of our Lord Jesus Christ, through which the world has been crucified to me, and I to the world. (Galatians 6:14)

One of the great dangers of our spiritual lives lies in our enthusiasm. This might sound strange to you, even paradoxical, yet it is nonetheless true and can lead to serious consequences in our witnessing for God.

So often we come across people in a church who wax lyrical about the music in their congregation or who take great satisfaction in the large number of people who attend the worship services. Beware of those who keep a sharp, watchful eye on the finances or those who regularly urge for more and more community activities for the different segments of their congregation.

These and many other activities might be very praiseworthy and in some instances even necessary. But it is of the utmost importance for your spiritual well-being that they should never be allowed to overshadow or eclipse the central focus of your faith: the anointed One of God, who saved us by His death on the cross at Golgotha.

No matter how laudable congregational projects and activities might be, enthusiasm for them must never be allowed to come between us and our commitment to the living Christ. Christ is all and in all!

When I survey the wondrous cross on which the Prince of Glory died, my richest gain I count but loss and pour contempt on all my pride. Amen.

 Read 2 Corinthians 8:1-12

Enthusiasm Is Not Enough

Now finish the work, so that your eager willingness to do it may be matched by your completion of it, according to your means. (2 Corinthians 8:11)

For many people the first experience of Christianity is unfortgettable: the most significant experience of their whole lives. Christ becomes a glorious reality, and the assurance that their sins have been forgiven brings about a joy that sets their souls on fire with the desire to share their experience with others.

To share your spiritual experiences with others strengthens your own spirit and faith, but this sharing requires much more than emotional involvement.

It is possible to talk about Jesus Christ and yet at the same time to lose your hold on Him. Enthusiasm must develop into a positive and practical faith that can bear reasonable testimony of what you believe.

When you become a Christian and your sins have been forgiven, when you experience peace with God and a sense of unity with the Father, you begin a pilgrimage that has many twists and turns. Your whole life—your body, mind and spirit—is involved. Your emotions are roused through experiencing the redeeming love of Christ; your mind is stirred in an attempt to try to understand such love; and the realization that you can be the dwelling place of God's Holy Spirit fills you with a positive, but not exclusively emotional, enthusiasm.

I praise and thank You, Lord Jesus, that my spiritual experience embraces every aspect of my life. Amen.

When He Returns

When Christ, who is your life, appears, then you also will appear with Him in glory. (Colossians 3:4)

The more some people think about life, the more puzzling it becomes for them. Most things are by no means what they appear to be on the surface.

In large sections of the Old Testament, people were looking forward to the coming of the Messiah. In the New Testament those who believed in Jesus knew that He had come. But they also knew that there was far more to the absolute rulership of God than what occurred with the coming of Jesus.

That is why they persevered in faith, believing that He would come again in a final revelation of glory and triumph. Then true peace will be in abundance, the secret things will be made known and the wickedness of this present world will be destroyed. Earthly things will be shown for what they really are. Then Jesus will truly be all and in all.

But Jesus will also not come alone in His glory. Those who believe in Him will be with Him when He comes. The important things such as love, peace, reconciliation, encouragement, joy and celebration will come to the fore.

Look forward to the return of Christ. Deepen your faith, extend your compassion in expectation of that glorious occasion. And keep your eyes fixed on Jesus—the Author and Perfecter of our faith.

Thank You, Lord Jesus, that I can look forward to Your future coming in glory and that I will be included in it. Amen.